Teach Yourself VISUALLY™

iMac®

2nd Edition

Visual™

Guy Hart-Davis

WILEY

John Wiley & Sons, Inc.

Teach Yourself VISUALLY™ iMac®, 2nd Edition

Published by
John Wiley & Sons, Inc.
10475 Crosspoint Boulevard
Indianapolis, IN 46256

www.wiley.com

Published simultaneously in Canada

Wiley also publishes its books in a variety of electronic formats and by print-on-demand. Some content that appears in standard print versions of this book may not be available in other formats. For more information about Wiley products, visit us at www.wiley.com.

Library of Congress Control Number: 2011937911

ISBN: 978-1-118-14762-7

Manufactured in the United States of America

10 9 8 7 6 5 4 3 2

Trademark Acknowledgments

Wiley, the John Wiley & Sons, Inc. logo, Visual, the Visual logo, Teach Yourself VISUALLY, Read Less - Learn More and related trade dress are trademarks or registered trademarks of John Wiley & Sons, Inc. and/or its affiliates. iMac is a registered trademark of Apple, Inc. All other trademarks are the property of their respective owners. John Wiley & Sons, Inc. is not associated with any product or vendor mentioned in this book. *Teach Yourself VISUALLY iMac, 2nd Edition* is an independent publication and has not been authorized, sponsored, or otherwise approved by Apple, Inc.

Contact Us

For general information on our other products and services please contact our Customer Care Department within the U.S. at 877-762-2974, outside the U.S. at 317-572-3993 or fax 317-572-4002.

For technical support please visit www.wiley.com/techsupport.

WILEY   **Sales** | Contact Wiley at (877) 762-2974 or fax (317) 572-4002.

Credits

Acquisitions Editor
Aaron Black

Sr. Project Editor
Sarah Hellert

Technical Editor
Dennis R. Cohen

Copy Editor
Scott Tullis

Editorial Director
Robyn Siesky

Business Manager
Amy Knies

Sr. Marketing Manager
Sandy Smith

Vice President and Executive Group Publisher
Richard Swadley

Vice President and Executive Publisher
Barry Pruett

Project Coordinator
Sheree Montgomery

Graphics and Production Specialists
Andrea Hornberger
Heather Pope
Julie Trippetti

Quality Control Technicians
Melissa Cossell
Lauren Mandelbaum

Proofreader
Tricia Liebig

Indexer
Potomac Indexing, LLC

Screen Artists
Ana Carrillo
Noah Hart
Mark Pinto
Jill A. Proll

Illustrator
Ronda David-Burroughs

About the Author

Guy Hart-Davis is the author of *iMac Portable Genius, 3rd Edition*, *iLife '11 Portable Genius*, and *iWork '09 Portable Genius*.

Author's Acknowledgments

My thanks go to the many people who turned my manuscript into the highly graphical book you are holding. In particular, I thank Aaron Black for asking me to write the second edition of the book; Sarah Hellert for keeping me on track and guiding the editorial process; Scott Tullis for skilfully editing the text; Dennis Cohen for reviewing the book for technical accuracy and contributing helpful sugggestions; and Andrea Hornberger, Heather Pope, and Julie Trippetti for laying out the book.

How to Use This Book

Who This Book Is For

This book is for the reader who has never used this particular technology or software application. It is also for readers who want to expand their knowledge.

The Conventions in This Book

① Steps

This book uses a step-by-step format to guide you easily through each task. **Numbered steps** are actions you must do; **bulleted steps** clarify a point, step, or optional feature; and **indented steps** give you the result.

② Notes

Notes give additional information — special conditions that may occur during an operation, a situation that you want to avoid, or a cross-reference to a related area of the book.

③ Icons and Buttons

Icons and buttons show you exactly what you need to click to perform a step.

④ Tips

Tips offer additional information, including warnings and shortcuts.

⑤ Bold

Bold type shows command names or options that you must click or text or numbers you must type.

⑥ Italics

Italic type introduces and defines a new term.

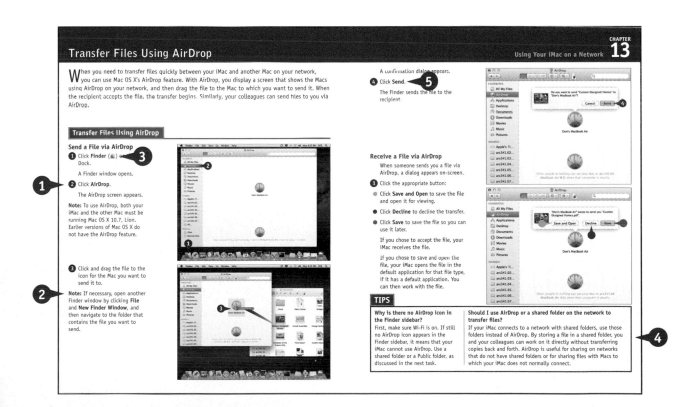

Table of Contents

Chapter 1   Getting Started with Your iMac

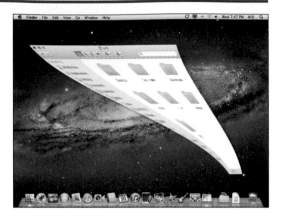

Chapter 2   Sharing Your iMac with Other People

Chapter 3 | Running Applications

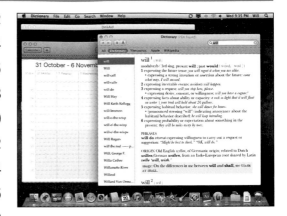

Chapter 4 | Managing Your Files and Folders

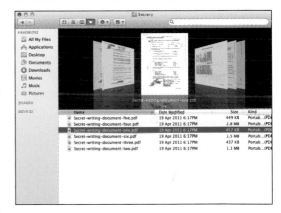

Table of Contents

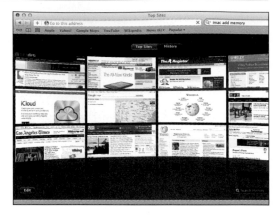
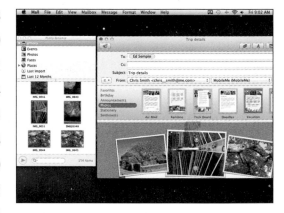

Chapter 7   Organizing Your Contacts and Schedule

Chapter 8   Chatting with iChat and FaceTime

Table of Contents

Chapter 9   Enjoying Music, Video, and DVDs

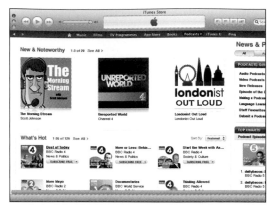

Chapter 10   Making the Most of Your Photos

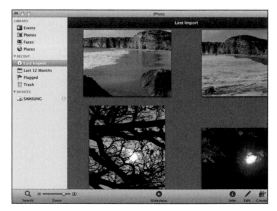

Table of Contents

CHAPTER 1

Getting Started with Your iMac

The iMac is a beautifully designed computer and comes with the powerful, easy-to-use Mac OS X operating system. In just a few minutes, you can set up your iMac and begin using it. This chapter shows you how to get started with your iMac, use the Mac OS X interface, and connect extra devices to the iMac.

Create Your Computer Account

Enter a name and password to create your computer account. You need this password to administer your computer, change settings, and install software.

Full Name: Will

Account Name: will
This will be used as the name for your home folder and can't be changed.

Password: ●●●●●●

Verify: ●●●●●●

☐ Allow my Apple ID to reset this user password.

☑ Require password when logging in.

Password Hint:

Enter a hint to help you remember your password. Anyone can see the hint, so choose a hint that won't make it easy to guess your password.

Back   Continue

Set Up Your iMac

If you have just bought your iMac, you need to connect its hardware and create your user account before you can use it. Your user account is where you store your files and settings on the iMac.

The first user account you create is the Administrator account, which can create other accounts later for other users. You may also choose to create a personal account for yourself, leaving the Administrator account strictly for administration.

Set Up Your iMac

Set Up Your iMac's Hardware

1 Unpack the iMac from its box.

2 Position the main unit on your desk or table.

3 If you have a wireless keyboard, turn it on by pressing the power button on its right side. If you have a wired keyboard, connect its cable to a USB port at the back of the iMac.

4 Optionally, connect external speakers to the audio out port.

5 Optionally, connect an external microphone to the audio in port.

6 If you have a Magic Mouse, turn it on by moving the on/off switch on its underside. If you have a Magic Trackpad, press the button at its upper-right corner.

7 Connect the power supply to the iMac and plug it into a power source.

8 Press the power button to start the iMac.

Note: On most iMacs, the power button is located at the back of the unit, at the lower-left corner looking from the front.

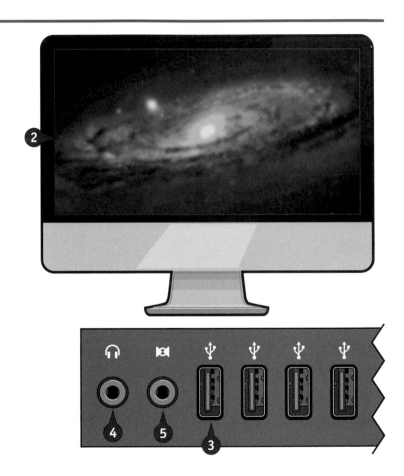

Create Your User Account

1 In the Welcome screen, click your country or region and then click **Continue**.

2 Follow through the registration information screens to the Create Your Computer Account screen.

3 Type the user's full name, or as much of it as you want to use.

4 Change the account name that Mac OS X suggests as needed.

5 Type a password.

6 Verify the Require Password When Logging In check box is selected (☑).

7 Optionally, type a password hint.

8 Click **Continue**.

9 If the Select a Picture for This Account screen appears, click **Take photo snapshot** to take a photo of yourself using the iMac's camera.

Note: You can also use a picture from the picture library. Click **Choose from the picture library**, and then click the picture you want.

10 Click **Continue**, and then finish the installation.

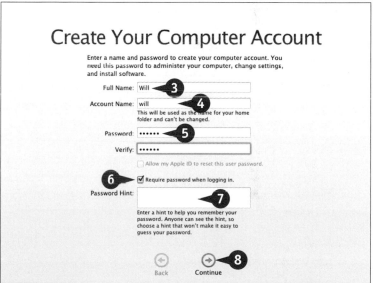

TIP

Can I use a USB mouse with Mac OS X?
Yes. Apple encourages you to get either the Magic Mouse or the Magic Trackpad — or both — with the iMac. But you can use any USB mouse for which Mac OS X has a software driver. To use a USB mouse, connect it to one of your iMac's USB ports. If you can then move the mouse pointer on the screen, the mouse is working.

Start Your iMac and Log In

When you are ready to start a computing session, start your iMac and log in to Mac OS X. When you log in, Mac OS X identifies you as the owner of your user account, and displays the Mac OS X desktop with your applications and settings.

Start Your iMac and Log In

1 Press the power button on the iMac.

Note: On most iMacs, the power button is located at the back of the unit, at the lower-left corner when you are looking from the front.

A window showing the list of users appears.

Note: Your iMac may not display the list of users and login window. Instead, it may simply log you in automatically or show a different login window. Chapter 2 shows you how to change this behavior.

2 Click your username.

The login window appears.

3 Type your password in the Password field.

● If you cannot remember your password, click ⬜.

● Mac OS X displays your password hint at the bottom of the login window.

4 Type your password.

5 Click ⊙.

Note: Instead of clicking ⊙, you can press Return.

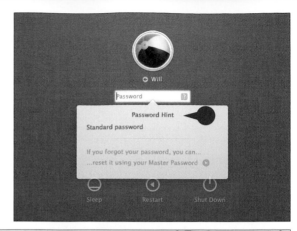

The iMac displays your desktop, the menu bar, and the Dock. You can now start using the iMac.

Why does my iMac not display the list of usernames but goes straight to the desktop?

If you do not see the list of names and then the login window, your iMac is set to log in automatically. Logging in automatically is convenient when you are the only user of your iMac, but it means that anyone who can start your iMac can log in. Chapter 2 shows you how to turn off automatic login.

Why does my iMac not show the list of usernames?

Rather than the list of usernames, you may see a window with a Name field and a Password field. Type your username and your password, and then click ⊙. Hiding the list of usernames gives extra security and is widely used in companies, but it is usually not necessary for iMacs used at home.

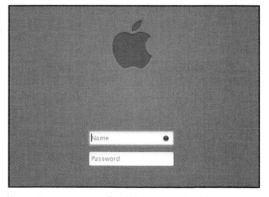

Connect Your iMac to the Internet

To browse the web and use email, you must connect your iMac to the Internet. This task shows general steps for using a DSL router or cable router connected directly to your iMac. The specifics depend on your Internet service provider and the equipment they supply; some providers install the router and make sure it works, whereas others provide a self-install kit. If you have a network that includes an Internet connection, see the next task, "Connect Your iMac to a Wired Network."

Connect Your iMac to the Internet

1 Connect the DSL router or cable router to your iMac with an Ethernet cable as instructed.

2 Click **System Preferences** (🖼) on the Dock.

Note: If System Preferences does not appear on the Dock, click 🍎 and **System Preferences**.

3 In the System Preferences window, click **Network**.

4 In the Network preferences pane, click **Ethernet**.

5 Open the Configure IPv4 pop-up menu and choose **Manually**.

6 Type the next IP address after the router's address. For example, if the router uses the IP address **10.0.0.2**, type **10.0.0.3**.

Note: Most DSL routers and cable routers use an address in the 192.168.0.*x* range, the 192.168.1.*x* range, the 10.0.0.*x* range, or the 10.0.1.*x* range, where *x* is a number between 1 and 255.

7 Type the subnet mask.

Note: Most DSL routers and cable routers use the subnet mask 255.255.255.0.

8 Click **Apply**.

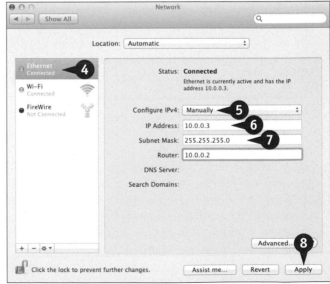

9 Click **Safari** (●) on the Dock.

10 In the Safari browser window, type the address for the router and press `Return`.

Note: If the router prompts you for a password, type the password provided in the documentation.

11 In the router's control screens, choose settings for the router following your ISP's instructions.

12 Click **Apple** to display the Apple website to test your Internet connection.

13 Click **Minimize** (●) to minimize the Safari window to the Dock.

14 In Network preferences, click the **Configure IPv4** ⬍ and choose **Using DHCP**.

15 Click **Apply**.

16 Click the **System Preferences** menu and click **Quit System Preferences** to close System Preferences.

17 Click **Safari** (●) on the Dock.

The Safari window reappears, and you can browse the Internet.

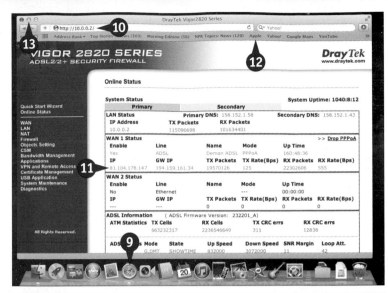

TIP

Which kind of Internet connection is better, DSL or cable?

A Digital Subscriber Line, or DSL, provides a high-speed Internet connection over a phone line. DSL divides the phone line into a data part and a voice part, so you can connect to the Internet even when the phone is in use. Cable Internet provides Internet access through your cable TV cabling. Both cable and DSL speeds depend on your location, so ask the providers what speeds are available and how much service costs. For cable, ask how many other users will share the same network circuit; the more users, the more the speed drops. If you cannot get either DSL or cable Internet service, look at satellite services, which are available in remote locations where DSL and cable are not. The other alternative is a dial-up connection using a modem and a phone line, but this is very slow compared to the other options.

Connect Your iMac to a Wired Network

If you have a wired network, you can quickly connect your iMac to it so that the iMac can use the network's Internet connection and share files and printers with other computers on the network.

Connect Your iMac to a Wired Network

1 Connect one end of a network cable to the Ethernet port on the back of your iMac.

2 Connect the other end of the network cable to an Ethernet port on your network switch or network router.

Note: If your Internet router includes a network switch, you can plug the network cable into an Ethernet port on the Internet router.

Your iMac automatically detects the network connection and tries to apply suitable settings.

3 Click ⌘.

The Apple menu opens.

4 Click **System Preferences**.

The System Preferences window opens.

5 Click **Network**.

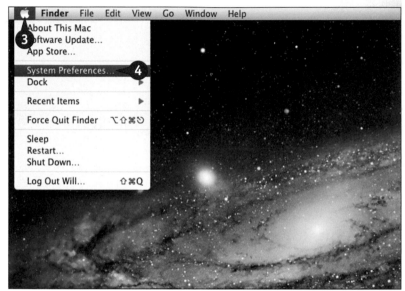

The Network preferences pane opens.

6 Click **Ethernet**.

7 Verify that your iMac has an IP address.

8 Click the **System Preferences** menu and click **Quit System Preferences**.

9 Click **Safari** (●) on the Dock.

A Safari browser window opens and displays your iMac's home page, the page Safari opens automatically.

You have now connected your iMac to the network and the Internet.

TIPS

How does a computer network work?

A wired network has a network switch or network router that directs the data around the network. Each computer connects to the switch or router via network cables. You typically connect your Internet router to the switch or router as well to share the Internet connection on the network; some Internet routers have a network router built in. Networked computers can also share files and printers with each other.

What is an IP address and what is DHCP?

An IP address is a number that identifies a computer on a network. An IP address consists of four groups of one, two, or three digits, such as 10.10.0.100 or 192.168.1.10. DHCP stands for Dynamic Host Configuration Protocol and is a way of providing IP addresses to computers on the network. When a computer joins the network, it requests an IP address and other connection information from the DHCP server. Most cable and DSL routers act as DHCP servers.

Connect Your iMac to a Wireless Network

If you have set up a wireless network, you can connect your iMac to it. Wireless networks are convenient for both homes and businesses because they require no cables and are fast and easy to set up.

Your iMac includes a wireless network card that Mac OS X refers to as Wi-Fi. You can control wireless networks directly from the Wi-Fi menu at the right end of the menu bar.

Connect Your iMac to a Wireless Network

1 Click the Wi-Fi status icon (🛜) on the menu bar.

The menu opens and displays a list of the wireless networks your iMac can detect.

Note: If the Wi-Fi menu shows Wi-Fi: Off, click **Turn Wi-Fi On** (🛜 changes to 🛜). Then open the menu again to see the available wireless networks.

● The networks in the No Network Selected part of the list are networks that connect using wireless access points. These are called *infrastructure wireless networks*.

● The networks in the Devices part of the menu are networks created by individual computers. These are called *ad hoc wireless networks* or *peer-to-peer wireless networks*.

● A lock icon (🔒) indicates that the network is secured with a password.

● The signal strength icon indicates the relative strength of the network's signal.

2 Click the network to which you want to connect your iMac.

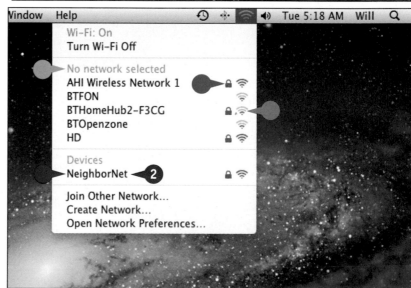

If the wireless network uses a password, your iMac prompts you to enter it.

③ Type the password in the Password field.

● If you want to see the characters of the password to help you type it, click **Show password** (□ changes to ☑).

● If you do not want your iMac to remember this wireless network for future use, click **Remember this network** (☑ changes to □).

④ Click **Join**.

Your iMac connects to the wireless network, and you can start using network resources.

● The Wi-Fi status icon on the menu bar changes from 📶 to 📶 when the connection is established. The number of arcs on the Wi-Fi status icon indicates the strength of the connection, from one arc to four arcs.

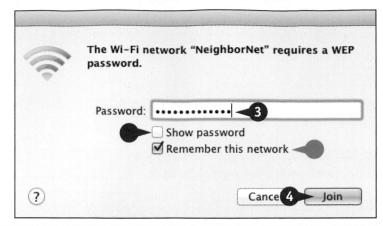

TIPS

How do I disconnect from a wireless network?
When you have finished using a wireless network, you can disconnect from it by turning Wi-Fi off. Click the Wi-Fi status icon (📶) on the menu bar and then click **Turn Wi-Fi Off**.

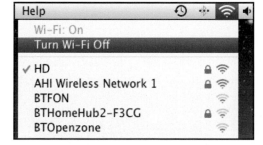

What kind of wireless network do I need for my iMac?
Wireless networks use several different standards. The latest standard is 802.11n, also called Wireless-N, and provides the fastest data rates. The best choice for a Mac wireless network is one of Apple's wireless access points, such as AirPort Extreme or Time Capsule, which includes backup capabilities.

Connect a Printer to Your iMac

To print from your iMac, you need to connect a printer and install a *driver*, the software for the printer. Mac OS X includes many printer drivers, so you may be able to connect your printer and simply start printing. But if your printer is a new model, you may need to locate and install the driver for it.

This task shows you how to connect a printer to your iMac with a USB cable. To connect to a printer on your network or shared by another computer, see Chapter 13.

Connect a Printer to Your iMac

1 Connect the printer to the iMac with a USB cable.

Note: If the printer is connected to another Mac, connect to it as explained in Chapter 13.

2 Plug the printer into an electrical socket and switch it on.

3 Click ⬛.

The Apple menu opens.

4 Click **System Preferences**.

The System Preferences window opens.

5 Click **Print & Scan**.

The Print & Scan preferences pane opens.

● If your printer appears in the list, you have connected it successfully. Go to step **12**.

6 If your printer does not appear, click **Add** (⊞).

14

The Add Printer dialog opens.

7 Click **Default**.

The Default pane opens.

8 In the Printer Name list field, click the printer.

9 If you want, change the printer's name.

Note: It is often helpful to use the name to make clear what kind of printer this is — for example, whether it prints in color or black and white.

10 Also optionally, change the description of the printer's location.

11 Click **Add**.

● Mac OS X adds the printer.

12 Click the **System Preferences** menu.

13 Click **Quit System Preferences**.

The System Preferences window closes.

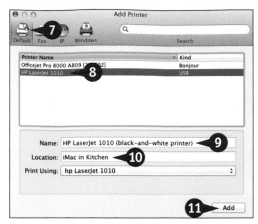

TIPS

What should I type in the Name field and Location field when adding a printer?

You can type anything you want in the Name field and the Location field. This information is to help you identify the printer. If you have many printers, and some are attached to different computers, making each printer's name and location descriptive helps you keep the printers straight.

My printer has the wrong sort of connector — it must be ten times bigger than a USB connector. How can I connect it?

The large connector is a parallel port, which some older printers have. To connect the printer to your iMac, buy a parallel-to-USB adapter cable. Before you do, make sure that Mac OS X has a printer driver for your printer.

Connect an iPhone, iPad, or iPod to Your iMac

If you have an iPhone, iPad, or iPod, you can connect it to your iMac to synchronize music, videos, and information such as appointments and addresses. To connect the iPhone, iPad, or iPod, you need the cable that came with the device. The cable has a USB connector at one end and a Dock connector at the other end.

Connect an iPhone, iPad, or iPod to Your iMac

Connect an iPhone or iPod

① Insert the cable's USB connector in a USB port on your iMac.

② Insert the cable's dock connector in the dock connector port on the bottom of the iPhone, iPad, or iPod, or in the device's dock.

Your iMac detects the device and launches iTunes for synchronizing it.

If you connect an iPhone, iPad, or iPod touch that contains photos you have not synchronized with iPhoto, iPhoto opens.

Note: If you have not used this version of iTunes yet on your iMac, you must agree to its license agreement and choose settings before you can synchronize the iPhone, iPad, or iPod. See Chapter 9 for information on iTunes.

Choose Synchronization Settings for the iPhone or iPod

1 Click the iPhone, iPad, or iPod in the Devices list.

Note: In the Devices list, the iPhone, iPad, or iPod appears with the name you gave it when setting it up. The example iPhone here is called simply iPhone.

2 Click each tab of the control screens in turn, and choose settings.

3 Click **Sync**.

Disconnect an iPhone or iPod

1 Click the eject button (⏏) for the iPhone or iPod in iTunes.

2 When the iPhone, iPad, or iPod's screen shows the message that it is okay to disconnect, pull out the dock connector.

TIPS

How can I tell when it is safe to disconnect my iPhone, iPad, or iPod?

You can safely disconnect an iPhone, iPad, or iPod touch unless the screen shows "Sync in Progress." To cancel a sync, drag your finger across the **Slide to Cancel** slider on the screen. Different iPod models use different messages, but see if either the iPod's screen or the iTunes readout displays "Do Not Disconnect" or "Eject Before Disconnecting." Also see if a rotating icon appears next to the iPod's listing in the Devices category of the Source list.

I am running out of USB ports on my iMac. Is there an alternative to unplugging cables and plugging them back in?

Buy a USB hub, a device that plugs into your iMac and provides extra ports. You can position the hub conveniently for your USB devices. You can find USB hubs at any good computer store, online or offline, including the Apple Store. Buy a powered hub for devices that do not have their own power supplies. Buy an unpowered hub for devices that do have power supplies.

Connect External Drives to Your iMac

Your iMac's built-in hard drive contains enough space for many files and applications, but you may need to connect an external drive to provide extra storage, a place for backup using Time Machine, or to transfer large files easily. You can connect an external drive to your iMac by using a Thunderbolt port, USB port, or FireWire port.

Connect External Drives to Your iMac

Connect an External Drive

1 On the back of your iMac, identify the port you need for the external drive.

● Use a USB port for a USB-connected external hard drive, a miniature drive, or a memory card reader.

Note: To connect a FireWire 400 drive to the FireWire 800 port, use a FireWire 400-to-FireWire 800 adapter.

● Use the FireWire 800 port to connect external hard drives that use the FireWire 800 standard.

Note: FireWire 800 is twice as fast as FireWire 400. So if your device can use either, choose FireWire 800.

● Use a Thunderbolt port to connect external hard drives that use the Thunderbolt standard.

2 Connect the external drive to the iMac using the right type of cable.

3 If the external drive needs a power supply, plug it in.

4 If the external drive has a power switch, turn it on.

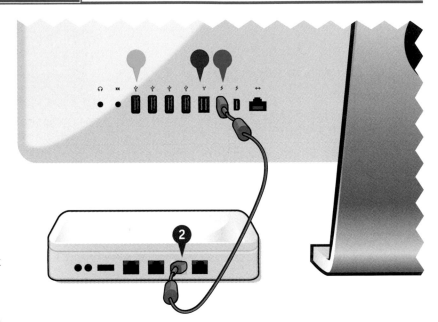

Use an External Drive

1 Click **Finder** () on the Dock to open a Finder window.

2 If the Devices list in the sidebar is hidden, position the mouse pointer over the Devices heading, and then click **Show**.

3 Click the drive in the Devices list.

You can then copy or move files to or from the drive or create new folders on it.

Disconnect an External Drive

1 Open a Finder window showing the drive.

2 Click the eject button () next to the drive.

Mac OS X dismounts the drive and removes it from the Finder window and from your desktop.

3 Disconnect the drive from the port.

Note: You must always eject a drive using these steps before you disconnect an external drive. Otherwise, you may corrupt or lose files on the drive or on your iMac.

TIP

Should I choose USB, FireWire, or Thunderbolt when I buy an external drive?

Thunderbolt is far faster than USB or FireWire, so it is the only choice if you need top performance and can afford to pay for it. Otherwise, choose FireWire 800 for high performance. But if you need to connect the drive to Windows PCs as well as to your iMac, USB is better because all PCs have USB ports but few have FireWire ports. You can also buy a drive that has both FireWire and USB. If you need to carry an external drive with you, a miniature USB drive is usually best. Also called "thumb drives" or "key drives," these are built to withstand life in a pocket and contain memory chips rather than delicate rotating platters.

Give Commands from the Menus and Toolbar

The easiest ways to give commands in Mac OS X are by using the menus and the toolbar. The menu bar at the top of the window shows the Apple menu () on the left followed by the menus for the active application. Any open window can have a toolbar, usually across its top but sometimes elsewhere in the window.

Give Commands from the Menus and Toolbar

Give a Command from a Menu

① On the Dock, click the application you want to activate, the Finder () in this example.

Note: You can also click in the application's window if you can see it.

② On the menu bar, click the menu you want to open.

The application opens the menu.

③ Click the command you want to give.

The application performs the action associated with the command.

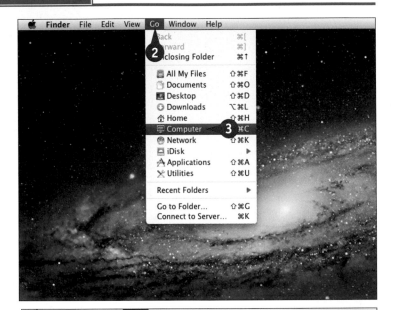

Choose among Groups of Features on a Menu

① On the Dock, click the application you want to activate, the Finder () in this example.

② On the menu bar, click the menu you want to open.

The application opens the menu.

③ Click the option you want to choose.

The application activates the feature you chose.

Give a Command from a Toolbar

1 On the Dock, click the application you want to activate, the Finder (⬛) in this example.

2 Click the button on the toolbar, or click a pop-up menu and then click the menu item for the command.

The application performs the action associated with the toolbar button or menu item.

Choose among Groups of Features on a Toolbar

1 On the Dock, click the application you want to activate, the Finder (⬛) in this example.

2 In the group of buttons, click the button you want to choose.

● The application highlights the button you clicked to indicate that the feature is turned on.

● The application removes highlighting from the button that was previously selected.

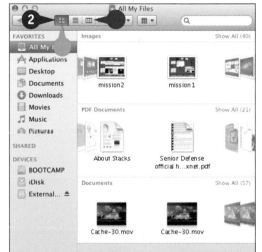

TIPS

Is it better to use the menus or the toolbar?

If the toolbar contains the command you need, using the toolbar is usually faster and easier than using the menus. You can customize the toolbar in many applications by opening the **View** menu and choosing **Customize Toolbar**. Use this command, or other similar commands, to put the buttons for your most-used commands just a click away.

Can I also give commands using the keyboard?

You can give many of the most widely used commands from the keyboard as well as from the menus or the toolbar. Each menu lists keyboard shortcuts next to their commands. This symbol (●) represents the Command key, (●) represents the Control key, (●) represents the Option key, and ⬆ represents the Shift key.

Open, Close, Minimize, and Hide Windows

Most Mac OS X applications use windows to display information so that you can see it and work with it. You can resize windows to the size you need, position them so that you can see the windows you require, minimize windows to icons on the Dock, or hide an application's windows from view.

Open, Close, Minimize, and Hide Windows

Open a Window

1 Click anywhere on the desktop.

Mac OS X activates the Finder and displays the menu bar for it.

Note: Clicking anywhere on the desktop activates the Finder because the desktop is a special Finder window. You can also click **Finder** ( ) on the Dock.

2 Click **File**.

The File menu opens.

3 Click **New Finder Window**.

A Finder window opens, showing your files in All My Files view.

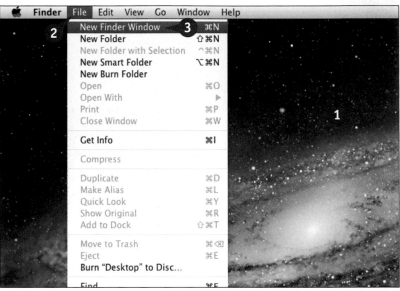

Move, Resize, and Zoom a Window

1 Click the window's title bar and drag the window to where you want it.

2 Click a border or corner of the window and drag until the window is the size and shape you want.

3 Click **Zoom** ( ).

The window zooms to its optimal size.

4 Click **Zoom** ( ) again.

The window zooms back to its previous size.

Close a Window

1 Click **Close** (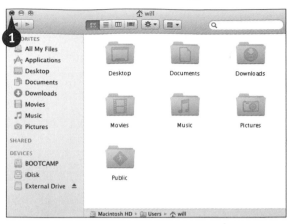).

The window closes.

Note: You can also close a window by pressing ⌘+W. If you need to close all the windows of the application, Option +click **Close** (⌐) or press ⌘+ Option +W.

Minimize or Hide a Window

1 Click **Minimize** (⌐).

Mac OS X minimizes the window to an icon on the right side of the Dock.

Note: You can also minimize a window by pressing ⌘+M.

2 Click the icon for the minimized window.

Mac OS X expands the window to its original size and position.

Note: Press and hold Shift while minimizing or restoring a window to see the animation in slow motion.

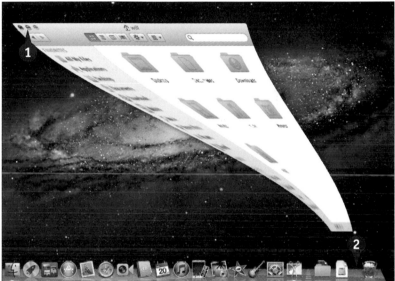

TIPS

What does zooming a window do?

Clicking **Zoom** (⌐) on a window changes its size to the size that Mac OS X judges best shows the window's contents. If this size does not show what you want to see, drag a border or corner of the window to change the size. Clicking ⌐ again returns the window to its previous size.

How can I find out where a window is located?

To quickly see what folder contains a file or folder, ⌘+click the window's name in the title bar. The window displays a pop-up menu showing the folder *path*, the sequence of folders to this folder. You

can click a folder in the path (●) to jump straight to that folder in the Finder, or click the title bar to hide the pop-up menu again. This works in any application, not just in the Finder.

Put Your iMac to Sleep and Wake It Up

When you are ready for a break but you do not want to end your computing session, put the iMac to sleep. Sleep keeps all your applications open and lets you start computing again quickly. When you wake your iMac up, your applications and windows are where you left them, so you can immediately resume what you were doing.

Put Your iMac to Sleep and Wake It Up

Put Your iMac to Sleep

1 Click .

The Apple menu opens.

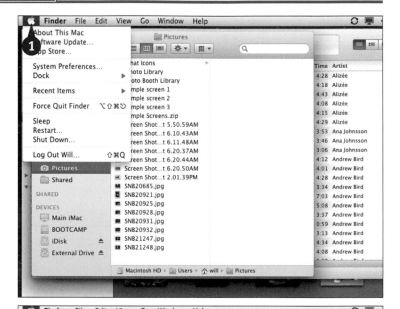

2 Click **Sleep**.

The iMac turns its screen off and puts itself to sleep.

Note: You can also put your iMac to sleep by pressing its power button for a moment.

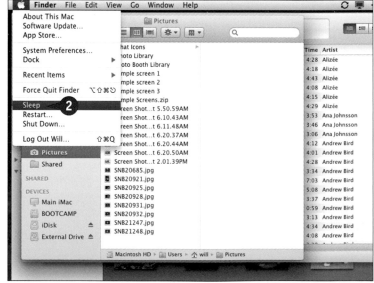

Wake Your iMac

1 Click the mouse button or press any key except **Fn** on the keyboard.

The iMac wakes up and turns on the screen. All the applications and windows that you were using are open where you left them.

The iMac reestablishes any network connections that it normally uses and performs regular tasks, such as checking for new email.

TIPS

What happens if a power outage occurs while my iMac is asleep?

If a power outage occurs while your iMac is asleep, the iMac loses power and crashes, and you lose any unsaved work. For this reason, you should save any unsaved work before putting your iMac to sleep. You may also want to consider buying an uninterruptible power supply, a battery-based device which enables a computer to ride out power outages.

When should I use sleep and when should I shut down my iMac?

Normally, it is better to put your iMac to sleep rather than shut it down. Sleep lets you start using your iMac again much more quickly than starting it from being off, and it uses only a minimal amount of power. Shut down your iMac only when you do not need to use it for several days.

Log Out, Shut Down, and Resume

When you have finished using your iMac for now, end your computing session by logging out. From the login screen, you can log back in when you are ready to use your iMac again. When you have finished using your iMac and plan to leave it several days, shut it down.

Whether you log out or shut down your iMac, you can choose whether to have Mac OS X reopen your applications and documents when you log back on. This helpful feature can help you get back to work — or play — quickly and easily.

Log Out, Shut Down, and Resume

Log Out from Your iMac

1 Click [Apple icon].

The Apple menu opens.

2 Click **Log Out**.

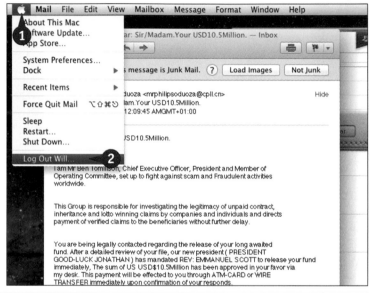

The iMac shows a dialog asking if you want to log out.

3 Make sure **Reopen windows when logging back in** is selected ([✓]) if you want to resume your applications and documents.

4 Click **Log Out**.

Note: Instead of clicking **Log Out**, you can wait for one minute. After this, the iMac closes your applications and logs you out automatically. To log out quickly, bypassing the dialog, click [Apple icon], press and hold Option, and click **Log Out**.

The iMac displays the window showing the list of users. You or another user can click your name to start logging in.

Are you sure you want to quit all applications and log out now?

If you do nothing, you will be logged out automatically in 57 seconds.

3 [✓] Reopen windows when logging back in

Cancel   Log Out **4**

Shut Down Your iMac

1 Click 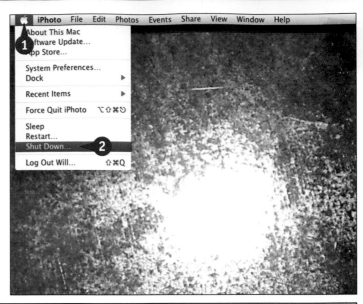.

The Apple menu opens.

2 Click **Shut Down**.

The iMac shows a dialog asking if you want to shut down.

3 Make sure **Reopen windows when logging back in** is selected (☑) if you want to resume your applications and documents.

4 Click **Shut Down**.

Note: Instead of clicking Shut Down, you can wait for one minute. After this, the iMac shuts down automatically. To shut down quickly, bypassing the dialog, click 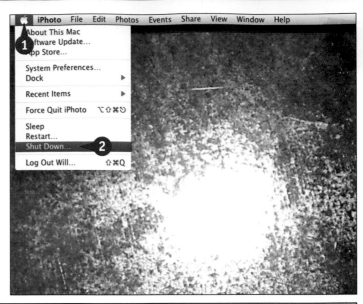, press and hold `Option`, and click **Shut Down**.

The screen goes blank, and the iMac switches itself off.

Are you sure you want to shut down your computer now?

If you do nothing, the computer will shut down automatically in 55 seconds.

3 ☑ Reopen windows when logging back in

Cancel | Shut Down **4**

TIPS

Do I need to save my documents before logging out?
If the applications you are using are designed to use Mac OS X's automatic-saving features, your iMac automatically saves any unsaved changes to your documents before logging you out. But because not all applications use these features, it is better to save all your documents yourself before you log out. Otherwise, an application may display a dialog prompting you to save unsaved changes, and this dialog may prevent logout or shutdown.

Must I log out, or can I stay logged in?
If you are the only user of your iMac, and you keep the iMac somewhere other people cannot get to it, you can stay logged in if you want. But if your iMac has other users, or other people can reach it, log out to ensure that other people cannot access or delete your files.

CHAPTER 2

Sharing Your iMac with Other People

Mac OS X makes it easy to share your iMac with other people. Each user needs a separate user account for documents, email, and settings.

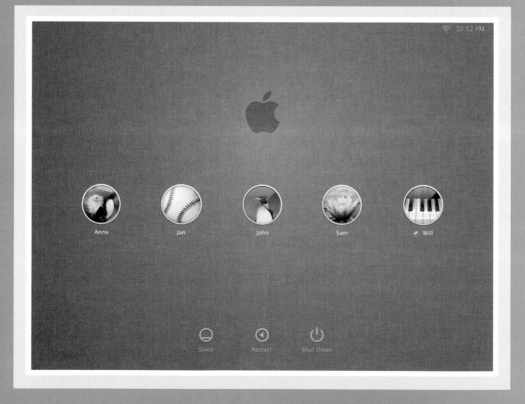

Create a User Account for Another Person

The first time you run your iMac, you set up an Administrator account for yourself, which means you can configure Mac OS X. You can then create a separate user account for each other person who uses your iMac regularly. You can also create a non-Administrator level account for yourself if you so choose. This is a good security measure, but many people find it inconvenient.

Creating separate accounts allows users to have their own folders for documents and use the settings they prefer.

Create a User Account for Another Person

1 Click the **Apple** menu (🍎).

2 Click **System Preferences**.

The System Preferences window opens.

3 In the System category, click **Users & Groups**.

Note: You must use Administrator credentials to create another account. The easiest way to do this is to use an Administrator account; you can also provide an Administrator name and password from another account. To check whether you are an Administrator, see if your account shows Admin in the Users & Groups pane.

The Users & Groups pane opens.

4 Click the lock icon (🔒) to unlock System Preferences.

System Preferences displays a dialog asking you to type your password or an Administrator name and password.

5 Type your password in the Password field.

6 Click **Unlock**.

The lock opens.

7 Click **Add** (⊞).

The New Account dialog opens.

8 In the New Account pop-up menu, choose **Standard**.

9 Type the username, such as John or John Brown, and short name, such as john.

10 Type the user's initial password in the Password field and the Verify field.

11 Click **Create User**.

The New Account dialog closes, and the new account appears in the Other Users list.

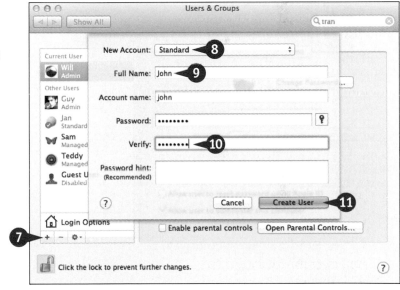

TIP

How do I choose a good password for a user?

For security, each user should choose his password after logging in. Only the user should know his password. Even you, the Administrator, should not know other users' passwords. When you create a new user account, set a password to secure the account against hackers. Tell the user the password, and ask the user to create a new password the first time he uses the account. To change the password, the user clicks the **Change Password** button in the Users & Groups window. The Change Password dialog opens, and the user types the new password. The user can click 🔑 in the Change Password dialog to open the Password Assistant, which produces hard-to-break passwords.

Configure Your iMac So Several People Can Use It

When you have created an account for each user, turn on Fast User Switching so that multiple people can use the iMac without logging out.

With Fast User Switching, your applications remain open in the background when another user logs in. When you switch back to your user session, you can resume where you left off.

Configure Your iMac So Several People Can Use It

1 In System Preferences, click **Users & Groups**.

The Users & Groups pane opens.

Note: To open the System Preferences window, see the task "Create a User Account for Another Person," earlier in this chapter.

2 Click the lock icon (🔒) to unlock System Preferences.

System Preferences displays a dialog asking you to type your password or provide Administrator credentials.

Type your password or credentials, and then click **Unlock**.

3 Click **Login Options**.

The login options pane appears.

④ In the Automatic Login pop-up menu, choose **Off**.

⑤ Click **Show fast user switching menu as** (☐ changes to ☑).

⑥ Click ⬍ .

The Show Fast User Switching Menu As pop-up menu opens.

⑦ Click **Full Name** if you want the Fast User Switching menu to show usernames. Click **Short Name** to use short names, or click **Icon** to use icons.

Note: Using full names for the Fast User Switching menu is clearest but takes the most space on the menu bar. Short names are more compact. Icons are more compact, but can be visually confusing.

Fast User Switching is now enabled.

TIPS

Why should I not use automatic login with Fast User Switching?
Automatic login lets anyone who can turn on your iMac use the account set for automatic login. So when you turn on Fast User Switching, choose **Off** in the Automatic Login pop-up menu to ensure that whoever logs in to the iMac uses his own user account.

Are there any disadvantages to Fast User Switching?
Fast User Switching saves time and effort when several users need to share your iMac, but it can make your iMac run more slowly because applications are open in both the current user's session and any sessions running in the background. If your iMac runs too slowly, try turning Fast User Switching off and see if performance improves. You may also be able to improve performance with Fast User Switching on by adding RAM to your iMac.

Share Your iMac with Fast User Switching

When Fast User Switching is turned on, two or more users can use your iMac without logging out. Only one user can use the keyboard, mouse, and screen at a time, but each other user's computing session keeps running in the background, with all of her applications still open.

Mac OS X automatically stops multimedia playing when you switch users. For example, if another user is still playing music in iTunes when you switch the iMac to your user account, iTunes stops playing the music.

Share Your iMac with Fast User Switching

Log In to the iMac

1 On the login screen, click your username.

Mac OS X prompts you for your password.

2 Type your password.

3 Click ⊙.

Your desktop appears.

Display the Login Window

1 When you are ready to stop using the iMac for now, but do not want to log out, click your username or icon on the menu bar.

2 Click **Login Window**.

● The login window appears. Your username shows a check mark icon (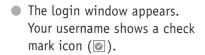).

Any of the iMac's users can log on by clicking his username.

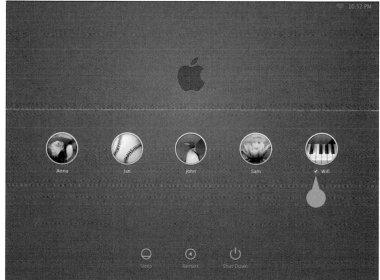

TIPS

What is the quickest way to switch to my user account?

If another user has left her user session displayed, you do not need to go to the login window. Click the current user's username or icon on the menu bar. Then click your username on the menu that appears.

How can I log another user out so that I can shut down?

From the Fast User Switching menu, you can see what other users are logged in to the iMac. If possible, ask each user to log in and then log out before you shut down. If you must shut down the iMac, and you are an Administrator, click **Shut Down** in the login window. Mac OS X warns you that there are logged-in users. Type your name and password, and click **Shut Down**.

Turn On Parental Controls for an Account

Parental controls are settings you, as an Administrator, can apply to limit the actions that a user can take on the iMac. For example, you can prevent the user from running certain applications, allow her only to email and chat with specific people, or prevent her from using the iMac at night.

Turn On Parental Controls for an Account

1 Click .

The Apple menu opens.

2 Click **System Preferences**.

The System Preferences window opens.

3 Click **Users & Groups**.

The Users & Groups preferences pane opens.

4 Click the lock icon ().

The Authenticate dialog opens.

5 Type your password or an Administrator's credentials.

6 Click **Unlock** or press **Return**.

● The Authenticate dialog closes, and 🔒 changes to 🔓.

7 Click the account to which you want to apply parental controls.

The settings for the account appear.

8 Click **Enable parental controls** (☐ changes to ☑).

You can now choose parental control settings as described in the following four tasks.

Note: When you select the Enable Parental Controls check box, the user type under the username in the list of users changes from Standard to Managed.

TIP

Can I apply parental controls to any user account?
You can apply parental controls to any Standard user account. To apply parental controls to an account, you must use an Administrator account or provide Administrator credentials. You cannot apply parental controls to an Administrator account, but you can downgrade an Administrator account to a Standard account, and then apply the controls to the Standard account. Your iMac must always have one Administrator account to manage the other user accounts.

Choose What Applications a User Can Run

An effective way of limiting the actions users can take is by letting them use only some of the applications and utilities installed on the iMac. Parental controls let you choose exactly which applications the user can run. For example, if you do not allow the user to play certain games, you can make those games unavailable.

For users who find the Mac OS X interface too complex, you can turn on the Simple Finder feature. Simple Finder presents a stripped-down version of the interface that makes the most important items easier to find and use.

Choose What Applications a User Can Run

1 In the Users & Groups preferences pane, click the user account you want to change.

Note: To open the System Preferences window and unlock the settings, see the task "Create a User Account for Another Person," earlier in this chapter.

2 Click **Open Parental Controls**.

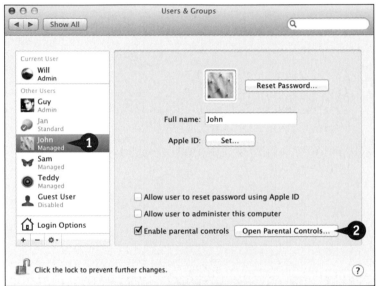

The Parental Controls preferences pane opens.

3 Click **Apps**.

The Apps pane appears.

4 Click **Use Simple Finder** (☐ changes to ☑) if you want to make the user use Simple Finder. See the tip for more information on Simple Finder.

5 Click **Limit Applications** (☐ changes to ☑).

6 Click the **Allow App Store Apps** ↕ and then click the level of apps to allow: **Don't allow, up to 4+, up to 9+, up to 12+, up to 17+,** or **All**.

7 In the Allowed Apps list, click ► next to a category of applications (► changes to ▼).

The list of applications appears.

8 Click ☑ for each application you want to prevent the user from using (☑ changes to ☐).

Note: To prevent the user from using an entire category of applications, click ☑ next to the category (☑ changes to ☐).

Note: If you plan to restrict the web content the user can access and the people she can contact, do not allow the user to use any browser other than Safari or any chat application other than iChat.

9 Click **Allow User to Modify the Dock** (☑ changes to ☐) if you want to prevent the user from rearranging the Dock icons, adding icons, or removing icons.

10 Set further parental controls as described in the next task.

TIP

What is Simple Finder and when should I make a user use it?

Simple Finder is a simplified version of the Finder designed for use by younger, older, or less-experienced computer users. Simple Finder provides a more streamlined look with fewer choices, making it easier to find applications and folders, and prevents the user from changing important settings. Some users benefit from using Simple Finder in the long term, whereas for others it is a step toward using the regular Finder after more computing experience.

Prevent a User from Seeing Inappropriate Content on the Web

The web includes sites containing almost every known depravity, so it is a good idea to use the web options in Parental Controls to restrict the websites that the user can access using Safari, the web browser that comes with Mac OS X.

You can set the web options to either try to limit access to adult websites or to allow the user to access only a list of websites that you approve. This limiting of access works only for Safari, not for any other browsers you may install on your iMac, so you should make Safari the only web browser the user is allowed to run, as described in the previous task.

Prevent a User from Seeing Inappropriate Content on the Web

1 In the Users & Groups preferences pane, click the user account you want to change.

Note: To open the System Preferences window and unlock the settings, see the task "Create a User Account for Another Person," earlier in this chapter.

2 Click **Open Parental Controls**.

The Parental Controls preferences pane opens.

3 Click **Web**.

The Web pane appears.

4 In the Website Restrictions area, click **Try to limit access to adult websites automatically** if you want to prevent access to adult websites (○ changes to ◉). For more control, go to step **9**.

5 Click **Customize**.

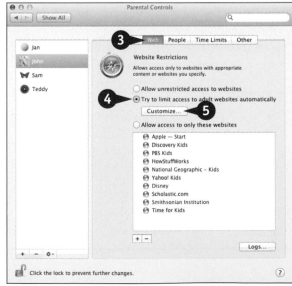

40

6 In the Customize dialog, click **Add** (⊞).

7 Type the web address to disallow and press Return.

Note: You can also add permitted addresses to the Always Allow These Websites field.

8 Click **OK**.

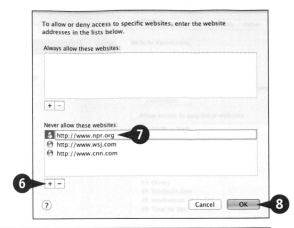

9 To allow the user to visit only certain websites, click **Allow access to only these websites** (○ changes to ◉).

● A list of inoffensive websites appears.

10 To add a site, click **Add** (⊞) and then click **Add Bookmark**.

11 In the dialog that appears, type a descriptive name for the website.

12 Type the website's address.

13 Click **OK**, and the site appears in the list.

14 To remove a site, click it and then click **Remove** (⊟).

Note: When you permit a user to visit only certain websites, those sites appear on the Bookmarks bar in Safari.

TIP

How effective is the blocking of adult websites?

The blocking of adult websites is only partly effective. Mac OS X can block sites that identify themselves as adult sites using standard rating criteria, but many adult sites either do not use ratings or do not rate their content accurately. Because of this, do not rely on Mac OS X to block all adult material. It is much more effective to choose **Allow access to only these websites** and provide a list of acceptable sites. You can add to the list by vetting and approving extra sites when the user needs to access them.

Control Whom a User Can Email and Chat With

When you have applied parental controls to an account, you can control the people with whom the user can exchange email messages and chat. This capability is useful for protecting children and other vulnerable individuals from unsuitable email messages and chat.

Control Whom a User Can Email and Chat With

1 In the Users & Groups preferences pane, click the user account you want to change.

2 Click **Open Parental Controls**.

Note: To open the System Preferences window and unlock the settings, see the task "Create a User Account for Another Person," earlier in this chapter.

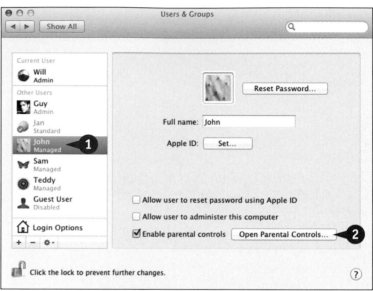

The Parental Controls preferences pane opens.

3 Click **People**.

The People pane appears.

4 Click **Limit Mail** (☐ changes to ☑) if you want to allow email to only the addresses you specify.

5 Click **Send permission requests to** if you want messages to nonallowed addresses to trigger a message to you.

6 Type your email address for the permission requests.

7 Click **Limit iChat** (☐ changes to ☑) if you want to allow chat only with addresses you specify.

8 Click **Add** (➕).

A dialog for adding allowed addresses appears.

9 If the address does not appear in your address book, add it like this:

● Type the first name.

● Type the last name.

● Type the address.

● Click ↕ and click the address type: **Email**, **AIM**, or **Jabber**.

Note: Choose **Jabber** for GoogleTalk.

● If you need to add another address, click **Add** (⊞) and repeat the steps.

● Click **Add person to my address book** if you want to add the person.

10 If the address appears in your address book, click ▾.

The dialog expands to show the addresses in your address book.

11 Click the address.

12 Click **Add**.

The name appears in the Allowed Contacts list.

Note: To remove a name from the Allowed Contacts list, click the name and then click **Remove** (⊟).

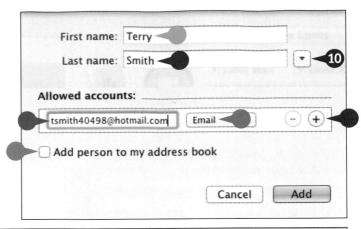

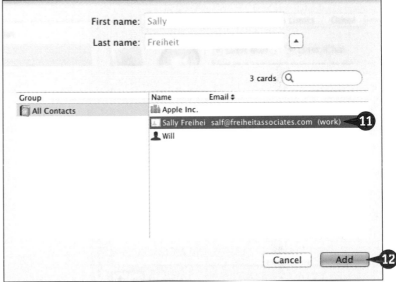

TIP

How effective is the blocking of email and chat?

Mac OS X's blocking of email and chat requests is highly effective for Mail and iChat. As long as you create a suitable list of allowed email and chat addresses, you can give the user solid protection against unwanted messages and chat requests. Mac OS X does not block other email and instant-messaging applications, however, so you must make sure that none are available for the user to circumvent the blocking.

Set Time Limits for Logging On

After turning on parental controls, you can limit the times during which a controlled user can log on to the iMac. You can set the permitted number of hours for weekdays and weekends and specify night hours when the user may not use the iMac.

You can set different limits for the nights before school days — Sunday through Thursday — than for Friday and Saturday nights.

Set Time Limits for Logging On

1 In the Users & Groups preferences pane, click the user account you want to change.

Note: To open the System Preferences window and unlock the settings, see the task "Create a User Account for Another Person," earlier in this chapter.

2 Click **Open Parental Controls**.

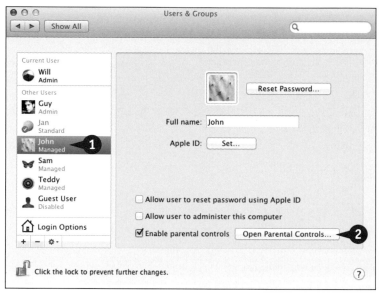

The Parental Controls preferences pane opens.

3 Click **Time Limits**.

The Time Limits pane appears.

4 To set a weekday time limit, click **Limit computer use to** in Weekday Time Limits (☐ changes to ☑).

5 Click and drag the slider to set the limit.

Note: You can set a weekday time limit of between 30 minutes and 8 hours a day.

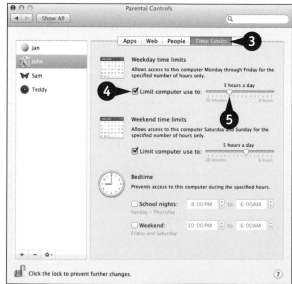

6 To set a weekend time limit, click **Limit computer use to** in Weekend Time Limits (☐ changes to ☑).

7 Click and drag the slider to set the limit.

Note: You can set a weekend time limit of between 30 minutes and 8 hours a day.

8 To set a block of time when the iMac is not available on school nights, click **School nights** (☐ changes to ☑).

Note: Parental controls go strictly by the days of the week and make no exceptions for holidays and vacations.

9 Set the start and end time for school nights.

10 To set a block of time when the iMac is not available on weekend nights, click **Weekend** (☐ changes to ☑).

11 Set the start and end time for weekend nights.

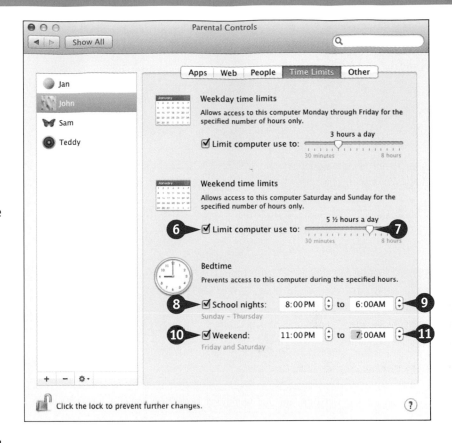

TIPS

What happens if a controlled user tries to log in outside the allowed times?

If a controlled user tries to log on during blocked night hours, Mac OS X displays the Computer Time Expired dialog. An Administrator can allow the user an extra period of time, from 15 minutes to the rest of the day, by typing the Administrator username and password.

What happens if a controlled user is still logged on when the time limit arrives?

Mac OS X displays the Your Computer Time Is Almost Up dialog to warn the user that he or she needs to log out. If the user does not have an Administrator add time, log out, or switch the user by the deadline, Mac OS X switches users if Fast User Switching is turned on, or logs the user out if it is not.

Apply Other Restrictions to What a User Can Do

After turning on parental controls, you can apply four other types of restrictions to the user. First, you can hide profanity in the Dictionary application, which can help prevent the user accessing inappropriate content. Second, you can prevent the user from changing printer settings, adding extra printers, or removing your existing printers. Third, you can prevent the user from burning CDs and DVDs in the Finder. This can help prevent the user from copying content to disc when you do not want him to copy it. And fourth, you can prevent the user from changing his password in the Users & Groups preferences pane.

Apply Other Restrictions to What a User Can Do

1 In the Users & Groups preferences pane, click the user account you want to change.

Note: To open the System Preferences window and unlock the settings, see the task "Create a User Account for Another Person," earlier in this chapter.

2 Click **Open Parental Controls**.

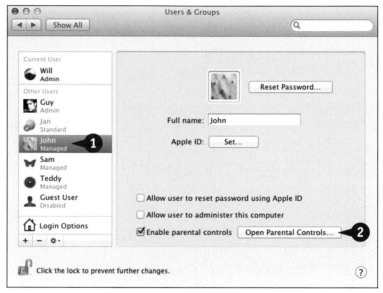

The Parental Controls preferences pane opens.

3 Click **Other**.

The Other pane appears.

4 If you want to suppress offensive words in the dictionary, click **Hide profanity in Dictionary** (☐ changes to ☑).

5 Click **Limit printer administration** (☐ changes to ☑) if you do not want to let the user administer printers.

Note: Printers can be awkward to set up, so it is a good idea to prevent Managed users from reconfiguring or removing them.

6 Click **Limit CD and DVD burning** (☐ changes to ☑) if the user may not burn discs from the Finder.

Note: Limiting the user's CD and DVD burning affects only the Finder. The user can still burn discs from iTunes, iPhoto, iDVD, and other applications. If necessary, you can prevent the user from running such applications, as discussed earlier in this chapter.

7 Click **Disable changing the password** (☐ changes to ☑) to prevent the user from changing her password.

Why should I prevent a Managed user from changing her password?

Normally, it is a good idea for each user to set her own password, and for only that user to know that password. This secrecy helps prevent anybody else from accessing the user's account without the user's consent.

But when you are dealing with a Managed user who tends to forget passwords, you will find it helpful to retain control of the user's password. By selecting the **Disable changing the password** check box (☐ changes to ☑), you can avoid the problem of the user changing her password, forgetting about the change, and then needing you to reset the password from an Administrator account.

See What a Controlled User Has Done on the iMac

Your iMac tracks the actions of each user to whose account you have applied parental controls. You can review the logs of each user's actions to decide whether the parental controls are effective, whether you need to adjust them, or whether it is time to remove them completely.

See What a Controlled User Has Done on the iMac

1 In the Users & Groups preferences pane, click the user account you want to change.

Note: To open the System Preferences window and unlock the settings, see the task "Create a User Account for Another Person," earlier in this chapter.

2 Click **Open Parental Controls**.

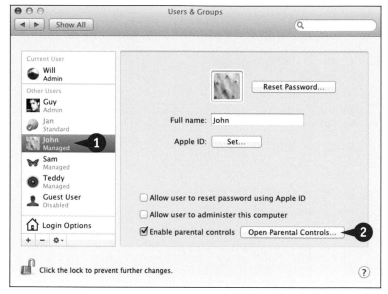

The Parental Controls preferences pane opens.

3 Click **Logs**.

④ In the Logs dialog, click **Websites Blocked**.

The list of blocked websites appears.

⑤ Click the **Show activity for** ✦ and choose the length of time.

⑥ Click the **Group by** ✦ and choose **Website** or **Date**.

⑦ Click ▣ to expand a category.

⑧ Click a site.

● Click **Allow** if you want to add the site to the Allowed list.

● Click **Open** to open the site in Safari.

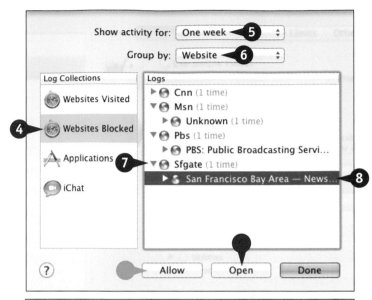

⑨ Click **Applications**.

The list of applications the user has run appears.

⑩ Click the **Show activity for** ✦ and choose the length of time.

⑪ Click the **Group by** ✦ and choose **Application** or **Date**.

⑫ Click ▣ to see the times the user used the application.

⑬ Click **Restrict** to restrict an application.

⑭ When you finish reviewing the logs, click **Done**.

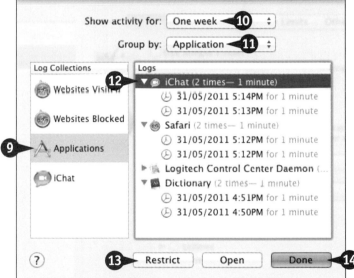

TIP

How do I use the iChat log collection?
Click **iChat** in the Log Collections pane, and then use the **Show activity** ✦ and the **Group by** ✦ to choose the activity period and how it appears. Double-click a contact in the log to view the contact's details. To view the transcript of a text chat, click the chat's date and time, and then click **Open**. To prevent the user from communicating with the contact, click the contact's name, and then click **Restrict**.

CHAPTER 3

Running Applications

Mac OS X includes many applications, such as the TextEdit word processor, the Preview viewer for PDF files and images, and the iTunes player for music and videos. You can use these applications to create and open documents, but you will very likely need to install other applications as well. Whichever applications you run, you can switch among them quickly and easily in several ways.

Open and Close an Application

To use an application, you must first open it. You can open an application from the Dock if the application's icon appears there, or from either Launchpad or the Applications folder if it does not. When you have finished using an application, you close it by giving a Quit command.

The Dock is the quickest way to launch applications you use frequently. Launchpad is a quick and easy way to see all the applications installed on your iMac. Because Launchpad shows all the apps, you will seldom need to use the Applications folder to launch an application.

Open and Close an Application

Open an Application from the Dock

1 Click the application's icon on the Dock.

Note: If you do not recognize an application's icon, position the mouse pointer over it to display the application's name.

● The application opens.

Open an Application from Launchpad

1 Click **Launchpad** ( ) on the Dock.

The Launchpad screen appears.

● To scroll to another screen, click and drag left or right, or press ⬅ or ➡. You can also click one of the dots above the center of the Dock to move to another screen.

2 Click the application you want to launch.

The application opens.

Open an Application from the Applications Folder

1 Click **Finder** ( ) on the Dock.

A Finder window opens.

2 Click **Applications** in the left column.

An icon appears for each application.

3 Double-click the application you want to run.

The application opens.

Close an Application

1 Click the application's menu, the menu with the application's name — for example, **Address Book**.

The menu appears.

2 Click the Quit command. This command has the application's name — for example, **Quit Address Book**.

Note: You can also quit the active application by holding down ⌘ and pressing Q.

TIPS

How do I add an application to the Dock?
You can click an application in Launchpad or the Applications folder and drag it to the Dock. Drop the application to the left of the divider line between applications and files. Alternatively, open the application, Control +click or right-click its Dock icon, highlight **Options** on the shortcut menu, and click **Keep in Dock**.

What happens if a document in the application I quit contains unsaved changes?
This depends on the application. Some applications automatically save your changes when you quit the application. Other applications display a dialog asking if you want to save the changes. Click **Save** to save the changes or **Don't Save** to discard the changes.

Install an Application from the App Store

Your iMac comes with many useful applications already installed, such as Safari for browsing the web, Mail for reading and sending email, and iTunes for enjoying music and video.

To get your work or play done, you will most likely need to install other applications on your iMac. You can install applications in three ways: by downloading them from Apple's App Store, as described in this task; by downloading them from other websites and then installing them, as described in the next task; or installing them from a CD or DVD, also described in the next task.

Install an Application from the App Store

1 Click **App Store** ( ) on the Dock.

● The App Store window opens.

The Featured screen shows a section of New & Noteworthy apps, a What's Hot section, and a Staff Picks section.

2 Click **Top Charts**.

The Top Charts screen appears, showing a Top Paid section, a Top Free section, and a Top Grossing section.

● You can also click Categories to browse applications by categories, such as Business and Entertainment.

3 Click the application you want to view.

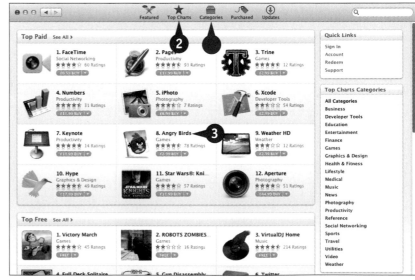

The application's screen appears.

④ Click **Buy**.

The Sign in to download from the App Store dialog appears.

⑤ Type your Apple ID.

Note: If you do not have an Apple ID, click **Create Apple ID** and follow the steps for creating one.

⑥ Type your password.

⑦ Click **Sign In**.

Note: If a dialog opens confirming the purchase, click **Buy**.

The download begins.

Launchpad appears and shows a Downloading indicator for the application.

⑧ Click the application's icon in Launchpad.

The application opens.

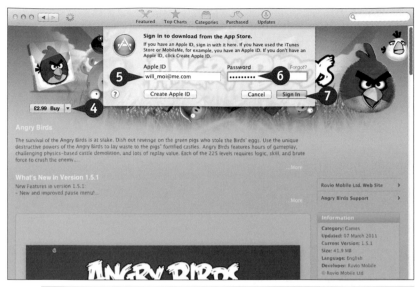

How do I update applications downloaded from the App Store?
Click **App Store** (⊙) on the Dock to open the App Store, and then click **Updates** on the title bar of the window to display the Updates screen. If any updates appear, click to download and install them.

Install an Application from a Disc or the Internet

Although many applications are available on Apple's App Store, others are not. Instead, you buy such applications either as a physical package containing one or more CDs or DVDs or as a file that you download from the Internet.

Whether you buy an application on a CD or DVD or as a downloaded file, you can install it as described in this task.

Install an Application from a Disc or the Internet

Install an Application

1 Open the disc or file that contains the application.

If the application is on a CD or DVD, insert the disc in your iMac's optical drive.

If the application is in a file you have downloaded, double-click the file.

A Finder window opens showing the contents of the disc or file.

2 If there is a file containing installation instructions, open it, read the instructions, and then follow them. Otherwise, double-click the Installer icon.

A dialog opens prompting you to type your password.

Note: To install most applications, you must have an Administrator account or provide an Administrator's name and password.

3 Type your password.

4 Click **Install Software**.

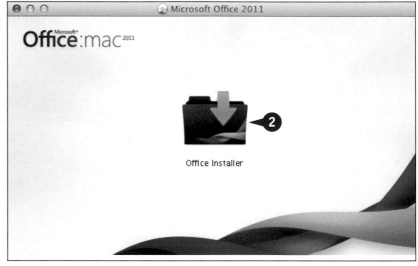

The installation continues. When it completes, Installer displays a screen telling you that the installation succeeded.

5 Click **Close**.

Installer closes.

Run the Application You Installed

6 If Installer has added an icon for the application to the Dock, click that icon to run the application.

7 If the application has no Dock icon, launch the application like this:

- Click **Launchpad** (⊘) on the Dock.

- Click the dot to display another Launchpad screen if necessary.

- Click the application's icon.

  The application opens.

Note: Installer places icons for some applications on the Dock. You can click the application's icon to open the application.

TIP

How do I install an application that has no installer or installation instructions?

If the application does not have an installer or specific installation instructions, such as those shown here, click the icon in the Finder window for the application's disc or file, and then drag the application's icon to the Applications folder in the sidebar.

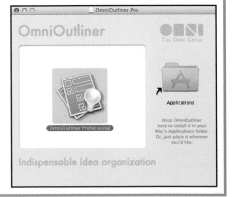

Run an Application Full Screen

Whative you need to concentrate on a single application, you can run it full screen instead of having it in a window competing with the Mac OS X user interface and other applications for your attention.

You can instantly switch the active application to full-screen display. When you need to use another application, you can switch to that app full screen as well — and then switch back to the previous application. When you finish using full-screen display, you can quickly switch back to displaying the application in a window.

Run an Application Full Screen

Switch the Active Application to Full Screen

1 Click **Full Screen** (🖼).

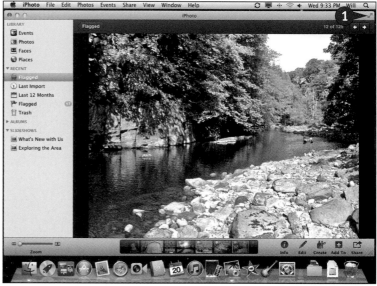

The application expands to take up the full screen.

Switch to Another Application

1 Swipe left or right with three fingers on the Magic Mouse or Magic Trackpad.

Note: You can also switch applications by using the techniques explained in the next two tasks.

The next application or previous application appears.

2 Swipe in the opposite direction.

The application you were using before you switched appears.

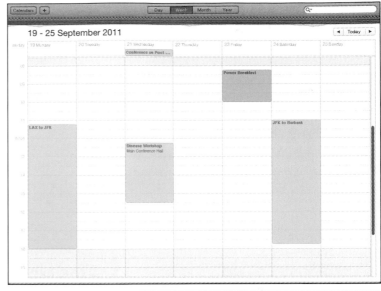

Return from Full-Screen Display to a Window

1 Move the mouse pointer to the top of the screen.

The menu bar appears.

2 Click **View**.

The View menu opens.

3 Click **Exit Full Screen**.

The application appears in a window again.

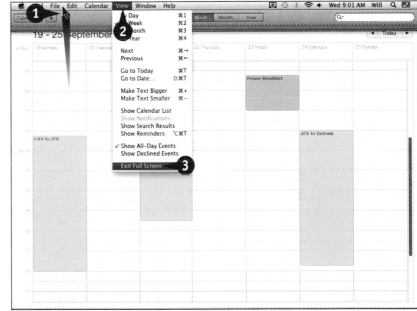

How do I display the Dock in full-screen view?

Move the mouse pointer to the bottom of the screen, and the Dock slides into view. If you have positioned the Dock at the left side or right side of the display, move the mouse pointer to that side to display the Dock.

Can I exit full-screen display by using the keyboard?

Yes. Press Esc twice to return from full-screen view to windowed view.

Switch Quickly to Other Applications

When you work with several applications at the same time, it is often useful to switch quickly from one application to another. In Mac OS X, you can switch quickly by using either the mouse or the keyboard.

You can also switch applications in full-screen view as described in the previous task or by using Mission Control, as explained in the next task.

Switch Quickly to Other Applications

Switch Applications Using the Mouse

1 If you can see a window for the application you want to switch to, click anywhere in that window.

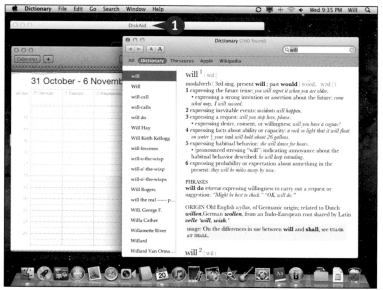

2 If you cannot see a window you want to switch to, click the application's icon on the Dock.

All the windows for that application appear in front of the other applications' windows.

3 Click **Window** on the menu bar.

The Window menu opens.

4 Click the window you want to bring to the front.

Switch among Applications Using the Keyboard

1 Press and hold ⌘ and press Tab.

Application Switcher opens, showing an icon for each open application.

2 Still holding down ⌘, press Tab one or more times to move the highlight to the application you want.

Note: Press and hold ⌘+Shift and press Tab to move backward through the applications.

3 When you reach the application you want, release ⌘.

Note: To return to the application that was active before you opened Application Switcher, press Esc or . while holding down ⌘. You can also keep pressing Tab until the application is selected again in Application Switcher.

Application Switcher closes, and the selected application comes to the front.

4 If necessary, switch to a different window in the application as described on the previous page.

TIPS

Are there other ways of switching among applications?

You can switch among applications by using the keyboard and the mouse together. Press and hold ⌘, press Tab once to open Application Switcher, and then click the application you want to bring to the front.

Can I do anything else with Application Switcher apart from switch to an application?

You can also hide an application or quit an application from Application Switcher. Press and hold ⌘, press Tab to open Application Switcher, and then select the application you want to affect. Press H to hide the application. Press Q to quit the application.

Switch Applications Using Mission Control

Another way of switching among windows is by using the Mission Control feature, which shrinks down open windows so that you can see all those you need. You can display all open windows in all applications or just the windows in a particular application. Mission Control also shows different desktop spaces, enabling you to switch among desktop spaces or move an application window from one desktop space to another.

Switch Applications Using Mission Control

See All Your Open Applications and Windows

① After opening various application windows, click **Mission Control** (▣) on the Dock or press **F3** to launch Mission Control and display all applications and windows.

Note: On some iMacs, you press **F9** to launch Mission Control.

Mac OS X shrinks and repositions each application and window so that you can see all applications and windows. Desktop spaces appear at the top. The desktop background darkens to make the windows more visible.

Note: To preview a window in an application, move the mouse pointer over the window so that a blue outline appears around it. Then press **Spacebar** to preview the window. Press **Spacebar** again to close the preview.

Note: To add a new desktop space, move the mouse pointer to the upper-right corner of Mission Control and click the + sign that appears.

② Click the window you want to use.

Mac OS X restores the windows to normal size and displays the window you clicked at the front.

You can now work with the window you clicked.

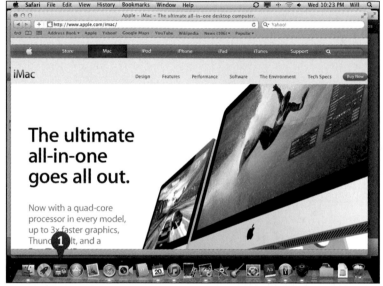

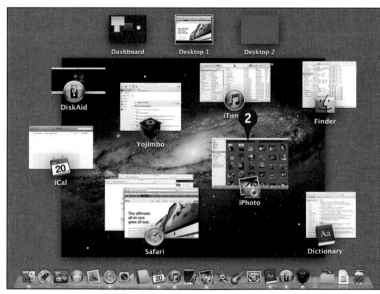

See All the Windows in the Active Application

1 Activate the application whose windows you want to see. For example, click the application's Dock icon, or click a window from that application.

2 Control +click **Mission Control** (▦) on the Dock and click **Show Application Windows**, or press Control + F3 .

Note: On some iMacs, you press F10 to display the windows of the active application.

Mac OS X tiles the windows of the application you chose so that you can see them all, and hides all other applications' windows.

3 Click the window you want to see.

Mac OS X restores all the windows from all the applications, placing the window you clicked at the front.

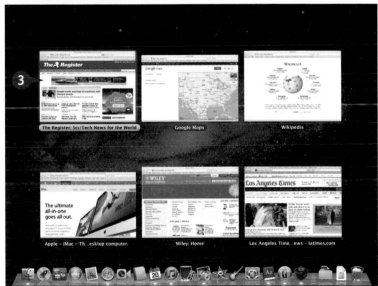

TIPS

Does Mission Control have any other tricks?

After pressing Control + F3 to show all windows of the current application, you can press Tab to show all windows of the next application. Press Shift + Tab to show all windows of the previous application. You can Control +click or right-click **Mission Control** (▦) on the Dock and click **Show Desktop**, or press ⌘ + F3 , to move all open windows to the sides of the desktop to reveal the desktop; on some keyboards, you press F11 . Press ⌘ + F3 or F11 when you want to see the windows again.

Is there any other way to launch Mission Control?

Yes. You can set up a hot corner on the screen for Mission Control. You then move the mouse pointer to that corner to launch Mission Control. See Chapter 12 for instructions.

Create and Save a Document

After opening an application, you can create a document and work with it. Mac OS X stores the document temporarily in your iMac's memory as you work. To keep the document permanently, save the document to your iMac's hard drive.

This example uses the TextEdit word processor that comes with Mac OS X. TextEdit automatically saves changes to your documents in case you forget, but it is best to save each document manually, assigning a name of your choice and selecting the folder in which to store the document.

Create and Save a Document

Create a Document

1 With the application open, click **File**.

The File menu opens.

2 Click **New**.

Note: Some applications display a New dialog to let you choose among different types of documents. Click the type you want, and then click **OK**.

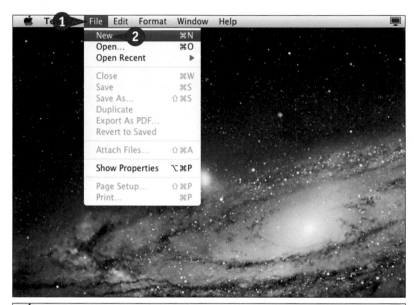

A new document opens.

3 Start working in the document. For example, start typing text in a TextEdit document.

Save a Document

1 Click **File**.

The File menu opens.

Note: You can also save a document by pressing ⌘+S. This shortcut is quick and convenient when you are working with the keyboard.

2 Click **Save**.

The Save As dialog appears.

Note: If the Save As dialog appears at a smaller size than shown here, click 🔽 to expand it.

3 In the Save As field, type the name you want to give the document.

4 If you want to change the folder, click the **Where** ⬍ and choose the folder.

5 Click **Save**.

The application saves the document.

TIP

When and how often should I save a document?

To avoid losing data, save each document as soon as you create it. After you have chosen the document's folder and given it a name, you can save it in moments by pressing ⌘+S or choosing **File** and then **Save**. In case your iMac has software or hardware problems, save every time you make changes to a document that you do not want to make again.

If the application you are using saves documents automatically, as TextEdit does, you will also have several automatically saved versions of the document from which to recover data if a problem occurs. But saving your documents manually is the best approach.

Close and Open a Document

After creating and saving a document, close it when you have finished working with it. You can then reopen the document whenever you need to work with it.

Some applications automatically reopen any document or documents that were open the last time you quit the application. With such an application, if you need to work with your last document, you do not need to open it manually.

Close and Open a Document

Close a Document

1 Click **File**.

The File menu opens.

2 Click **Close**.

Note: You can also press ⌘+W to close a document.

If you have named the document but it contains unsaved changes, what happens next depends on the application. Some apps, such as TextEdit, automatically save your changes. Other applications, such as TextWrangler, display a dialog asking if you want to save changes.

3 Click **Save** if you want to save the changes. Click **Don't Save** if you want to discard the changes.

The document closes.

Note: If you tell an application to quit, the application automatically closes each open document. If any document contains unsaved changes, the application either automatically saves the changes or displays a dialog asking if you want to save the changes.

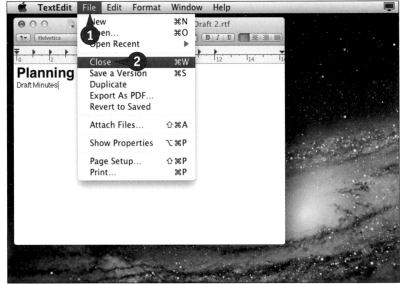

Open a Document

1 In the application you will use to view or edit the document, click **File**.

The File menu opens.

Note: You can also press ⌘+O to display the Open dialog.

2 Click **Open**.

The Open dialog appears.

3 Click the document.

● If the document is in a different folder, go to the Favorites list and click the folder that contains the document. For example, click **All My Files** to view all your files.

4 Click **Open**.

A window opens showing the document.

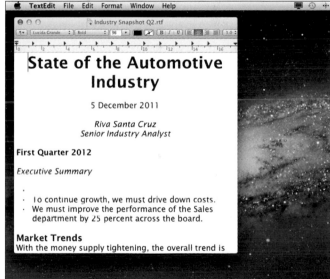

TIP

Are there other ways of opening documents?
If you have opened the document recently, choose **File** and then **Recent Files**, and then click the document. In a Finder window, double-click the document, or select it and press ⌘+O, to open the document in the default application. To use another application, Control+click or right-click a document in a Finder window, highlight **Open With**, and then click the application.

Edit a Document

Many types of documents are based on text — for example, word processing documents, text files, and emails. To edit such documents, you can use standard techniques of selecting, copying, moving, and deleting text.

Edit a Document

Select Text

1 Click at the beginning of the text you want to select, and then drag to the end.

Note: You can also select by clicking at the end of the text and dragging to the beginning. Sometimes this is easier.

2 When you have selected all the text you want, release the mouse button.

The application highlights the selected text, and you can then work with it.

Delete a Selection

1 Select the text you want to delete.

2 Press **Delete**.

The text disappears.

Note: To delete text without selecting it first, click after the last character of the text, and then press **Delete** until the text disappears.

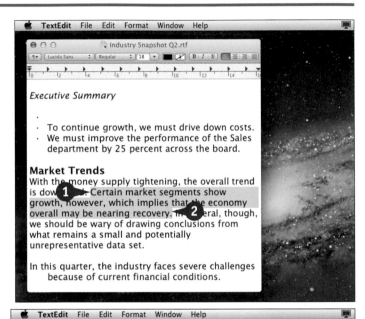

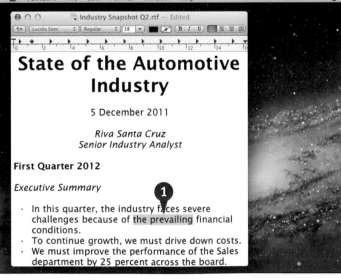

Copy or Move Text

1 Select the text you want to copy or move.

Note: You can also press ⌘+C to copy or ⌘+X to cut.

2 Control+click or right-click anywhere in the selection.

3 Click **Copy** if you want to copy the text. Click **Cut** if you want to move it.

Note: The Cut and Copy commands both place the text on the Mac OS X *clipboard*, an area of memory that can hold one item at a time. Cut also removes the text from the document.

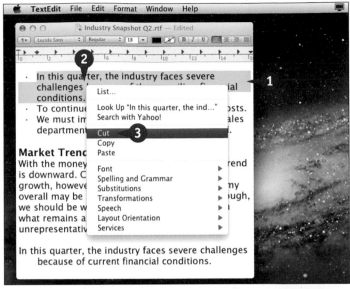

4 In the document, Control+click or right-click where you want to insert the text.

Note: You can also click to place the insertion point where you want it and press ⌘+V to paste where the insertion point is.

The shortcut menu opens.

5 Click **Paste**.

The application inserts the text where you clicked.

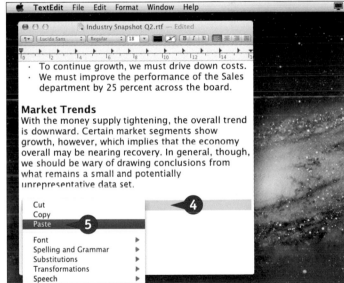

TIP

Is there a way to control scrolling when I click and drag to select text that continues off the screen?
When you need to select past the end of the text on the screen, it is usually easier to use a different method than clicking and dragging. Click to place the insertion point where you want to begin selecting. Scroll until you can see the end of the text you want to select. Press and hold Shift and click. The application selects from where you placed the insertion point to where you Shift+click.

Use Mac OS X's Help System

Mac OS X includes a built-in help system that you can use to solve problems that this book does not cover. You can launch the help system from the menu bar of the Finder. You can then either browse or search to find the information you need.

Each application has its own Help menu, which you can access from within the application. See the tips for details.

Use Mac OS X's Help System

1 Click anywhere on the desktop.

The Finder becomes active.

2 Click **Help**.

The Help menu opens.

3 Click **Help Center**.

The Help Center window opens and displays the Welcome screen.

4 Click the search box.

5 Type a question or some keywords.

6 Press Return.

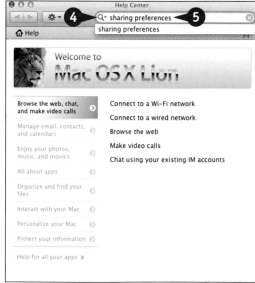

The Mac Help window shows a list of topics related to what you searched for.

⑦ Click the topic you want to view.

Help Center displays the detailed help for the topic.

● Click a link to open another topic, an application or utility, or a web page.

● Click **Home** (⌂) to return to the Help Center screen.

● Click **Back** (◄) to return to the previous screen you viewed.

⑧ When you have finished using Mac Help, click ⊗.

The Mac Help window closes.

TIPS

Can I print out a help topic for reference?

To print the current topic, click **Action** (✿▾), and then click **Print** on the pop-up menu. This menu also includes commands for making the text in the Help Center window larger or smaller and for searching for text in the current topic.

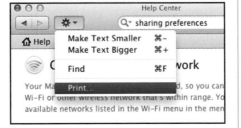

How do I get help for other applications?

Each application has its own Help menu. Activate the application, click **Help** to open the Help menu, and then click the help topic for the application or type your search terms and press Return.

CHAPTER 4

Managing Your Files and Folders

The Finder is Mac OS X's built-in tool for managing files, folders, and drives. This chapter shows you how to perform tasks in the Finder.

Understanding Where to Store Files on Your iMac

For each user account you set up, Mac OS X automatically creates a structure of folders for storing files. Your home base is the Home folder, which contains the Desktop, Documents, Downloads, Movies, Music, Pictures, Public, and Sites folders. The Finder automatically puts the most widely used folders in the Favorites category, giving you instant access to them.

You can create extra folders of your own as needed, but for most people the built-in folders are plenty to start with. To help you find your files, the Finder also includes a view called All My Files, which shows your files by their type or another attribute you choose.

Understanding Where to Store Files on Your iMac

View All Your Files

1 Click **Finder** (🙂) on the Dock.

A Finder window opens to your default folder or view.

Note: The default view in a standard installation of Mac OS X is the All My Files view. If Finder displays the All My Files view, skip step **2**.

2 Click **All My Files**.

The Finder window displays the All My Files view, which shows all your files.

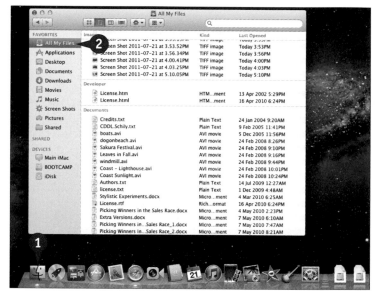

The Documents Folder

1 Click **Documents**.

The contents of the Documents folder appear.

The Finder switches to Column view. The next task explains views.

Note: The Documents folder is your storage place for word processing documents, spreadsheets, and similar files.

2 Click a file.

● A preview of its contents appears.

3 Click ◀.

The Finder window displays the previous view, the All My Files view.

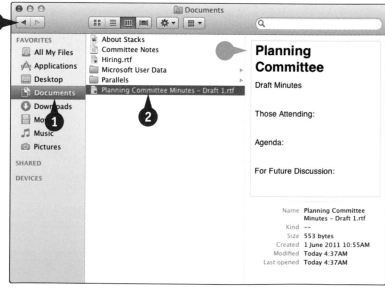

The Music Folder

1 Click **Music**.

The contents of the Music folder appear.

● The GarageBand folder appears if you have used GarageBand, the music-composition application.

● The iTunes folder is where iTunes stores songs you buy or import from CD.

2 Click **iTunes**.

The contents of the iTunes folder appear.

The Movies and Pictures Folders

1 Click **Movies**.

The contents of the Movies folder appear.

● The iMovie Projects folder is where iMovie stores your movie projects.

Note: If you have not yet used iMovie, the iMovie Projects folder does not appear in the Movies folder.

2 Click **Pictures**.

The Pictures folder appears. It contains your iPhoto Library and an alias to your iChat Icons folder.

3 Click 🔘.

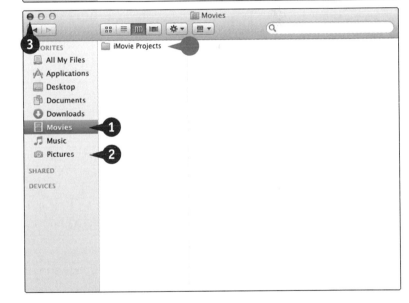

TIPS

What is the Downloads folder?
The Downloads folder is the folder in which Mac OS X and the Safari web browser automatically store files you download from the Internet. You can choose to store files you download using Safari in a different folder if you prefer.

What is the Desktop folder in the Favorites section of the sidebar?
Your Desktop folder shows you the files and folders on your iMac's desktop. The desktop can be a handy place to store files and folders, but if you store many of them, you may find viewing them in a Finder window easier than viewing them on the desktop itself.

Using the Finder's Four Views Effectively

To help you find and identify your files, the Finder has four different views. Icon view shows each file or folder as a graphical icon, whereas List view shows folders as a collapsible hierarchy. Column view lets you navigate quickly through folders and see where each item is located, and Cover Flow view is great for identifying files visually by looking at their contents.

Using the Finder's Four Views Effectively

Icon View

1 Click **Finder** ( ) on the Dock.

A Finder window opens showing your default folder or view.

2 Click **Documents**.

The Documents folder appears.

3 Click **Icons** ( ) on the toolbar.

The files and folders appear in Icon view.

List View

1 In the Finder window, click **List** ( ) on the toolbar.

The files and folders appear in List view.

2 Click (changes to) next to a folder.

The folder's contents appear.

Note: In List view, you can expand the contents of multiple folders at the same time and select files from multiple folders.

3 When you need to hide the folder's contents again, click (changes to).

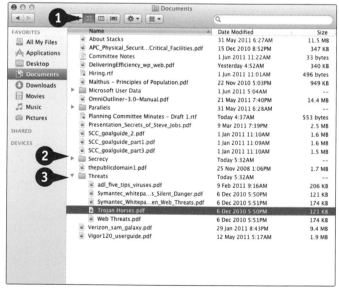

Column View

1 In the Finder window, click **Columns** (▥) on the toolbar.

The files and folders appear in Column view.

2 Click a folder in the first column after the sidebar.

The folder's contents appear in the next column.

3 Click a document.

● A preview of the document appears.

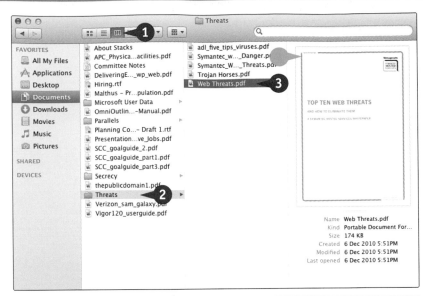

Cover Flow View

1 In the Finder window, click **Cover Flow** (▤) on the toolbar.

The files and folders appear in Cover Flow view.

2 Click a file.

A preview or icon appears in the Cover Flow area.

● Click to display the previous document.

● Click to display the next document.

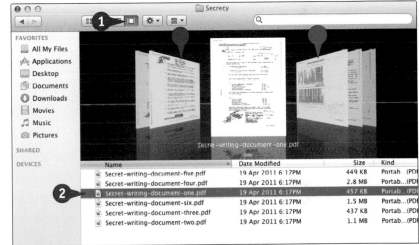

TIPS

Can I change the size of icons used in Icon view?
If the status bar and toolbar are displayed, you can change icon size by dragging the slider on the right side of the status bar. If the toolbar is hidden, the status bar appears below the window's title bar. To set a default size in Icon view, choose **View** and **Show View Options**. The View Options window opens, showing the folder's name in the title bar. Click and drag the **Icon size** slider until the icons are the size you want. Click **Use as Defaults**. Click ◉ to close the View Options window.

Is there an easy way to use different views for different folders?
You can tell the Finder to use a particular view for any folder. Click the folder and choose **View** and **Show View Options**. The View Options window opens. In the main window, click the view icon you want and then click the **Always open** option (☐ changes to ☑) — for example, **Always open in icon view**. Repeat the process for other folders whose default views you want to set.

Look Through a File without Opening It

When you have many files with similar names or contents, it can be difficult to identify the document you need without opening the document and looking at its contents. To help you find the right document, Mac OS X's Quick Look feature enables you to look quickly inside many widely used types of documents right from the Finder without opening the document in an application.

Look Through a File without Opening It

1 Click **Finder** (🖐) on the Dock.

A Finder window opens to your default folder or view.

2 Click the file you want to look through.

3 Click ☀▾.

The Action pop-up menu opens.

4 Click **Quick Look**.

A Quick Look window opens showing a preview of the file or the file's icon.

Note: When you use Quick Look on a video file, Mac OS X starts playing the file.

5 If you need to scroll to see more of the file, click and drag the scroll bar.

● If you want to open the file in the default application, click the **Open with** button — for example, the **Open with Preview** button.

6 To see the file full screen, click ⬚.

The Quick Look window expands to fill the screen.

Note: To see more of the file in full-screen view, click and drag the scroll bar, or press Page down.

⑦ Click ⬛ when you have finished using full-screen view.

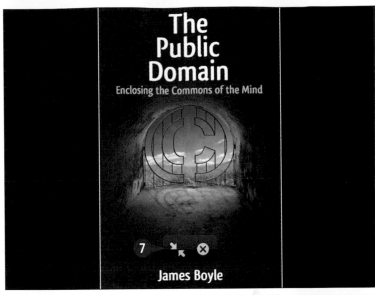

⑧ Click ⬛ to close the Quick Look window.

Note: Instead of closing the Quick Look window, you can press ▶, ◀, ▲, or ▼ to display another file or folder.

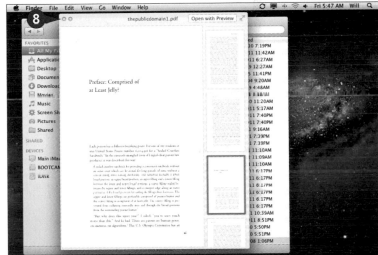

TIPS

Why does the Quick Look preview of a file look different from the actual file?

Quick Look does not actually open the file fully, so the Quick Look preview of the file may look somewhat different from the actual file. Normally, all text and objects such as graphics are visible, but the layout and formatting may be different. When Quick Look is not accurate enough to identify a file visually, open the file in an application to see it better.

Can I use Quick Look on more than one file at a time?

You can use Quick Look on as many files as you want. Select the files, launch Quick Look, and click ⬛ to enter full-screen view. Click ▶ to play each preview for a few seconds, or click ◀ and ▶ to move from preview to preview. Click ⊞ to see the index sheet showing all previews, and then click the item you want to see.

Search for a File or Folder

To help you find the files and folders you need to work with, Mac OS X includes a powerful search feature called Spotlight. You can search quickly from the desktop or from a Finder window, using either straightforward search keywords or complex search criteria.

Search for a File or Folder

Search Quickly from the Desktop

1 Click 🔍.

The Spotlight search field opens.

2 Type one or more keywords in the search field.

Note: Spotlight searches automatically for the keywords within the contents of most files as well as in the names of files.

Spotlight displays a list of matches as you type.

3 Position the mouse pointer over a result.

● A preview of the file appears.

4 Click the file you want to see.

The file opens in the application associated with it.

Search from a Finder Window

1 Click **Finder** (🙂) on the Dock.

A Finder window opens to your default folder or view.

If you want to search a different folder, click it.

2 Click in the search field.

3 Type the keywords for your search.

The Finder window's title bar changes to Searching, and the list of search results appears.

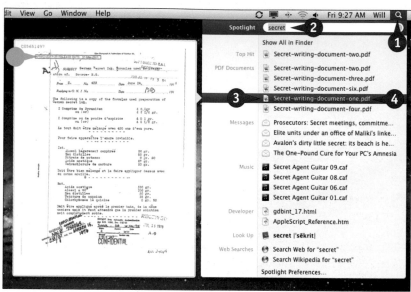

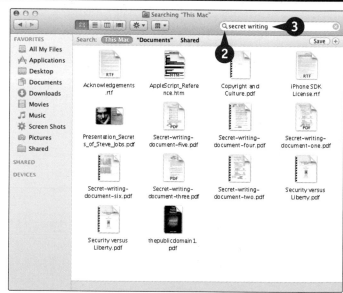

④ To change where Spotlight is searching, click a button.

⑤ To quickly view a file, **Control** + click or right-click it and choose **Quick Look**.

⑥ To open a file, double-click it.

⑦ To refine the search, click **Add** (⊕).

A line of controls appears.

⑧ Click ↕ and choose **Kind, Last opened date, Last modified date, Created date, Name,** or **Contents**.

⑨ Click ↕ and choose search criteria — for example, *Kind is PDF* or *Created date is within last 3 days*.

⑩ If you need to add more search criteria, click **Add** (⊕), and another line of controls appears.

⑪ Set up another condition as described in steps **8** and **9**.

The search results appear.

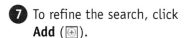

Can I change where Spotlight searches for files?
You can customize the list of folders that Spotlight searches. See Chapter 12 for instructions on customizing Spotlight.

Save a Search in a Smart Folder

After a successful search, you can save the search as a Smart Folder so that you can use it again quickly and easily. Unlike a regular folder, a Smart Folder does not actually contain the items it shows because each item remains in its original folder. The Smart Folder gives you a way to locate items swiftly by their characteristics.

Save a Search in a Smart Folder

1 Click **Finder** (🙂) on the Dock.

A Finder window opens.

2 Set up a search as described in the previous task.

Your search results appear in the Finder window.

3 Click **Save**.

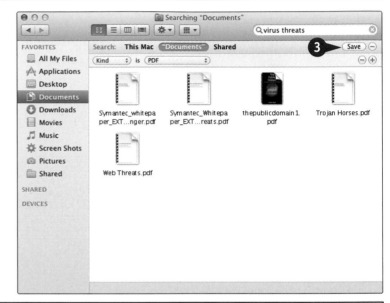

The Specify a Name and Location for Your Smart Folder dialog opens.

Note: Mac OS X automatically saves your Smart Folders in the Saved Searches folder in your Library folder. You can choose another folder if you want. The Library folder is hidden, but you can display it by clicking **Go**, pressing and holding Option, and clicking **Library**.

4 Type the Smart Folder name.

5 Click **Add To Sidebar** (☑ changes to ☐) if you do not want to add the Smart Folder to the sidebar.

6 If you want to save the search in a different folder, click ▾.

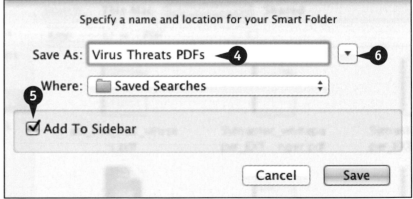

The Specify a Name and Location for Your Smart Folder dialog expands.

7 Choose the folder in which to store the Smart Folder.

8 Click **Save**.

The Specify a Name and Location for Your Smart Folder dialog closes.

If you left Add To Sidebar selected, Mac OS X adds the Smart Folder to the Favorites category in the Finder's sidebar.

9 Click the Smart Folder when you need to display matching items.

Note: To use a Smart Folder that you did not add to the sidebar, open a Finder window to the folder in which you stored the Smart Folder.

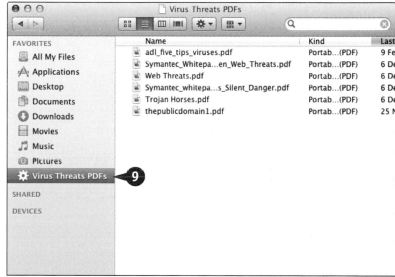

Should I add my Smart Folders to the sidebar?
If you create only a few Smart Folders, adding them to the sidebar is usually helpful. If you create many Smart Folders, you may prefer to keep them in different folders. Alternatively, add each Smart Folder to the sidebar, and then remove those you do not need to keep. To remove a Smart Folder from the sidebar, Control+click or right-click the folder, and then click **Remove from Sidebar**.

How do I change a Smart Folder?
Control+click or right-click the Smart Folder in the sidebar or in the folder in which you saved it, and then click **Show Search Criteria**. The controls for changing the criteria appear. You can then change the Smart Folder by using the same techniques you used to set it up.

Create and Name a New Folder

Mac OS X builds a hierarchy of folders in your user account, but you will normally need to create other folders to keep different types of files or different projects organized.

You can create as many folders as needed, and you can create subfolders within other folders.

Create and Name a New Folder

1 Click **Finder** (😊) on the Dock.

A Finder window opens to your default folder.

2 Click or double-click, depending on the view you are using, the folder in which you want to create the new folder.

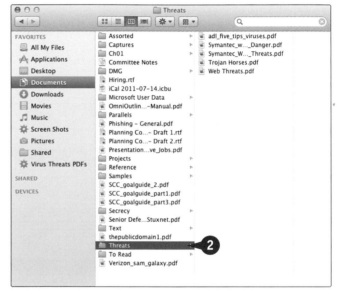

3 Click ✿▾ on the toolbar.

The Action pop-up menu opens.

4 Click **New Folder**.

● A new folder appears in the
Finder window.

The new folder shows an edit
box around the default name,
Untitled Folder.

⑤ Type the name you want to
give the folder.

⑥ Press Return.

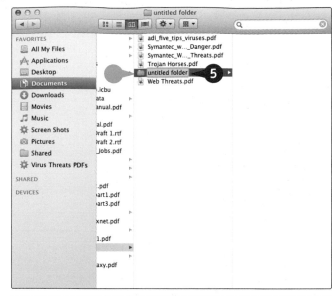

The folder takes on the new
name.

⑦ Click or double-click the
folder, depending on the
view you are using.

The folder opens. You can
now add files to the folder or
create subfolders inside it.

TIPS

Are there other ways of creating a new folder?
You can also create a new folder in three other ways.
In a Finder window in any view, press ⌘+Shift+N
or choose **File** and **New Folder** from the Finder menu
bar. In Icon view or Column view, Control+click or
right-click in open space inside the folder and then
click **New Folder** on the shortcut menu.

**Why can I not create a new folder inside some
other folders?**
Most likely, you do not have permission to create a
folder in that folder. Each user can create new items
in the folders in his user account, and Administrators
can create folders in some other folders. But Mac OS X
protects other folders, such as the System folder and
the Users folder, from anybody creating new folders.

Copy a File from One Folder to Another

Mac OS X makes it easy to copy a file from one folder to another. Copying is useful when you need to share a file with other people or when you need to keep a copy of the file safe against harm.

You can copy one or more files at a time either by clicking and dragging or by using the Copy and Paste commands.

Copy a File from One Folder to Another

Copy a File by Clicking and Dragging

1 Click **Finder** (◻) on the Dock.

A Finder window opens to your default folder.

2 Open the folder that contains the file you want to copy.

3 Choose **File** and **New Finder Window**.

A new Finder window opens.

4 In the second Finder window, open the folder to which you want to copy the file.

5 Click and drag the Finder windows so that you can see both.

6 Select the file or files you want to copy.

7 Press and hold **Option** while you click the file and drag it to the destination folder.

Note: When you **Option**+drag a file, ⬧ changes to ⬧ to indicate that you are making a copy.

A copy of the file appears in the folder.

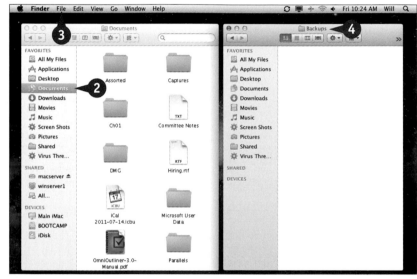

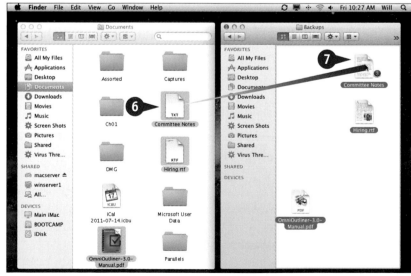

Copy a File by Using Copy and Paste

1. Click **Finder** (🙂) on the Dock.

   A Finder window opens to your default folder.

2. Open the folder that contains the file you want to copy.

3. Click the file to select it.

4. Click ⚙️▾.

   The Action pop-up menu opens.

5. Click **Copy**.

   Mac OS X copies the file's details to the clipboard.

6. Open the folder in which you want to create the copy.

7. Click ⚙️▾.

   The Action pop-up menu opens.

8. Click **Paste Item**.

   A copy of the file appears in the destination folder.

Note: You can use the Paste command in either the same Finder window or another Finder window — whichever you find more convenient.

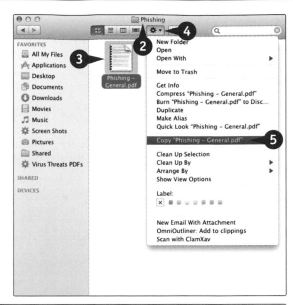

TIPS

How do I copy a folder?

You can copy one or more folders by using either of the techniques for copying files: Either Option +click and drag the folder or folders to the destination folder, or use the Copy command to copy the folder and the Paste command to paste it into the destination folder.

Can I make a copy of a file in the same folder as the original?

To make a copy of a file in the same folder as the original, click the file, click ⚙️▾, and then click **Duplicate** (●) from the Action pop-up menu. Finder automatically adds *copy* to the end of the copy's filename to distinguish it from the original.

Move a File from One Folder to Another

When organizing your files, you will often need to move a file from one folder to another. You can move files quickly by selecting the file or files and then clicking and dragging. But you must use a different technique if the destination folder is on a different drive from the source folder than if it is on the same drive.

Move a File from One Folder to Another

Move a File between Folders on the Same Drive

1 Click **Finder** (🔵) on the Dock.

A Finder window opens to your default folder.

2 Open the folder that contains the file you want to move.

3 Choose **File** and **New Finder Window**.

A new Finder window opens.

4 In the second Finder window, open the folder to which you want to move the file.

5 Click and drag the Finder windows so that you can see both.

6 Click the file and drag it to the destination folder.

The file appears in the destination folder and disappears from the source folder.

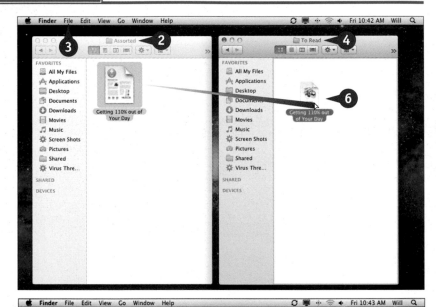

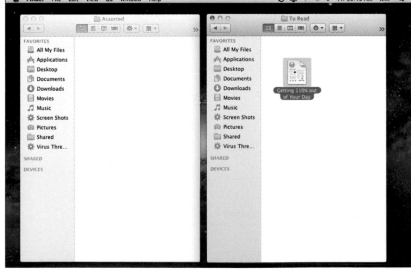

Move a File from One Drive to Another

1 Click **Finder** (![icon]) on the Dock.

A Finder window opens to your default folder.

2 Open the folder that contains the file you want to move.

3 Choose **File** and **New Finder Window**.

A new Finder window opens.

4 In the second Finder window, open the drive to which you want to copy the file.

5 Open the destination folder on that drive.

6 Click and drag the Finder windows so that you can see both.

7 Select the file or files you want to move.

8 Press and hold ⌘ while you click the file or files and drag them to the destination folder.

The file appears in the destination folder and disappears from the source folder.

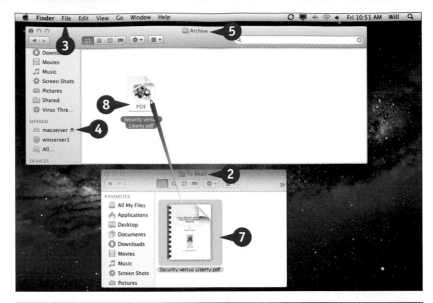

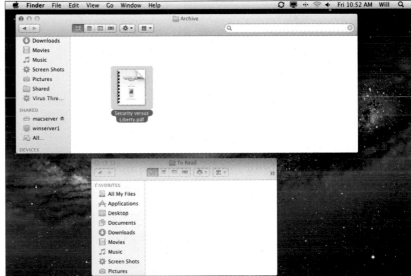

TIP

Can I move files by using menu commands rather than clicking and dragging?
If you find it awkward to click and drag files from one folder to another, you can use menu commands instead. Select the file or files you want to move, and then click **Edit** and **Copy** to copy them. Open the destination folder and click **Edit** to open the Edit menu. Press and hold **Option** and click **Move Item Here** or **Move Items Here**.

Rename a File or Folder

When you create a new file or folder, you normally give it a name that describes its contents or what you intend it to be.

To keep your iMac's file system well organized, you will often need to rename files and folders after creating them. You can rename a file or folder in seconds by using the Finder.

Rename a File or Folder

1 Click **Finder** (🖼) on the Dock.

A Finder window opens to your default folder or view.

2 Open the folder that contains the file you want to rename.

3 Click the file to select it.

4 Press **Return**.

Note: You can also display the edit box by clicking the file's name again after selecting it. Be careful to pause between the clicks, or Mac OS X registers a double-click and opens the file.

An edit box appears around the file name.

5 Edit the file's current name, or simply type the new name over the current name.

6 Press **Return**.

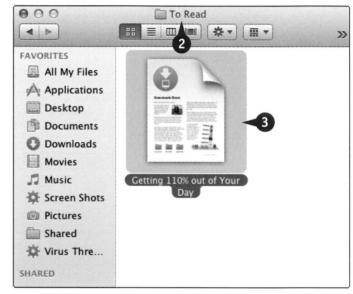

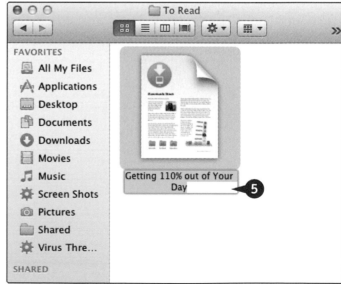

● The file takes on the new name.

You can now open the file by double-clicking it or pressing ⌘+O, or rename another file or folder.

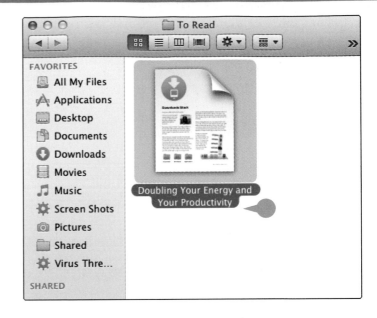

TIPS

Can I rename any file or folder in Mac OS X?

You can rename many items within your Home folder. It is best not to rename the folders that Mac OS X creates for you, such as Desktop, Documents, and Downloads, but you can freely rename any folders you create. In addition, you can safely rename your iMac's hard disk, but do not rename any of the system folders. For example, do not rename the Applications folder, the System folder, the Users folder, or your Home folder, because renaming these folders may cause Mac OS X problems.

Can I rename several files at once?

There is no convenient way to rename several files at once from the Finder manually. Each file in a folder must have a unique name, so you cannot apply the same name to two or more files at once. Some applications and scripts have features for renaming multiple files at once, usually by giving them sequential names using numbers appended to a base name — for example, Photo01, Photo02, Photo03, and so on.

View the Information about a File or Folder

When you click a file or folder in a Finder window, the Finder displays its filename in all views. In all views but Icon view, the Finder displays basic information, such as the file's kind, size, and date last modified. To see extra information about the file or folder, and to add information, you can open the Info window.

View the Information about a File or Folder

1. Click **Finder** ( ) on the Dock.

2. In the Finder window, open the folder that contains the file whose info you want to view.

3. Click the file.

4. Click ☀▾.

5. Click **Get Info**.

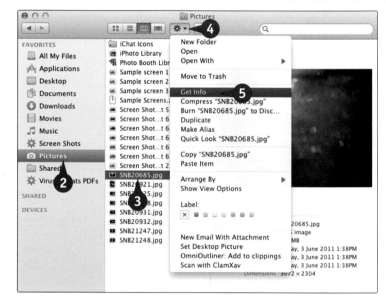

The Info window for the file opens.

Note: The Info window has several sections. You can expand each section by clicking ▶ or collapse it by clicking ▼.

6. Click ▶ next to General.

7. Review the general information for the file:

   Kind shows the file's type. *Size* shows the file's size on disk. *Where* shows the folder that contains the file. *Created* shows when the file was created. *Modified* shows when the file was last changed.

8. Click ▶ next to Spotlight Comments.

9. To make the file easier to find with Spotlight, type keywords in the Spotlight Comments field.

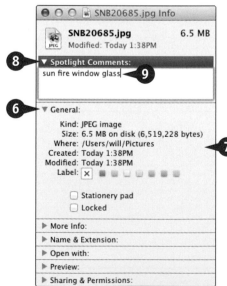

10 Click ▶ next to Open With.

The Open With area appears.

11 To change the application with which this file opens when you double-click it in the Finder, click ⬍, and then click the application.

12 Click ▶ next to Preview.

The Preview area appears, and you can see a preview of the file.

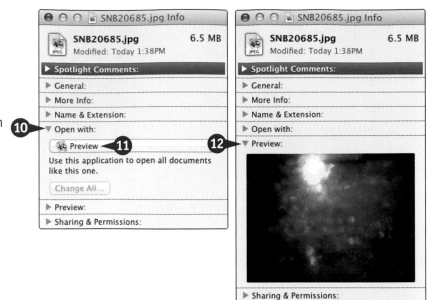

13 Click ▶ next to Sharing & Permissions.

The Sharing & Permissions area appears.

14 If necessary, click the lock icon (🔒), type your password, and then change the permissions.

Note: Normally, it is best not to change the permissions Mac OS X has set for a file.

15 Click 🔴.

The Info window closes.

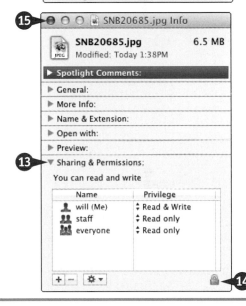

TIPS

What does the Locked setting in the Info pane do?

You can click **Locked** (☐ changes to ☑) in the General section of the Info window to lock the file against changes. When someone tries to save changes to the file, a dialog opens to warn him that the file is locked. The user can overwrite the lock, so locking provides only modest protection against changes.

What does the More Info section of the Info window contain?

The information in the More Info section of the Info window depends on the type of file or folder you have selected. For example, the More Info section for a photo contains details of the photo's dimensions, the make and model of the camera that took the photos, and the aperture used for the lens.

Compress Files for Easy Transfer

To transfer files faster and more easily across the Internet, or to fit more files onto a CD, DVD, or removable disk, you can compress the files. Compressing creates a compressed file in the widely used zip format, often called a "zip file," that contains a copy of the files. The original files remain unchanged in their folder.

Compress Files for Easy Transfer

Compress Files to a Zip File

1 Click **Finder** ( ) on the Dock.

A Finder window opens to your default folder.

2 Open the folder that contains the file or files you want to compress.

3 Select the file or files.

4 [Control]+click or right-click in the selection.

The shortcut menu opens.

5 Click **Compress**.

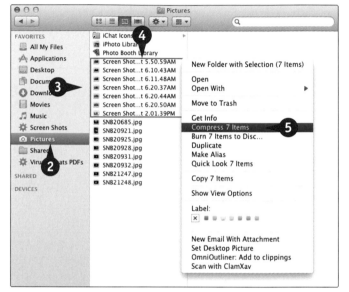

● The compressed file appears in the folder.

Note: If you selected one file, Mac OS X gives the file the same name with .zip added to the end. If you selected two or more files, Mac OS X names the zip file Archive.zip.

6 If you want to rename the file, click it and press [Return].

An edit box opens around the filename.

7 Type the new name and press [Return].

The file takes on the new name.

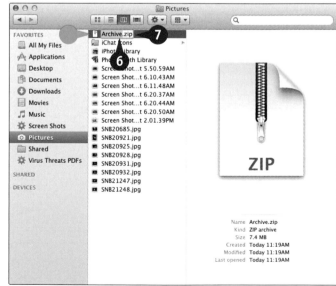

Extract Files from a Zip File

1 Open a Finder window to the folder that contains the zip file.

Note: If you receive the zip file attached to an email message, save the file as explained in Chapter 6.

2 Double-click the zip file.

Archive Utility unzips the zip file, creates a folder with the same name as the zip file, and places the contents of the zip file in it.

3 Double-click the new folder to see the files from the zip file.

TIPS

Can I exchange zip files with Windows users?

The zip file is a standard format used by Macs, Windows PCs, and other operating systems. This means that you can normally exchange zip files with users of Windows or other operating systems without needing to worry about compatibility.

When I compress a music file, the zip file is bigger than the original file. What have I done wrong?

You have done nothing wrong. Compression removes extra space from the file, and can squeeze some graphics down by as much as 90 percent. But if you try to compress an already compressed file, such as an MP3 audio file or an MPEG video file, Archive Utility cannot compress it further — and the zip file packaging adds a small amount to the file size.

Burn Files to a CD or DVD

A CD or DVD is a useful means of storing files and folders, either for transferring them to another computer or keeping a copy as a backup. Mac OS X enables you to easily copy files and folders to a CD or DVD. The process of creating a CD or DVD is called *burning*.

Burn Files to a CD or DVD

1 Insert a blank CD or blank DVD in your iMac's optical drive.

A dialog opens asking what you want to do with the disc.

Note: If you always want to burn this type of disc using the Finder, click **Make this action the default** (☐ changes to ☑).

2 Click ↕.

The Action pop-up menu opens.

3 Click **Open Finder**.

4 Click **OK**.

● The blank CD or blank DVD appears on your desktop, with a name such as Untitled CD.

5 Double-click the icon for the CD or DVD.

● A Finder window opens showing the CD's or DVD's contents — nothing so far.

6 Choose **Finder** and **New Finder window**.

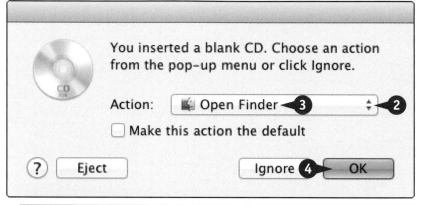

7 Position the new Finder windows so that you can see both of them.

8 Drag files from the new Finder window to the CD or DVD window.

Note: When you drag files to the CD or DVD, Mac OS X adds aliases, or shortcuts, to the files. It does not add the files to the CD or DVD yet.

9 Click **Burn**.

10 Type a name in the dialog that opens.

11 Click ↕ and choose the speed at which to burn the disc. Maximum Possible is usually the best choice.

12 Click **Burn**.

The iMac starts burning the CD or DVD. The Burn dialog shows you the progress of the burn.

When the burn has completed, your iMac ejects the disc.

Note: Before labeling and storing the disc, it is a good idea to reinsert it in your iMac and check that the disc's contents are as you intended them to be.

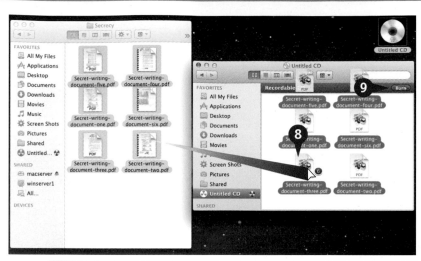

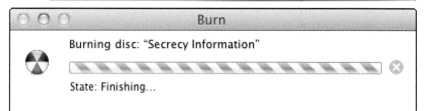

TIPS

Should I use a CD or a DVD for my files?
Use a CD when you have only a modest amount of data to store. Most recordable CDs can hold 640MB or 700MB. Use a DVD when you need to store more data than this. A single-layer DVD holds 4.7GB, whereas a dual-layer DVD holds 8.5GB.

Is it better to use rewriteable discs or single-use discs?
Use single-use recordable discs when you want to make a permanent copy of data — for example, on a backup that you intend to keep indefinitely. Use rewriteable discs for data you plan to store for only a short time. For example, if you back up documents to DVD each day, keep a rewriteable DVD for each day of the week.

Erase a CD or DVD

After you have burned a rewriteable CD or DVD, you can erase its contents so that you can use the disc again. To erase a rewriteable disc like this, you use the Disk Utility tool, which also works with hard disks and removable disks.

Erase a CD or DVD

1 Insert the CD or DVD in your iMac's optical drive.

● The CD or DVD appears on your desktop.

2 Click the desktop.

The Finder becomes active.

3 Choose **Go** and **Utilities**.

A Finder window opens showing the Utilities folder.

4 Press and hold Option and double-click **Disk Utility**.

Note: Pressing and holding Option while you double-click a file makes the Finder window close when the file opens.

The Finder window closes and Disk Utility opens.

5 Click the CD or DVD in the sidebar.

6 Click **Erase**.

The Erase pane opens.

7 If the disc has not been working normally, click **Completely** (○ changes to ◉). Otherwise, leave **Quickly** selected.

8 Click **Erase**.

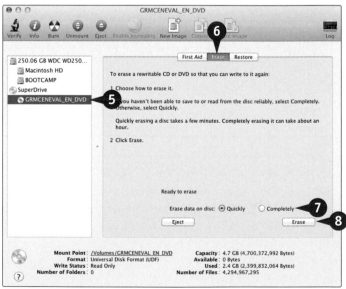

A dialog opens to confirm that you want to erase the disc.

9 Click **Erase**.

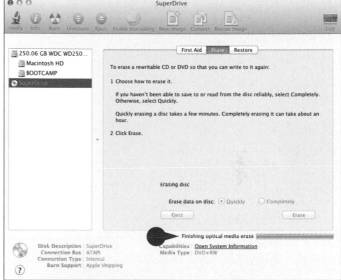

Are you sure you want to erase the disc in the SuperDrive drive?

All data on the disc will be lost.

9 ➞ Erase   Cancel

● Disk Utility erases the disc and shows a readout of its progress.

When Disk Utility finishes erasing the disc, a dialog opens.

10 Click ⬍ and choose the application to open. For example, choose **Open Finder** if you want to burn files to the disc.

11 Click **OK**.

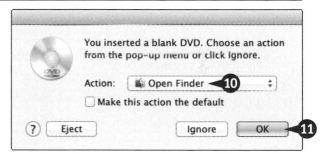

You inserted a blank DVD. Choose an action from the pop-up menu or click Ignore.

Action: Open Finder **10**

☐ Make this action the default

(?) Eject   Ignore   OK **11**

TIP

How many times can I reuse a rewriteable CD or DVD?
You should be able to reuse a rewriteable CD or DVD several dozen times before needing to replace it. However, if the disc suffers wear and tear, or if it is several years old, it is better to err on the side of caution and replace the disc. Similarly, if the disc gives errors but is not scratched, try using the Completely option in Disk Utility to erase it thoroughly and make it work properly again — but if your data is valuable, replacing the disc instead is safer.

Throw a File in the Trash

When you do not need a file any more, you can throw it in the Trash. The Trash is a special folder in which Mac OS X keeps files and folders you intend to dispose of.

Like a real-world trash can, the Trash retains files until you actually empty it. So if you find you have thrown away a file that you need after all, you can recover the file from the Trash.

Throw a File in the Trash

Throw a File in the Trash

1 Click **Finder** () on the Dock.

A Finder window opens to your default folder or view.

2 Open the folder that contains the file you want to throw in the Trash.

3 Click the file you want to delete.

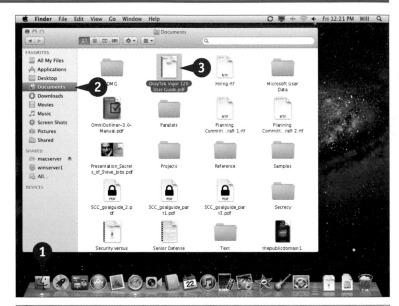

4 Click .

The Action pop-up menu opens.

5 Click **Move to Trash**.

● The file disappears from the folder and moves to the Trash.

Note: You can also throw a file in the Trash by clicking and dragging it to the Trash icon on the Dock. From the keyboard, click the file, and then press ⌘+Delete.

Recover a File from the Trash

1 Click **Trash** (🗑) on the Dock.

The Trash window opens.

2 Choose **File** and **New Finder window**.

Note: If you want to restore the file to the folder it was in, you do not need to open a new Finder window. Just click the file in the Trash and then choose **File** and **Put Back**.

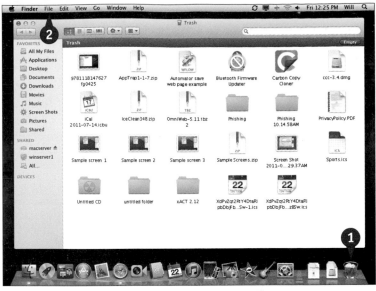

A new Finder window opens.

3 Open the folder to which you want to restore the file or files.

4 Position the Finder windows so that you can see both the Trash and the destination folder.

5 Select the file or files in the Trash.

6 Click and drag the file or files from the Trash to the destination folder.

You can now work with the file again.

TIPS

When and how do I get rid of the Trash?
You can empty the Trash at any time you find convenient. Chapter 15 shows you how to empty the Trash. Unless you need to dispose of sensitive files immediately, leaving files in the Trash until you are certain that you never need them again is normally a good idea.

What else do I need to know about the Trash?
When you click a CD, DVD, or removable disk and drag it toward the Trash, the Trash icon changes to an Eject icon (⏏). Drop the item on the Eject icon to eject it. When you click and drag a recordable CD or DVD to which you have added files toward the Trash, Mac OS X displays a Burn icon (☢). Drop the disc on the Burn icon to start burning it.

CHAPTER 5

Surfing the Web

If your iMac is connected to the Internet, you can browse or *surf* the sites on the World Wide Web. For surfing, Mac OS X provides a web browser application called Safari. Using Safari, you can quickly move from one web page to another, search for interesting sites, and download files to your iMac.

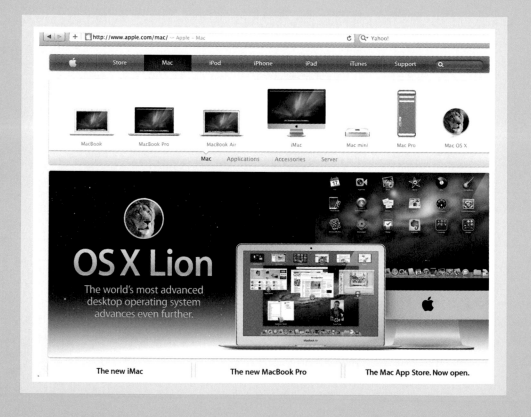

Open and Close Safari

To start surfing the web, you open the Safari browser. Because Safari is a widely used application, its icon appears in the Dock by default.

If you surf the web often, as many people do, you may want to set Safari to open automatically when you log in.

Open and Close Safari

Open Safari

1 Click **Safari** ( ) on the Dock.

Note: If the Safari icon does not appear on the Dock, click **Launchpad** ( ) on the Dock, and then click **Safari**.

The Safari window opens and shows your default page.

Note: The default page may be the Top Sites page (which shows the pages you have visited most recently), your home page, or another page.

You can then browse to another page as explained later in this chapter.

● Click if you want to switch to full-screen view. Press Esc twice when you want to return to a window.

Close Safari

1 Click **Safari**.

The Safari menu opens.

2 Click **Quit Safari**.

The Safari window closes.

TIPS

Are there quicker ways of opening and closing Safari?

The quickest way to launch Safari is to have your iMac launch it when you log in. `Control`+click or right-click **Safari** (🧭) on the Dock, highlight **Options**, and then click **Open at Login**. Mac OS X puts a check mark next to this option to show it is on. To quit Safari quickly, press ⌘+Q when Safari is active.

Can I use other another web browser instead of Safari?

Safari is a fast and responsive browser, but you can use another web browser instead if you prefer. The next most popular browser for Macs is Firefox, which you can download for free from www.mozilla.com. Camino, free from www.caminobrowser.org, is another fast and easy-to-use browser for Macs. Chrome, free from www.google.com/chrome, is a stable and easy-to-use browser.

Firefox

Open a Web Page

Each web page has a unique address called a *uniform resource locator* or *URL*. The most straightforward way to go to a particular web page is by typing its URL into the address box in Safari.

This technique works well for short addresses but is slow and awkward for complex addresses. Instead of typing a URL, you can click a link to a web page, as explained in the next task. Or you can create a bookmark for a web page you want to return to, as explained later in this chapter.

Open a Web Page

1 In Safari, triple-click anywhere in the address box.

Safari selects all of the current address.

Note: If you find triple-clicking difficult, press ⌘+L to select the whole address.

2 Type the URL of the web page you want to visit.

Note: You do not need to type the http:// part of the address. Safari adds this automatically for you when you press Return.

3 Press Return.

Safari opens the web page and displays its contents.

Follow a Link to a Web Page

Once you have opened a page in Safari, you can use the easier way of navigating to a web page: Clicking a link on a page to go to another page.

Most web pages contain links to other pages. Some links are underlined, whereas others are attached to graphics or to different-colored text. When you position the mouse pointer over a link, the pointer changes from ▸ to 🖑.

Follow a Link to a Web Page

① In Safari, position the mouse pointer over a link (▸ changes to 🖑).

● The address of the linked web page appears in the status bar.

Note: If the Safari window is not showing the status bar, choose **View** and **Show Status Bar** to display it.

② Click the link.

Safari shows the linked web page.

● The address of the linked web page appears in the address box.

Open Several Web Pages at Once

To browse quickly and easily, you can open multiple web pages at the same time. In Safari, you can open multiple pages on separate tabs in the same window or in separate windows.

Use separate tabs when you need to see only one of the pages at a time. Use separate windows when you need to compare two pages side by side.

Open Several Web Pages at Once

Open Several Pages on Tabs in the Same Safari Window

1 Go to the first page you want to view.

Note: You can also click **Add** (⊞) or press ⌘+**T** to open a new tab showing your default page. Type a URL in the address box, and then press **Return** to go to the page.

2 **Control**+click or right-click a link.

The shortcut menu opens.

3 Click **Open Link in New Tab**.

● Safari opens the linked web page in a new tab.

Note: You can now repeat steps **2** and **3** to open further pages on separate tabs.

4 To change the page Safari displays, click the tab for the page you want to see.

Open Several Pages in Separate Safari Windows

1 Go to the first page you want to view.

2 Control +click or right-click a link.

The shortcut menu opens.

3 Click **Open Link in New Window**.

Note: You can also open a new window by pressing ⌘+T.

● Safari opens the linked web page in a new window.

4 To move back to the previous window, click it.

Note: You can also move back to the previous window by closing the new window you just opened.

Can I change the way that Safari tabs and windows behave?
Choose **Safari** and **Preferences** to open the Preferences window, and then click **Tabs**. Click the **Open pages in tabs instead of windows** ⟐ and then click **Never**, **Automatically**, or **Always**, as needed. Select ⌘**-click opens a link in a new tab** (☐ changes to ☑) to use ⌘+click for opening a new tab. Select **When a new tab or window opens, make it active** (☐ changes to ☑) if you want to switch to the new tab or window on opening it. Click ⊙ to close the Preferences window.

A s you browse, Safari tracks the pages that you visit, so that the pages form a path. You can go back along this path to return to a page you viewed earlier; after going back, you can go forward again as needed.

Safari keeps a separate path of pages in each open tab or window, so you can move separately in each.

Find Your Way from One Page to Another

Go Back One Page

1 Click **Previous Page** (◄).

Safari displays the previous page you visited in the current tab or window.

Go Forward One Page

1 Click **Next Page** (►).

Note: The Next Page button is available only when you have gone back. Until then, there is no page for you to go forward to.

Safari displays the next page for the current tab or window.

Go Back Multiple Pages

1 Click **Previous Page** (◄) and keep holding down the mouse button.

A pop-up menu opens showing the pages you have visited in the current tab or window.

2 Click the page you want to display.

Safari displays the page.

Go Forward Multiple Pages

1 Click **Next Page** (►) and keep holding down the mouse button.

A pop-up menu opens showing the pages further along the path for the current tab or window.

2 Click the page you want to display.

Safari displays the page.

TIP

Can I navigate from page to page, or tab to tab, by using the keyboard?

You can use the following keyboard shortcuts to move quickly from page to page and from tab to tab in Safari:

- Press ⌘+[to display the previous page.
- Press ⌘+] to display the next page.
- Press ⌘+Shift+H to display your home page.
- Press ⌘+Shift+[to display the previous tab.
- Press ⌘+Shift+] to display the next tab.

- Press ⌘+W to close the current tab and display the previous tab. If the window has no tabs, this command closes the window.
- Press ⌘+Shift+W to close the current window and display the previous window, if there is one.

Return to a Recently Visited Page

To help you return to web pages you have visited before, Safari keeps a History list of all the pages you have visited recently.

Normally, each person who uses your iMac has a separate user account, so each person has his own History. But if you share a user account with other people, you can clear the History list to prevent them from seeing what web pages you have visited. You can also shorten the length of time for which History tracks your visits.

Return to a Recently Visited Page

Return to a Page on the History List

1 In Safari, click **History**.

The History menu opens.

2 Highlight or click the day on which you visited the web page.

Note: If the item for the web page you want appears on the top section of the History menu, before the day submenus, simply click the item.

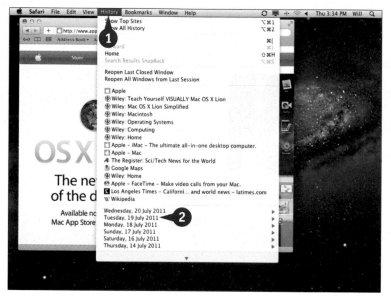

The submenu opens, showing the sites you visited on that day.

3 Click the web page to which you want to return.

Safari displays the web page.

Clear Your Browsing History

1 Click **History**.

The History menu opens.

2 Click **Clear History**.

The Are You Sure You Want to Clear History? dialog opens.

3 Click **Also reset Top Sites** (☐ changes to ☑) if you want to reset the list of sites you visit most frequently.

4 Click **Clear**.

Safari clears the History list.

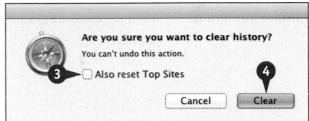

TIP

What does the Show All History command do?

Choose **History** and **Show All History** to open a History window for browsing and searching the sites you have visited. Type a term in the search box (●) to search. In the preview area (●), scroll left or right with two fingers on the Magic Mouse or Magic Touchpad, or click and drag the slider (●) on the scroll bar, to preview other pages. Click a page in the Bookmark list (●) to bring it to the front. Double-click a page to open it.

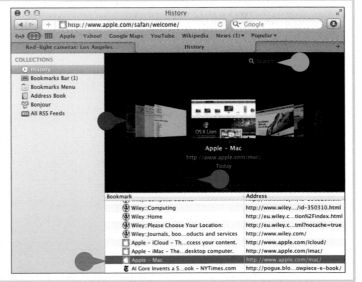

Change the Page Safari Opens at First

When you open a new window in Safari, it automatically opens a page called your *home page*, the page from which it is set to start.

You can set your home page to any web page you want by using the technique explained here. You can also set Safari to display the Top Sites screen or an empty page when you open a new window or tab.

Change the Page Safari Opens at First

1 In Safari, navigate to the web page that you want to make your home page.

2 Click **Safari**.

The Safari menu opens.

3 Click **Preferences**.

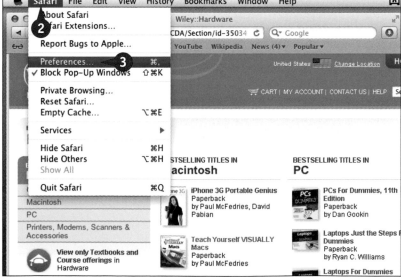

The Preferences window opens.

4 Click **General**.

The General pane opens.

5 Click **Set to Current Page**.

Safari changes the Home Page text field to show the page you chose.

6 Optionally, choose other General preferences as discussed in the tip.

7 Click 🔘.

The Preferences window closes.

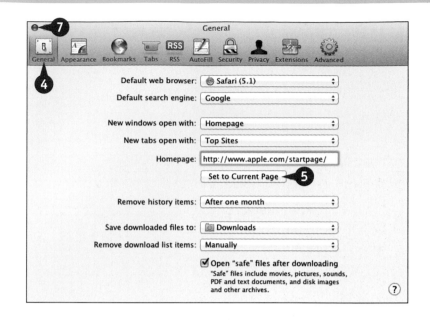

TIP

Are there other General preferences I can benefit from changing?

In the New Windows Open With pop-up menu (●), choose what you want new windows to show. A good choice is **Empty Page** because you can then choose the History item or bookmark you want. You can also choose **Same Page** if you want a new window showing the same page that your current window shows. The New Tabs Open With pop-up menu (●) gives you similar choices for when you open a new tab. The Remove History Items pop-up menu (●) lets you tell Safari when to delete History items: **After one day**, **After one week**, **After two weeks**, **After one month**, **After one year**, or **Manually**. If you choose Manually, click **History** and **Clear History** to clear your History items.

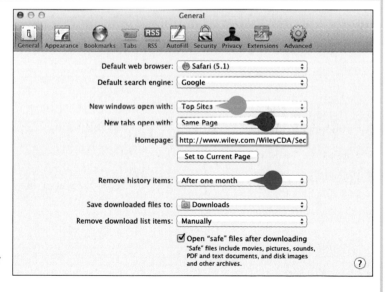

Keep Bookmarks for Web Pages You Like

History is handy for revisiting web pages, but you can also create markers called *bookmarks* for sites you want to revisit. The advantage of bookmarks over History is that you can organize your bookmarks and put the ones you use most frequently on the Bookmarks bar so that you can access them with a single click.

Keep Bookmarks for Web Pages You Like

Create a New Bookmark

1 In Safari, navigate to a web page you want to bookmark.

2 Click **Bookmarks**.

The Bookmarks menu opens.

3 Click **Add Bookmark**.

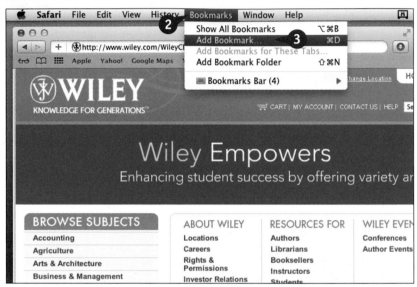

The Add Bookmark dialog opens, with the web page's title added to the upper box.

Note: If the Add This Page To pop-up menu shows Reading List, click ⇳, and then click **Bookmarks Menu**.

4 Type a new name for the bookmark if you want.

5 Click ⇳.

The pop-up menu opens.

6 Click the location or folder in which to store the bookmark.

7 Click **Add**.

Safari closes the Add Bookmark dialog and adds the bookmark to the location or folder you chose.

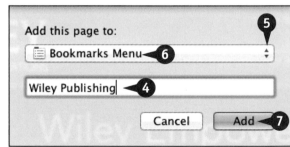

Organize Your Bookmarks

① Click **Show All Bookmarks**
(📖).

Safari opens a list of all your
bookmarks.

② Click the bookmarks
collection you want to
organize.

Note: The Bookmarks bar
collection contains the
bookmarks that appear on the
Bookmarks bar below the
address bar.

③ Click **Add** (➕).

Safari adds a new bookmarks
folder to the list.

④ Type the name for the new
folder and press Return.

⑤ Click and drag a bookmark to
the new folder.

Note: You can click and drag the
bookmark folders into a different
order. You can also place one
folder inside another folder.

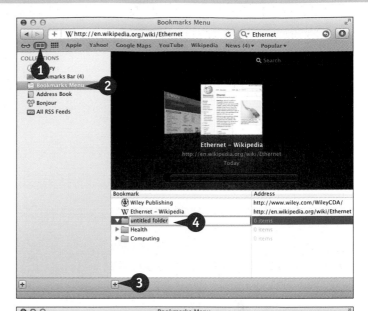

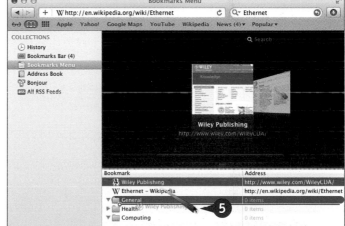

 TIP

How do I go to a bookmark I have created?

If you placed the bookmark on the Bookmarks bar, click
the bookmark. If you put the bookmark on the Bookmarks
menu, click **Bookmarks**, and then click the bookmark on
the Bookmarks menu or one of its submenus (●). Otherwise,
click **Show All Bookmarks**, locate the bookmark, and then
double-click it.

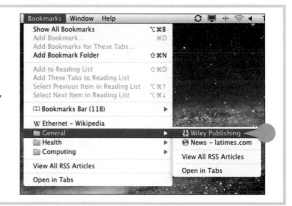

Find Interesting Websites

erhaps the best aspect of the web is that you can search it for exactly the information you need. Safari has a built-in search capability for searching with Google, the Internet's biggest search engine, Yahoo!, or Bing.

Find Interesting Websites

Search with the Built-In Google Search Feature

1 Click in the search box.

2 Type keywords, a phrase, or a whole question into the search box.

3 Press **Return**.

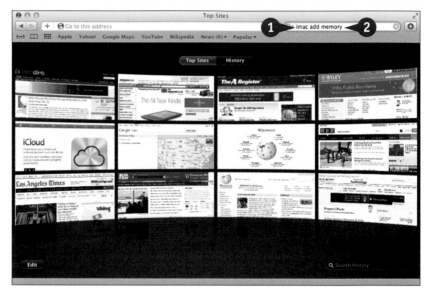

Safari displays a page of search results from the Google search engine.

4 Click a link to open a web page.

The web page opens.

Note: When examining search results, it is often useful to **Control**+click or right-click a link and choose **Open in New Tab** or **Open in New Window**. This way, the page of search results remains open, and you can follow other linked results as needed.

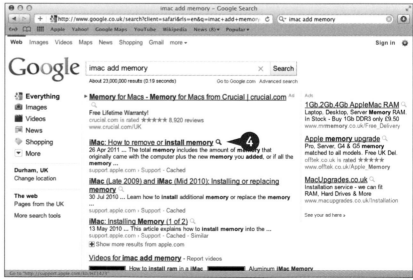

Search with a Search Engine Other Than Google

1 Click in the search box.

2 Type your search terms.

3 Click Q▾.

The search options pop-up menu opens.

4 Click the search engine you want to use. For example, click **Yahoo!**.

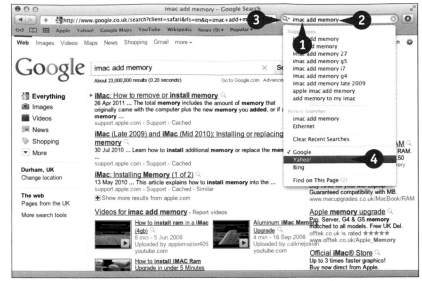

Safari displays results from the search engine you chose.

5 Click a link you want to open.

Safari opens the linked web page.

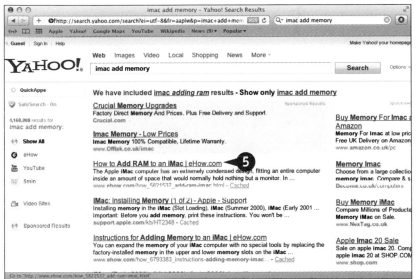

TIP

How can I get more useful search results?

Here are three ways to make your search results more accurate and helpful:

- To keep two words together as a phrase instead of searching for them separately, put them in double quotes. For example, use "add memory" to search for that phrase rather than for "add" and "for memory" separately.

- To exclude a word from a search, put a – sign before it. For example, –g5 tells Google not to return search results that include the term "G5."

- To make sure each search result includes a particular term, put a + sign before it. For example, +upgrade tells Google to return only search results that include the term "upgrade."

Download a File from the Internet

Many websites contain files that you can download and use on your iMac. For example, you can download applications to install on your iMac, pictures to view on it, or songs to play.

Mac OS X includes applications that can open many file types, including music, graphic, movie, document, and PDF files. To open other file types, you may need to install extra applications.

Download a File from the Internet

1 In Safari, go to the web page that contains the link for the file you want to download.

2 Click the link.

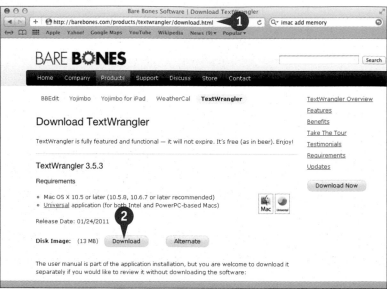

Safari starts the download.

● The indicator on the Downloads button shows the progress of the download.

3 Click **Downloads** to open the Downloads window to view the progress in detail.

4 When the download is complete, Control +click or right-click the file in the Downloads window.

The shortcut menu opens.

5 Click **Open**.

Note: Depending on the file type and the preferences you have set, Safari may open the file automatically for you.

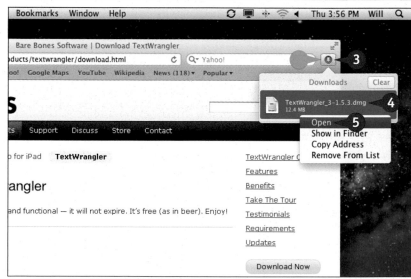

The file opens.

Depending on the file type, you can then work with the file, enjoy its contents, or install it.

Note: If the file is an application, you can install it as discussed in Chapter 3. If the file is a data file, such as a document or a picture, Mac OS X opens the file in the application for that file type.

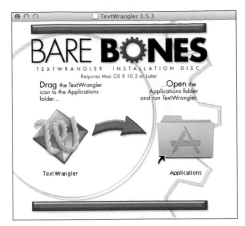

6 If the file disappears from the Downloads window and Safari does not open the file for you, click **Downloads** on the Dock.

The Downloads stack opens.

7 Click the file you downloaded.

The file opens.

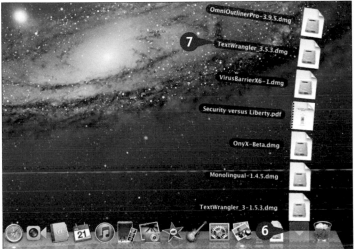

Can downloading files from the Internet be dangerous to my iMac?

Files available on the Internet for download can contain software that attempts to attack your iMac or compromise your privacy. For safety, download files only from websites that you trust, and use antivirus software as discussed in Chapter 14.

What should I do when clicking a download link opens the file instead of downloading it?

If clicking a download link on a web page opens the file instead of downloading it, `Control`+click or right-click the link, and then click **Download Linked File** (●). To save the file in a different folder or under a different name of your choice, click **Download Linked File As**. Safari opens a dialog in which you can choose the folder and filename.

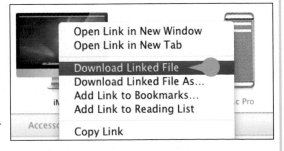

Keep Up to Date with News Feeds

I f you like to keep up to the minute with what is happening, use Safari's news feeds to bring you the latest news. The news feeds use a technology called *Really Simple Syndication*, or *RSS*, to enable you to subscribe to websites and to receive the latest information when it becomes available.

Keep Up to Date with News Feeds

Open a News Feed from Safari

1 In Safari, click **News**.

The News pop-up menu opens.

2 Click **View All RSS Articles**.

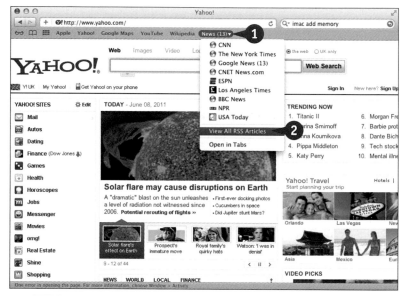

Safari displays a page showing the headlines of the available articles.

3 Click and drag the **Article Length** slider if you want to change the amount of information displayed for each article.

4 Click the article you want to read.

Safari opens the article.

Note: To find articles on a particular topic, click in the Search Articles box and type one or more keywords.

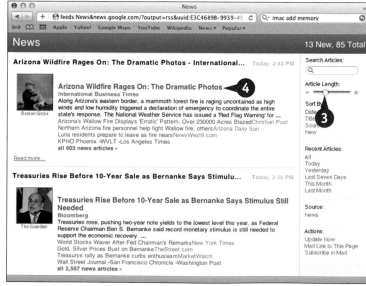

Open a News Feed from a Website

1 On a page that shows the RSS button (RSS) in the address box, click the button.

Note: If multiple news feeds are available, a menu opens. Click the news feed you want.

Safari opens the news feed.

2 Click the article you want to read.

Note: You can bookmark a news feed by choosing **Bookmarks** and **Add Bookmark**.

TIP

How can I get the latest news feeds in Safari?
Choose **Safari** and **Preferences**. The Preferences window opens. Click **RSS** (●) to display the RSS pane. In the Automatically Update Articles In area, select **Bookmarks bar** (☐ changes to ☑) to update news feeds on the Bookmarks bar or **Bookmarks menu** (☐ changes to ☑) to update news feeds on the Bookmarks menu. Click the **Check for updates** ↕ and choose how often to check for updates — **Every 30 minutes**, **Every hour**, or **Every day**. Click ● to close the Preferences window.

Choose Essential Security Settings

The web is packed with fascinating sites and useful information, but it is also full of criminals who want to attack your iMac and steal your valuable data.

Safari comes with several important security settings. To keep your iMac as safe as possible, make sure all the protective settings you need are turned on.

Choose Essential Security Settings

① Click **Safari**.

The Safari menu opens.

② Click **Preferences**.

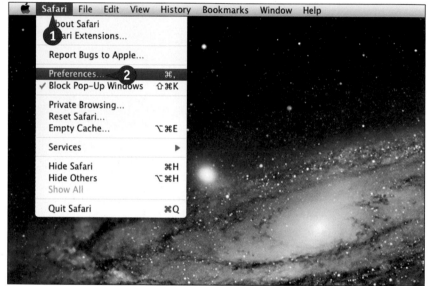

The Preferences window opens.

③ Click **Security**.

The Security pane opens.

④ Make sure that **Warn when visiting a fraudulent website** is checked (☑).

⑤ Make sure that **Block pop-up windows** is checked (☑).

⑥ Make sure that **Ask before sending a non-secure form from a secure website** is checked (☑).

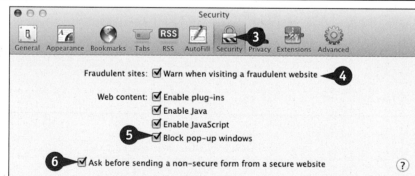

7 Click **Privacy**.

The Privacy pane opens.

8 In the Block Cookies area, click **From third parties and advertisers** (○ changes to ◉).

9 In the Limit Website Access to Location Services area, click **Prompt for each website once each day** (○ changes to ◉).

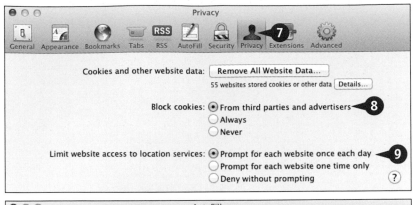

10 Click **AutoFill**.

The AutoFill pane opens.

11 Make sure that **User names and passwords** is cleared (☐).

12 Click ◉.

The Preferences window closes.

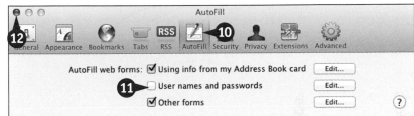

Should I allow pop-up windows for certain websites?

Pop-up windows can be dangerous. Some shopping sites need pop-up windows to function properly, but many malicious websites use pop-up windows to distribute malevolent software. For safety, keep pop-up windows blocked until you know a particular site requires them. Then choose **Safari** and **Block Pop-up Windows** to temporarily allow pop-ups, removing the check mark from the command. When you have finished, click the command again to restore the blocking.

What are cookies, and should I accept them?

A *cookie* is a small text file that a website uses to store information about what you do on the site — for example, what products you have browsed or added to your shopping cart. Cookies from sites you visit are usually helpful to you. Cookies from third-party sites, such as those that advertise on sites you visit, may threaten your privacy. For this reason, choose From Third Parties and Advertisers rather than **Never** in the Block Cookies area of the Privacy pane.

CHAPTER 6

Sending and Receiving Email

Apple Mail is a powerful email application. After setting up an email account, you can send and receive email messages and files.

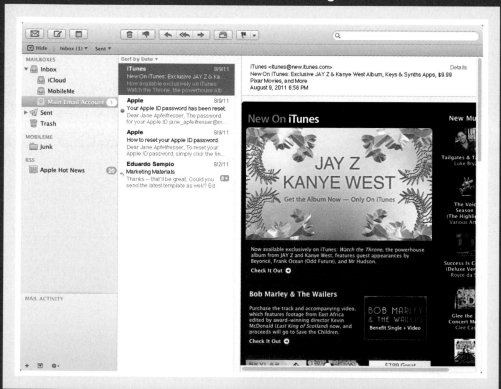

Open and Close Apple Mail

To use Mail, you must first open the application either from the Dock or from Launchpad. Unless you entered your email account information when setting up Mac OS X, you must set up an email account the first time you open Mail. See the next task for details of the setup process.

Open and Close Apple Mail

Open Mail

1 Click **Mail** (⬛) on the Dock.

Note: If Mail does not appear on the Dock, click **Launchpad** (🚀) on the Dock, and then click **Mail**.

2 The Mail window opens.

Close Mail

1 Click **Mail**.

The Mail menu opens.

2 Click **Quit Mail**.

Mail closes.

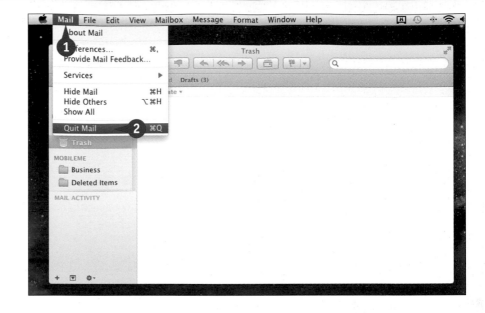

How can I make my iMac open Mail automatically for me?

You can make your iMac open Mail automatically each time you log in.

To do so, Control +
click or right-click
the **Mail** icon (■)
on the Dock,
highlight or click
Options, and then
click **Open at
Login**. Mac OS X
puts a check mark
next to Open at
Login. Next time
you log in,
Mail opens
automatically.

**Is it okay to leave Mail
running all the time?**

Many people like to leave
Mail running all the time
that they are using their
Macs. If you set Mail to
check automatically for new
messages, you receive the
messages soon after they
reach your ISP's mail server.
The disadvantage to keeping
Mail running is that new
messages may distract you
from your other tasks.

Set Up Your Email Account

Unless you gave the Mac Setup Assistant your account information while setting up Mac OS X, you must set up Mail with your email account. Mail works with most types of email accounts, including Apple's iCloud service and industry-standard POP mail servers and IMAP mail servers.

Mail is able to set up email accounts with major providers such as Apple's iCloud service, Google's Gmail, and Yahoo! Mail by using only your email address and password. For other accounts, you also need to enter the addresses and types of your provider's mail servers.

Set Up Your Email Account

Set Up an Email Account with a Major Provider

1 Click **Mail** (🖼) on the Dock.

The first time you open Mail, the Welcome to Mail assistant opens to its first screen.

2 Change the name if necessary. Mail uses your Mac OS X account name.

3 Type your email address.

4 Type your email account password.

5 Click **Create**.

Mail contacts the email servers and verifies the account.

The Account Summary screen appears.

6 If the Calendars check box appears, select it (☐ changes to ☑) to set up your calendars automatically.

7 If the Chat check box appears, select it (☐ changes to ☑) to set up iChat automatically.

8 Click **Create**.

Mail finishes setting up the account.

The Mail window opens.

Set Up an Email Account with Another Provider

1 Perform steps **1** to **4** of the list on the previous page and click **Continue**.

2 In the Incoming Mail Server screen, click the **Account Type** ‡ and choose the account type; this example uses **POP**.

3 Type a name for this email account.

4 Type the name of your provider's incoming mail server.

5 Verify your username and password and click **Continue**.

6 Check **Use Secure Sockets Layer (SSL)** if your ISP uses SSL.

7 Click the **Authentication** ‡ and choose the authentication for receiving messages, usually **Password**, and click **Continue**.

8 In the Outgoing Mail Server screen, type a name for this outgoing server.

9 Type the server address.

10 If your provider requires authentication for sending messages, click **Use Authentication** (☐ changes to ☑). Type your email username and password and click **Continue**.

11 In the Outgoing Mail Security screen, choose SSL and authentication settings.

12 In the Account Summary screen, click **Continue**, and Mail sets up the email account.

TIP

Which account type should I choose for my incoming mail server?

If you do not know which type of email server your ISP uses, check the ISP's website or call customer service to find out. Most ISPs use POP (Post Office Protocol) servers for incoming mail, but some use IMAP (Internet Mail Access Protocol). Exchange 2007 and Exchange IMAP are mostly used within companies rather than by ISPs that provide accounts to consumers.

Send an Email Message

After setting up an email account, you can send an email message to anybody whose email address you know. You can either type the email address directly into the message or pick it out of your Address Book.

You can create either unformatted text messages or messages that include formatting and pictures. Mail includes stationery templates for creating graphical messages.

Send an Email Message

Create and Send a Text-based Email Message

1 In Mail, click **New Message** (✐).

2 In the message window, type the name or address of the recipient.

Note: To send the message to two or more recipients, type a comma after the first address, and then type the next address.

3 To send a copy of the message to another person, type the email address in the Cc field.

Note: If you start typing an email address that is in Address Book, Mail offers to complete the address for you.

4 Type the subject or heading of the message.

5 Type the body of the message.

6 Click **Send** (✈).

Mail sends the message and stores a copy in your Sent folder for reference.

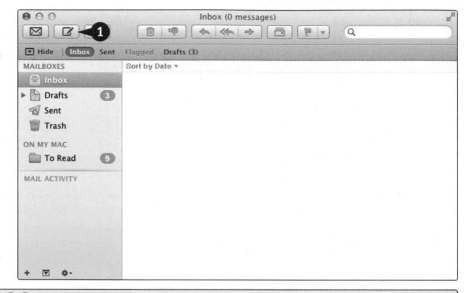

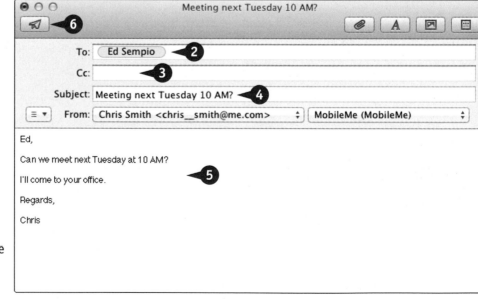

Create a Formatted Message Using Stationery

1 Click **Show Stationery** (▦).

2 In the Stationery pane, click a category of stationery.

3 Click a stationery design.

Mail applies the stationery design to the message.

4 Click **Hide Stationery** (▦) to close the Stationery pane.

5 Type the recipient's name or address.

6 Type the subject of the message.

7 Replace the sample text with your own text.

Note: You can change the font formatting of the message by clicking **Fonts** (**A**) and using the Font panel.

8 If the stationery includes photo placeholders, click **Photo Browser** (▣).

9 In the Photo Browser, click and drag a photo to each placeholder.

10 Click ▣ to close the Photo Browser.

11 Click **Send** (✈) to have Mail send the message.

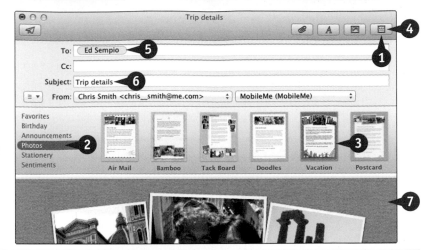

TIP

How do I send a message to many people at once?

To send the same message to many people at once, you can simply add each name to the To field. When you are sending a message to people who may not know each other, be discreet. Type your own email address in the To field. Then click **Customize** (▤▾), and click **Bcc Address Field** on the pop-up menu. A Bcc field appears below the Cc field. Add each address to the Bcc field, and then send the message. Each recipient then sees only your address in the To field, not the addresses of the other recipients.

Get Your Messages and Read Them

When someone sends you an email message, it goes to your mail provider's email server. To receive the message, you make Mail connect to the email server and retrieve the message.

Mail comes set to check for new messages when you launch the application and at five-minute intervals after that. You can set Mail to check at different intervals if you prefer.

Get Your Messages and Read Them

Get Your Messages from the Email Server

1 In Mail, click **Get Mail** (✉).

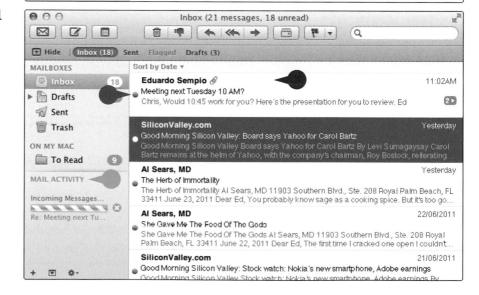

Mail connects to the email server and downloads any messages.

● The Mail Activity pane shows information about incoming messages.

● The new messages appear in your Inbox.

● A blue dot indicates that you have not read a message yet.

Open a Message for Reading

1 Double-click the message in the message list.

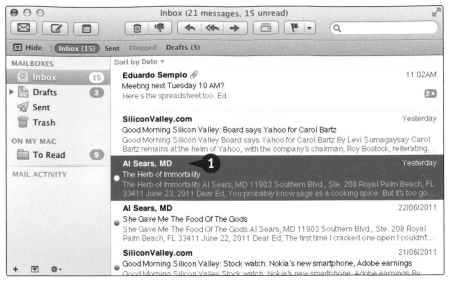

The message's text and contents appear in a separate window.

2 Read the message.

3 Click 🔘.

The message window closes.

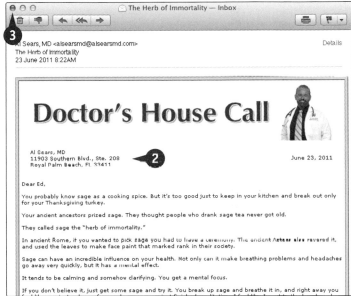

TIPS

Is there an easy way to tell whether I have new messages?

If you have unread messages, the Mail icon on the Dock shows a red circle containing the number of messages. If you usually read all your email messages, you can use this telltale as a quick way of checking whether you have new messages.

How can I change Mail's frequency of checking for new messages?

Choose **Mail** and **Preferences** to open the Preferences window, and then click **General**. Click the **Check for new messages** ⬍, and then click the interval: **Every minute**, **Every 5 minutes**, **Every 15 minutes**, **Every 30 minutes**, **Every hour**, or **Manually**. Click 🔘 to close the Preferences window.

Reply to a Message

After reading an email message you receive, you can reply to it. If you are one of several recipients of the message, you can choose between replying only to the sender or replying to the sender and the other recipients.

Reply to a Message

1 In the Inbox, click the message to which you want to reply.

Note: You can also double-click the message to open it in a message window, and then start the reply from there.

2 Click **Reply** (↰).

Note: If the message has multiple recipients, you can click **Reply All** (↞) to reply to the sender and to all the other recipients.

Mail creates the reply and opens it in a window.

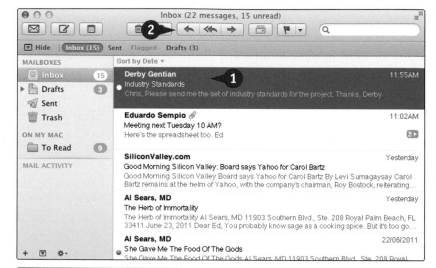

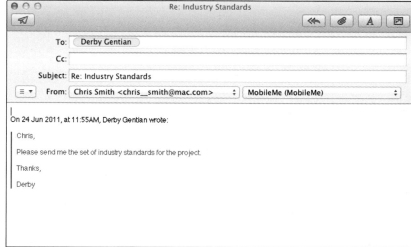

3 Type the text of your reply.

It is usually best to type your text at the beginning of the reply rather than after the message you are replying to.

Note: You can also add other recipients to the message as needed. If you have chosen to reply to all recipients, you can remove any recipients as necessary.

4 Click **Send** (✈).

Mail sends the reply and saves a copy in your Sent folder.

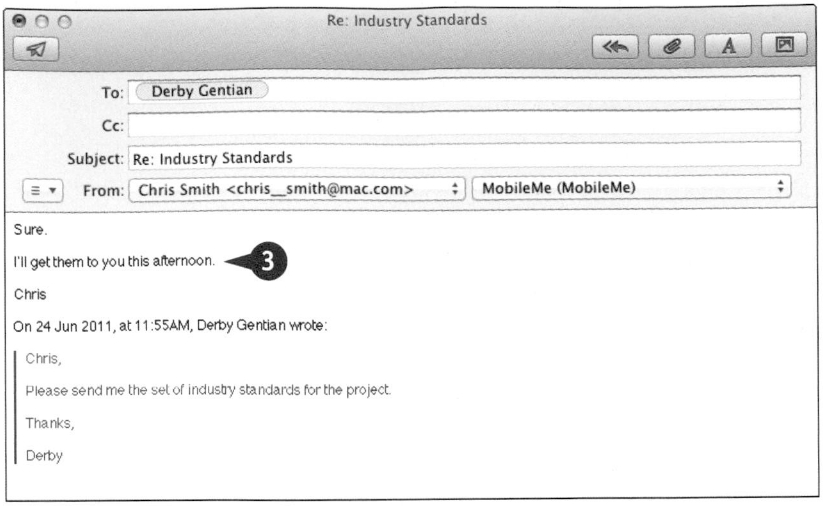

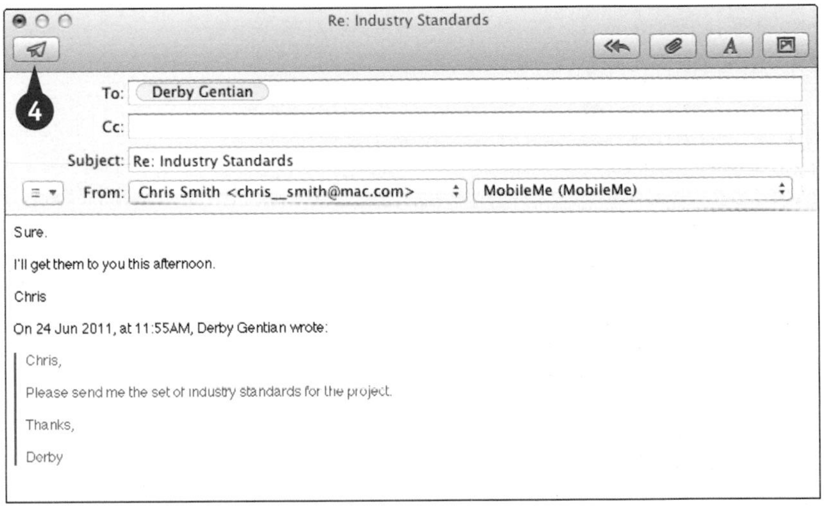

TIPS

Can I reply to only part of a message rather than send the whole of it?

To reply to only part of a message, select the part you want to include, and then click **Reply** (↩) or **Reply All** (↩↩), as appropriate. Mail creates a reply containing only the part you selected. Use this technique to keep replies concise and make them easy to read.

What are the Send Again and Redirect commands on the Message menu for?

Choose **Message** and **Send Again** to send the same message again — for example, because a mail server returns it. Choose **Message** and **Redirect** if you receive a message in error; this command lets you send it on to the correct recipient, if you know who that is.

Send a Message on to Someone Else

When you receive a message that you want to share with someone else, you can forward it to that person. You can add your own comments to the forwarded message — for example, to explain to the recipient who sent the original message or why you are forwarding it.

Send a Message on to Someone Else

1 In the Inbox, click the message you want to forward.

The preview pane shows the contents of the message.

Note: You can also forward a message that you have opened in a message window.

2 Click **Forward** (➡).

A window opens showing the forwarded message.

The subject line shows Fwd: and the message's original subject, so that the recipient can see it was forwarded.

3 Type the recipient's name or address.

4 Edit the subject line of the message if necessary.

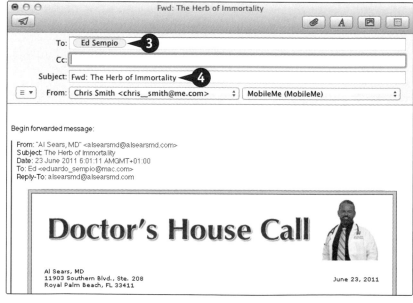

5 Optionally, edit the forwarded message to make it more useful to the recipient.

6 Type any message you want to include to the recipient.

7 Click **Send** (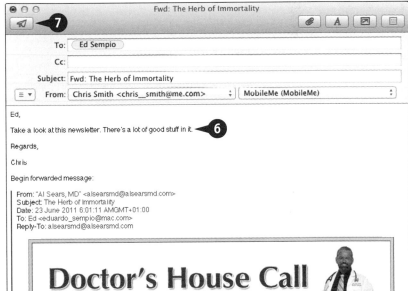).

Mail sends the forwarded message to the recipient.

What does the Forward as Attachment command on the Message menu do?

The Forward as Attachment command enables you to send a copy of a message as an attachment to a message rather than in the message itself. This command is useful when you want to send a forwarded message that includes formatting in a plain text message.

Can I forward only part of a message rather than all of it?

To forward only part of a message, select the part you want to forward, and then click **Forward** (➡). Mail includes only the part you selected. This trick is often quicker than creating a forwarded message containing the full text of the message and then deleting the parts you do not want to send.

Send a File via Email

Email also provides an easy way to send files to other people. You can attach one or more files to an email message so that the files travel as part of the message.

You can send any kind of file, from a document to a photo or movie. The recipient can then save the file on her computer and open it.

Send a File via Email

1 In Mail, click **New Message** (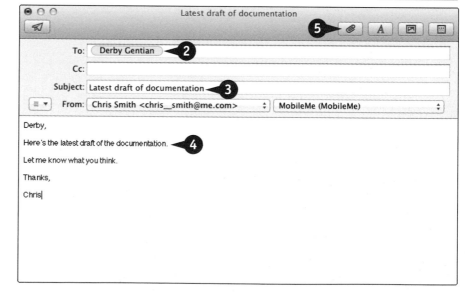).

A new message window opens.

2 Add the recipient's name or address.

3 Type the subject for the message.

4 Type any message body that is needed.

5 Click **Attach** ().

A dialog opens.

6 Click the file you want to attach to the message.

7 Click **Choose File**.

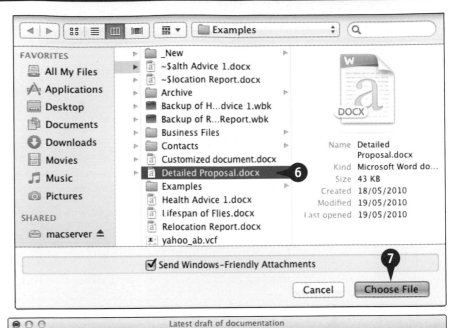

● The dialog closes, and Mail attaches the file to the message.

Note: Depending on the file type, the attachment may appear as an icon in the message or as a picture.

8 Click **Send** (✈).

Mail sends the message with the file attached.

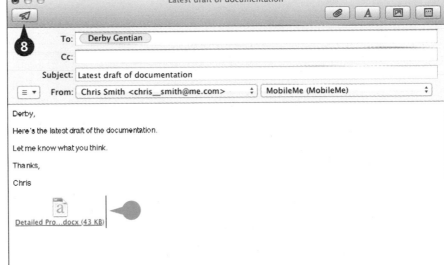

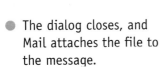

TIPS

How big a file can I attach to a message?
The size limit is hard to determine because it depends on your email provider and the recipient's email provider. Generally, it is wise to limit attachments to 5MB total, either a single file or multiple files. If you need to transfer many files, use a file transfer site such as Dropbox (www.getdropbox.com) or an FTP server.

Are there other ways to attach files to a message?
You can also attach a file to a message by clicking the file in a Finder window and then dragging it to the message window. To attach photos from iPhoto, select the photos in iPhoto, click **Share** (▣) on the toolbar, and then click **Email**. Mail then creates a new message containing the photos.

Receive a File via Email

A file you receive via email appears as an attachment to a message in your Inbox. You can use Quick Look to examine the file and decide whether to keep it or delete it. Quick Look can display the contents of many types of files, but not all.

To keep the file, you can save it to your iMac's hard drive. From there, you can open it in a suitable application.

Receive a File via Email

1 In your Inbox, double-click the message.

A message window opens showing the message.

● The attachment appears where the sender positioned it in the message.

2 Click **Details**.

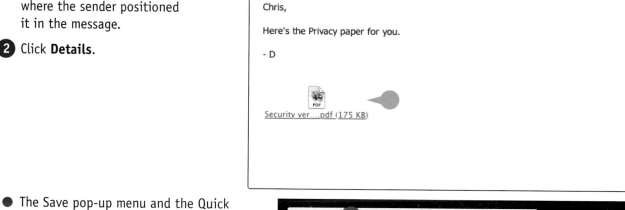

● The Save pop-up menu and the Quick Look button appear.

3 Click **Quick Look**.

● A Quick Look window opens showing the attachment's contents.

Note: Click **Full Screen** (⬛) if you want to view the document full screen. Click **Open With** to open the file in a suitable application — for example, click **Open with Preview** to open a PDF in Preview.

4 When you finish previewing the file, click ⊗.

The Quick Look window closes.

⑤ Click **Save** and keep pressing and holding the mouse button until the Save menu appears.

⑥ Click the file's name.

Note: If the message has multiple attachments, you can save them all in the same folder by clicking **Save All**.

The Save As dialog opens.

⑦ Navigate to the folder in which you want to save the files.

⑧ Click **Save**.

The Save As dialog closes.

⑨ If you want to remove the attachment from the message, choose **Message** and **Remove Attachments**.

Note: After saving the attachment, you should remove it from the message if you plan to keep the message. If you leave the attachment in the message, your mailbox can quickly grow to a large size.

TIPS

Do I need to check incoming files for viruses and malevolent software?

Yes, you should always check incoming files with antivirus software. Even though Mac OS X generally has fewer problems with viruses and malevolent software than Windows PCs, it is possible for a file to cause damage, steal data, or threaten your privacy.

Is there a quick way to see which messages have attachments?

In the Inbox, click the **Sort by** pop-up menu, and then click **Attachments**. Mail sorts the Inbox so that the messages with attachments appear first.

View Email Messages by Conversations

If you exchange email messages on the same topic with your colleagues, you can benefit from Mail's ability to display each exchange as a conversation instead of handling each message as a separate item. Conversations are also called *threads*.

Mail lets you choose whether to organize your messages by conversations. If you do so, you can expand or collapse all conversations to see the messages you want.

View Email Messages by Conversations

1 In Mail, click your Inbox or the folder you want to use.

● The messages in the folder appear.

2 Click **View**.

The View menu opens.

3 Click **Organize by Conversation**.

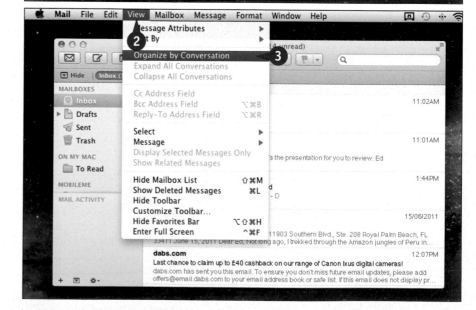

Mail organizes the messages into conversations, so that each exchange appears as a single item rather than as separate messages.

The number to the right of a conversation indicates how many messages it contains.

4 Click the number for the conversation you want to expand.

Note: You can expand all conversations in the folder by clicking **View** and **Expand All Conversations**. Similarly, you can collapse all conversations in the folder by clicking **View** and **Collapse All Conversations**.

● Mail expands the conversation, so that you can see each of the messages it contains.

5 Double-click the message you want to open.

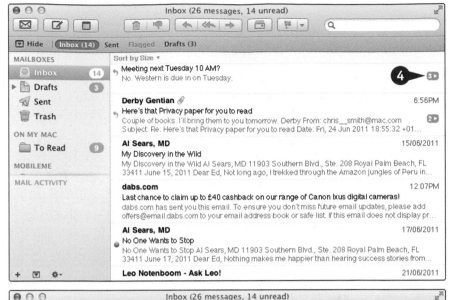

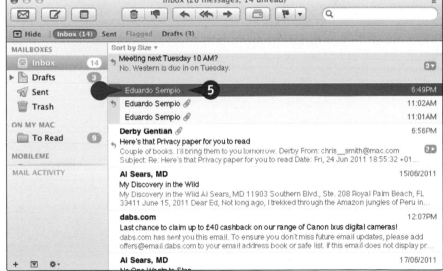

TIP

Are there other advantages to viewing an exchange as a conversation?
When you view an exchange as a conversation, you can manipulate all the messages in a single move instead of having to manipulate each message individually. For example, click the conversation and drag it to a folder to file all its messages in that folder, or click the message and press ⌘+Delete to delete the entire conversation.

Get Your Email on Any Computer

If you have an account on Apple's iCloud service, you can send and receive email using any computer — not just your iMac but any Mac; any iPad, iPhone, or iPod touch; or any PC.

To use iCloud, all you need is an Internet connection and a full-featured web browser, such as Safari or Internet Explorer.

Get Your Email on Any Computer

Log In to iCloud Mail and Read Your Mail

① Open your web browser. For example, on a Mac, click **Safari** (◉) on the Dock.

② Select the address in the address box. For example, in Safari, triple-click in the address box.

③ Type the address **icloud.com** and press **Return**.

The iCloud Login page opens.

④ Type your login name.

⑤ Type your password.

⑥ Click **Sign In**.

iCloud shows your Inbox.

Note: If iCloud shows another part of your user account, such as your contacts or calendar, click **iCloud** (△), and then click **Mail** (✉).

⑦ Click a message header.

iCloud displays the message's content.

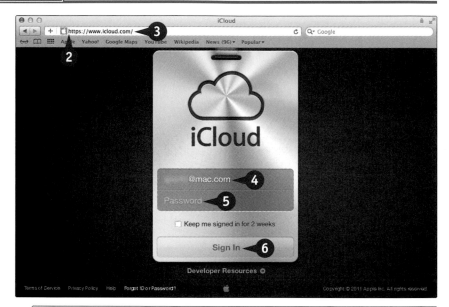

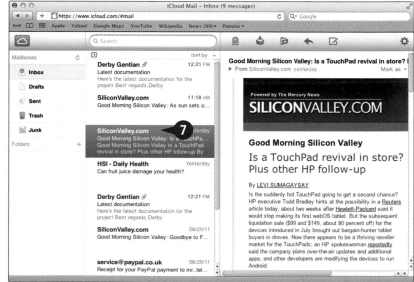

Send an Email Message

1 Click **Compose new message** ().

A New Message window opens.

2 In the To field, type the recipient's name or address.

3 Type the subject for the message.

4 Type the body text of the message.

5 Click **Send**.

iCloud sends the message.

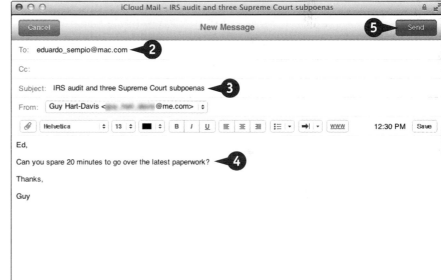

TIPS

Should I check the Keep Me Signed In for 2 Weeks box when I log into iCloud?

Check the **Keep me signed in for 2 weeks** check box (□ changes to ☑) only when you are using one of your own Macs to access iCloud. Using this setting on another computer increases the risk that someone else can access your iCloud mail.

How can I get an iCloud account?

You can sign up for an iCloud account on the iCloud website, www.icloud.com.

Create Notes

As well as email messages, Mail also enables you to create notes. Notes are useful for jotting down information or for planning what you need to do.

You can paste a note's contents into another document, or you can create an email from the contents of a note.

Create Notes

Create a Note

1 In Mail, click **New Note** (▣).

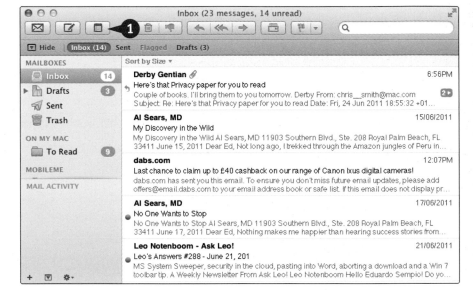

Mail opens a note window.

2 Type the text of the note.

Note: You can also paste text into the note window.

3 When you have finished creating the note, click ▣.

Mail closes the note window.

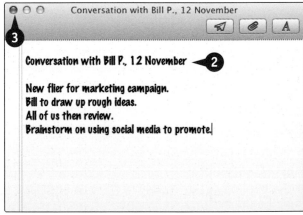

View Your Notes

1 If the Reminders category is collapsed, position the mouse pointer over it, and then click **Show** to expand the category.

2 Click **Notes**.

● The list of notes appears.

3 Click a note to display it in the preview pane, or double-click a note to display it in a window.

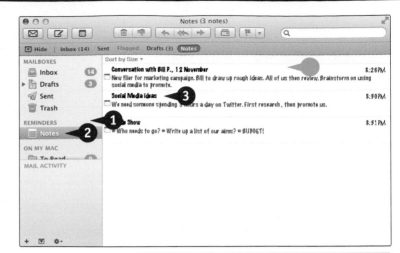

Send a Note

1 In Mail, double-click the note to open it in a note window.

2 Click **Send** ( ).

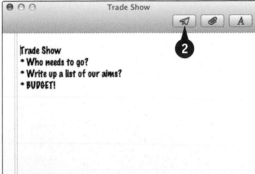

Mail opens a new message containing the note.

3 Type the recipient for the note.

4 Edit the subject as needed. Mail inserts the note's title as the subject.

5 Edit the note if necessary.

6 Click **Send** ( ).

Mail sends the note.

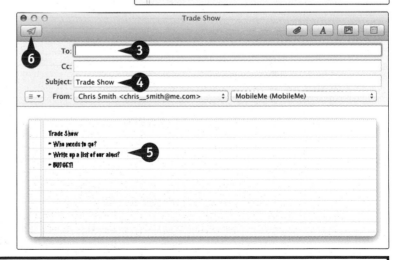

TIP

How can I send just the text of a note?

After creating a message containing the note, choose **Format** and **Make Plain Text**. Mail removes the note formatting, leaving only the text.

Reduce the Amount of Spam You Receive

Spam is unwanted email messages, also called *junk mail*. Spam ranges from messages offering stimulating pharmaceuticals — real or fake — to attempts to steal your financial details, passwords, or identity.

Avoiding spam completely is almost impossible, but you can reduce the amount you receive by setting Mail to identify junk mail automatically and by learning to spot identifying features of spam messages.

Reduce the Amount of Spam You Receive

Set Mail to Identify Junk Mail Automatically

1 Click **Mail**.

2 Click **Preferences**.

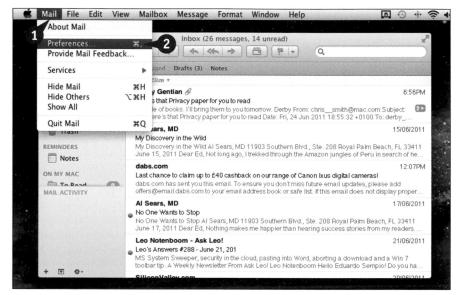

The Preferences window opens.

3 Click **Junk Mail**.

4 In the Junk Mail pane, make sure **Enable junk mail filtering** is checked (☑).

5 Click **Mark as junk mail, but leave it in my Inbox** (○ changes to ●) if you want to review junk mail in your Inbox. Click **Move it to the Junk mailbox** if you prefer to review it in your Junk mailbox.

6 Make sure **Sender of message is in my Address Book**, **Sender of message is in my Previous Recipients**, and **Message is addressed using my full name** are all checked (☑).

7 Verify that **Trust junk mail headers in messages** is checked (☑).

8 Click ⬤ to close the Preferences window.

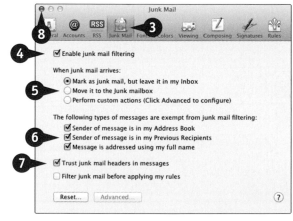

Review Your Junk Mail

1 Click **Inbox** or **Junk Email** — wherever you told Mail to put your junk mail in step **5**.

The list of messages in the mailbox appears.

2 Double-click a message.

A message window opens showing the message.

3 Look to see whether Mail has identified the message as junk mail.

4 Look at the To field to see if the message is addressed to you. In the sample message, the To field does not appear.

5 Check whether the message greets you by name or with a generic greeting, such as "Dear customer."

6 Read the message's content and see if it is obviously spam or an offer too good to be true.

7 If the message appears to be spam, and Mail has not identified it as junk, click **Junk** ( ).

8 Click **Delete** ( ) to delete the message.

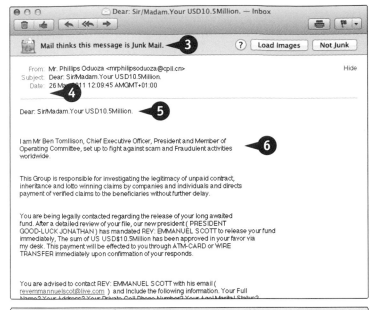

TIPS

How can I tell whether a message is genuine or spam?
Does the message show your email address and your name? If not, it is most likely spam. If it does, read the content and decide whether it is likely true. If the message calls for action, such as reactivating an online account that you have, do not click a link in the message. Instead, open Safari, type the address of the website, log in as usual, and see if an alert is waiting for you.

How can I make a spammer remove me from his mailing list?
You cannot make a spammer remove you from his mailing list. Never click a "Remove Me" link in a message because it confirms to the spammer that your email address is "live" and makes it worth selling to other spammers. For the same reason, never reply to spam either.

CHAPTER 7

Organizing Your Contacts and Schedule

To help you keep your daily life organized, your iMac includes iCal for appointments and Address Book for contacts.

Open and Close iCal

iCal is a sleek and streamlined calendar application that makes it easy to enter and track your appointments and events. You can launch iCal either from the Dock or from Launchpad.

Open and Close iCal

Open iCal

1 Click **iCal** (📅) on the Dock.

Note: If iCal does not appear on the Dock, click **Launchpad** (🚀) on the Dock, and then click **iCal**.

The iCal window opens, showing your existing calendars.

Close iCal

1 Click **iCal**.

The iCal menu opens.

2 Click **Quit iCal**.

iCal closes.

TIP

How can I make iCal run each time I log in?
If you use iCal in every computing session, set the application to launch automatically when you log in to your iMac. **Control** +click or right-click **iCal** (📅) on the Dock, highlight or click **Options**, and then click **Open at Login**. Mac OS X puts a check mark next to this item to indicate it is turned on. Next time you log in, iCal opens automatically.

Find Your Way around the Calendar

iCal has a streamlined user interface that makes it easy to move among days, weeks, months, and years. You can click the **Today** button to instantly display the current day, or use the Go to Date dialog to jump directly to a specific date.

Find Your Way around the Calendar

View and Navigate by Days

1 Click **Day**.

iCal displays the current day, including a schedule of upcoming events.

2 Click **Next** (▶) to move to the next day or **Previous** (◀) to move to the previous day.

iCal displays the day you chose.

View and Navigate by Weeks

1 Click **Week**.

iCal displays the current week.

2 Click **Next** (▶) to move to the next week or **Previous** (◀) to move to the previous week.

iCal displays the week you chose.

View and Navigate by Months

1 Click **Month**.

iCal displays the current month.

2 Click **Next** (▶) to move to the next month or **Previous** (◀) to move to the previous month.

iCal displays the month you chose.

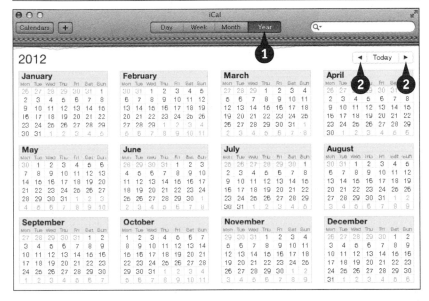

View and Navigate by Years

1 Click **Year**.

iCal displays the current year.

2 Click **Next** (▶) to move to the next year or **Previous** (◀) to move to the previous year.

iCal displays the year you chose.

Note: In Week view, Month view, or Year view, double-click a day to display it in Day view. Click **Today** when you want to switch to today's date.

TIPS

Which keyboard shortcuts can I use to navigate in iCal?

Press ⌘+**1** to display the calendar by day, ⌘+**2** by week, ⌘+**3** by month, or ⌘+**4** by year. Press ⌘+**→** to move to the next day, week, month, or year, or ⌘+**←** to move to the previous one. Press ⌘+**Shift**+**T** to open the Go to Date dialog, discussed next. Press ⌘+**T** to jump to today's date.

How can I jump to a specific date?

To jump to a specific date, click **View** and **Go to Date**. In the Go to Date dialog, click the day, month, or year, and then click ⬍ to increase or decrease the number. Click **Show**, and iCal displays the date.

Create a New Calendar

iCal comes with two calendars already created for you, the Home calendar and the Work calendar. You can create new calendars as needed. For example, you can create a calendar specifically for sports or for family events.

Create a New Calendar

1 In iCal, click **File**.

The File menu opens.

2 Click **New Calendar**.

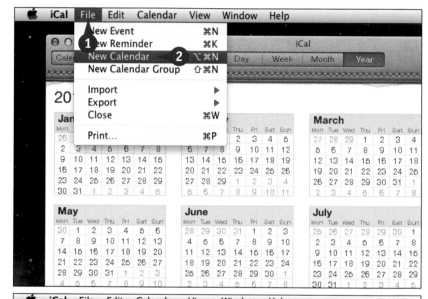

iCal displays the Calendars pop-up panel, creates a new calendar, and displays an edit box around its default name, Untitled.

3 Type the name for the calendar and press **Return**.

iCal applies the name to the calendar.

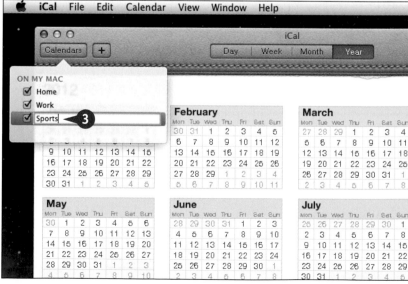

④ **Control**+click or right-click the calendar's name.

The shortcut menu opens.

⑤ Click **Get Info**.

A dialog opens showing information for the calendar.

⑥ Click ⬍.

The pop-up menu opens.

⑦ Click the color you want the calendar to use.

⑧ Type a description for the calendar.

Note: Click **Ignore alerts** (☐ changes to ☑) if you want to suppress alerts for the calendar.

⑨ Click **OK**.

The dialog closes.

You can now add events to the calendar.

TIPS

What do the check boxes in the Calendars pop-up panel do?

The check boxes control which calendars iCal displays. Deselect a check box (☑ changes to ☐) to remove a calendar's events from display.

How can I organize my many calendars?

You can organize your calendars by creating calendar groups. Click **Calendars** to open the Calendars pane, and then **Control**+click or right-click in it and click **New Group**. Type the name for the new group and press **Return**. You can then click a calendar and drag it into the group, so that it appears in a collapsible list under the group (●).

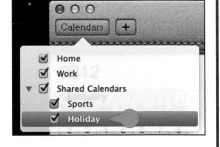

Create an Appointment

To organize your time commitments, create an *event* in iCal for each appointment, meeting, or trip. iCal displays each event as an item on its grid, so you can easily see what is supposed to happen when.

You can create an event either for a specific length of time, such as one or two hours, or for an entire day. And you can create either an appointment that occurs only once or an appointment that repeats one or more times, as needed.

Create an Appointment

1 Navigate by days, weeks, months, or years to reach the day on which you want to create the event.

2 If the appointments area is in Month view or Year view, click **Day** to switch to Day view or **Week** to switch to Week view.

3 In the appointments area, click the time the event starts, and then drag to the time at which it ends.

iCal creates an event where you clicked and selects its default name, New Event.

4 Type the name for the event and then press **Return**.

5 Double-click the event.

A panel opens showing the details of the event.

6 Click **location** and type the location for the event.

7 Click **calendar** and then click the calendar to which the event belongs.

8 If you want a reminder, click **alert** and choose the details of the alert.

Note: You can create multiple alerts for the same event if you need to.

9 To add further information, click **note** and type the note.

10 Click **Done**.

The panel closes.

TIPS

How do I create an all-day event?
To create an all-day event, double-click in the all-day area at the top of the day. iCal creates a new event, gives it the name New Event, and displays an edit box around the name. Type the name for the event and press Return.

How do I create a repeating appointment?
In the panel showing the appointment's details, click **repeat** (●) and click **Every day**, **Every week**, **Every month**, or **Every year**. Use the controls that appear for setting the details of the repetition — for example, click **end**, click **After**, and specify **8 times**. For other options, choose **Custom** and set the repetition in the dialog that opens.

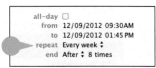

Share Your Calendar with Other People

As well as keeping your calendar on your iMac, iCal enables you to share your calendar with other people so that they know when you are busy.

If you store your calendar on iCloud, you can share it by simply turning on sharing and specifying whom you want to share it with. If you store your calendar on your iMac, you can share that calendar with others by publishing it to your MobileMe account or to a private server — for example, a server that your company runs.

Share Your Calendar with Other People

1 Click **Calendars**.

The Calendars pop-up panel appears.

2 In one of the iCloud sections, Control+click or right-click the calendar you want to share.

3 Click **Share Calendar**.

The Share Calendar dialog appears.

4 Type the name under which you want to publish the calendar.

Note: Make your calendar's name descriptive so that people can identify it easily. For example, publish it as John Brown's Work Calendar rather than just Work.

5 In the Share With area, click **Everyone** (○ changes to ◉) if you want to share the calendar publicly on iCloud. If you want to choose who can view your calendar, click **Only the people you invite** (○ changes to ◉).

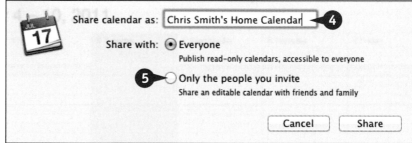

- If you click **Only the people you invite**, the dialog expands to reveal a box for selecting the people.

6 To add a person, click in the box and type the email address.

7 Click the **Privilege** ↕ and choose **Read & Write** if you want the person to be able to change your calendar. Choose **Read only** if you want the person to be able to view your calendar but not change it.

Note: To remove a person from the box, click the person's name, and then click **Remove** (⊟).

8 When you have created the list of people, or if you have chosen to share the calendar with everyone, click **Share**.

iCal shares the calendar.

Note: To stop sharing a calendar, click **Calendars**, Control +click or right-click the calendar, and then click **Stop Sharing**. In the confirmation dialog that opens, click **Stop Sharing**.

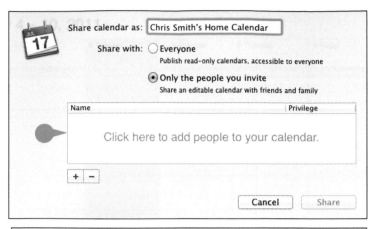

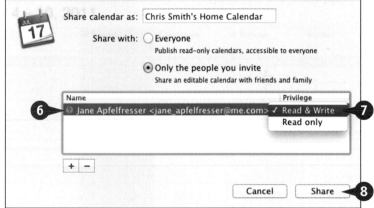

TIP

How do I publish a calendar to a private server?

Ask your network administrator for the server's base URL and your login name and password. Then click the calendar and choose **Calendar** and **Publish** to open the Publish Calendar dialog. Click the **Publish on** ↕ , and then click **A private server** in the pop-up menu. An extra section appears in the dialog. Type the server's address in the Base URL field. Type your login name and password. Choose what items to publish (☐ changes to ☑), and then click **Publish**.

Subscribe to a Calendar Someone Is Sharing

To learn the details of someone else's schedule, you can subscribe to a calendar that person is sharing. After subscribing, you can view the other person's calendar in iCal.

You can subscribe to a calendar either by entering its URL in iCal or by clicking a link in a message that you have received.

Subscribe to a Calendar Someone Is Sharing

1 In iCal, click **Calendar**.

The Calendar menu opens.

2 Click **Subscribe**.

The Enter the URL of the Calendar You Want to Subscribe To dialog opens.

3 Type or paste in the calendar's URL.

Note: If you receive a link to a shared calendar, click the link in Mail. iCal opens and displays the Enter the URL of the Calendar You Want to Subscribe To dialog with the URL inserted. Click **Subscribe**.

4 Click **Subscribe**.

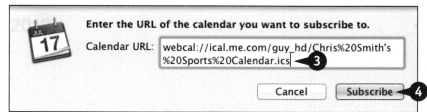

A dialog opens showing the details of the calendar.

5 Type the name you want to see for the calendar.

6 Click ⬍ and pick the color with which to code the calendar.

7 Choose whether to remove alarms, attachments, and reminders from the calendar.

8 Click ⬍ and choose whether to automatically refresh the calendar: **No**, **Every 5 minutes**, **Every 15 minutes**, **Every hour**, **Every day**, or **Every week**.

9 Click **OK**.

● The calendar appears in the Subscriptions list, and you see its contents.

How do I update a shared calendar?

To update a shared calendar with the latest information the sharer has published, click **Calendars**, `Control`+click or right-click the calendar, and then click **Refresh**. If you subscribe to two or more calendars, you can click **Refresh All** on the shortcut menu to update them all.

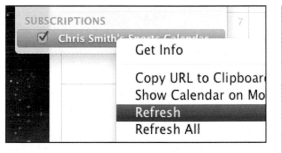

How do I unsubscribe from a shared calendar?

Instead of unsubscribing, you delete the calendar from the list. Click **Calendars**, `Control`+click or right-click the calendar, and then click **Delete**.

Open and Close Address Book

Address Book is a powerful but easy-to-use application for tracking and managing your contacts. You can launch Address Book either from the Dock or from Launchpad.

Open and Close Address Book

Open Address Book

① Click **Address Book** (📖) on the Dock.

Note: If Address Book does not appear on the Dock, click **Launchpad** (🚀) on the Dock, and then click **Address Book**.

The Address Book window opens.

Note: Even though Address Book's window is different from regular windows, you can resize it by dragging its borders.

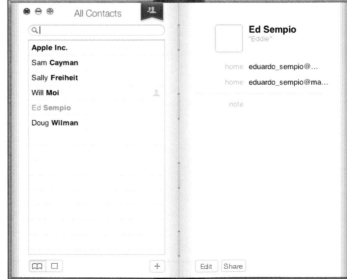

Close Address Book

1 Click **Address Book**.

The Address Book menu opens.

2 Click **Quit Address Book**.

Address Book closes.

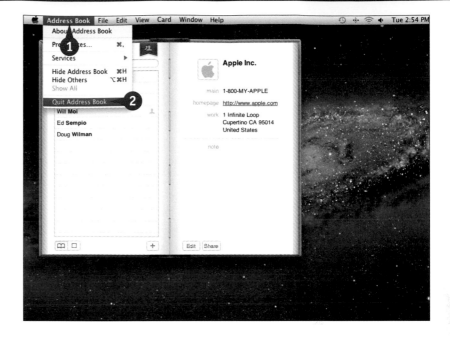

How can I start an email message to a contact in Address Book?

You can do this in either of two ways.

- In Address Book, click the contact's card (●), and then click the button before the email address — for example, **Work** (●). On the pop-up menu, click **Send Email** (●).

- In Mail, click **New Message** to start a new message, and then click **Addresses**. The Addresses window opens, showing the contacts in

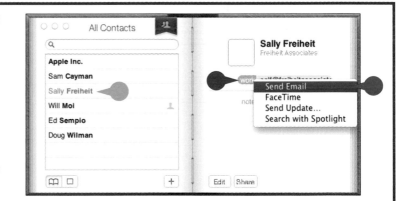

Address Book. You can then add one or more contacts to the message. Alternatively, start a new message, start typing a contact's name or email address, and then click the contact in the matches on the pop-up list that appears.

Add Someone to Your Address Book

To add someone to your Address Book, you create a new card and enter the person's data on it. Address Book provides storage slots for many different items of information, from the person's name, address, and phone numbers to the email addresses, website URL, and photo.

Add Someone to Your Address Book

1 In Address Book, click **New Card** (+).

Note: You can also add a card by pressing ⌘+N or choosing **File** and **New Card**.

Address Book adds a new card with placeholders for the information.

2 Click the first placeholder and type the person's first name.

Note: Press Tab to move the selection from the current field to the next. You can also click another field to move to it.

3 Type the person's last name.

4 If the person is with a company, type the company name.

● When creating a card for a company or organization rather than a person, click **Company** (□ changes to ☑).

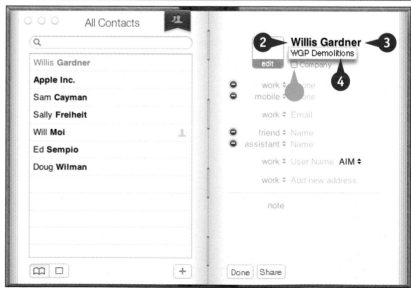

5 Click ▦ next to the first Phone field.

The pop-up menu opens.

6 Click the type of phone number — for example, **work**, **home**, or **mobile**.

7 Type the phone number.

8 Add other phone numbers as needed.

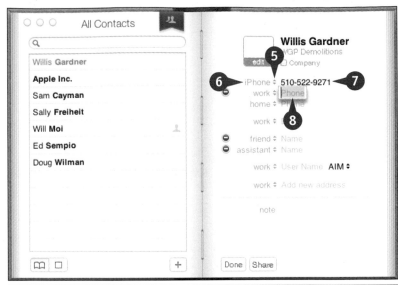

9 Click ▦ next to the first Email field.

10 Click the type of email address — for example, **work** or **home**.

11 Type the email address.

12 Add the physical address and other information.

13 Click **Done** to stop editing the card.

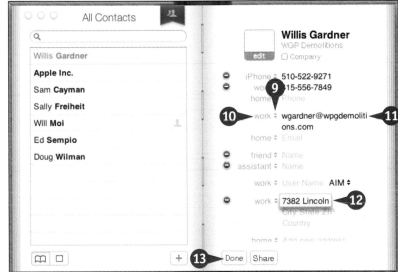

TIPS

Is there a quicker way of adding a contact to Address Book than typing all the information?

Many people include virtual address cards called vCards with email messages. If you receive a vCard in

Mail, Control +click or right-click it, highlight **Open With**, and choose **Address Book**. A dialog opens confirming that you want to import the card into Address Book. Click **Import**.

How do I delete a contact from Address Book?

To delete a contact, click the card, and then choose **Edit** and **Delete Card** or press Delete . A confirmation dialog opens. Click **Delete**.

Change the Information for a Contact

People frequently change their phone numbers, email addresses, and even their names, so you will often need to edit your contacts to update their information.

You can add extra fields to a contact record as needed, enabling you to store additional phone numbers, email addresses, or physical addresses. You can even add a photo for a contact.

Change the Information for a Contact

1 On the left page of Address Book, click the contact you want to change.

2 Click **Edit**.

Address Book opens the contact's card for editing.

The Done button replaces the Edit button.

3 To change an existing field, click it and then type the updated information.

Note: To add a field, click **Card**, **Add Field**, and then the field type — for example, **Phone**.

4 To remove an existing field, click ⊖ next to it.

5 To add a photo for the contact, double-click the picture placeholder.

● Address Book opens a dialog for adding a photo.

6 Click **iPhoto** (🖼) on the Dock.

The iPhoto window opens.

7 Click and drag a photo from iPhoto to the Address Book dialog.

Note: You can also click and drag a photo from a Finder window to the Address Book dialog.

8 Choose **iPhoto** and **Quit iPhoto**.

iPhoto closes.

9 Click and drag the slider if you want to zoom the photo.

10 Click and drag the photo if you want to reposition it.

11 Click **Set**.

Address Book closes the dialog and adds the photo to the contact.

TIP

How can I add information that does not fit in any of Address Book's fields?

The Notes field is useful for adding extra information, but you can also create a custom field name. Click ⊕ next to an empty field. On the pop-up menu that opens, click **Custom**. The Add Custom Label dialog opens. Type the label you want to use, and then click **OK**. Address Book adds the label to the field. Type the data for the field.

Add custom label:

Interests

Cancel   OK

Organize Your Contacts into Groups

Like most people, you probably have several different types of contacts — family, friends, colleagues, companies, and so on. Address Book enables you to organize your contacts into separate groups, making it easier to find the contacts you need.

After creating groups, you can view a single group at a time or search within a group. You can also send an email message to all the members of a group.

Organize Your Contacts into Groups

Create a Group of Contacts

1 In Address Book, click **Groups**.

The Groups page appears.

2 Click **New Group** (+).

Address Book adds a group named Untitled Group and displays an edit box around it.

3 Type the name for the group and press **Return**.

The group takes on the name.

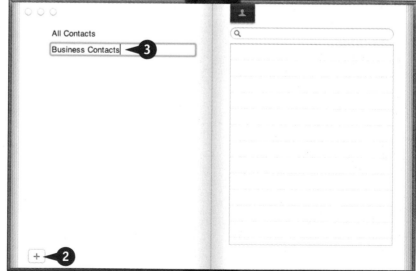

Add Contacts to the Group

① Click **All Contacts**.

Address Book displays all your contacts.

② Click and drag a contact to the new group.

Note: To add multiple contacts to the group, click the first, and then ⌘+click each of the others. Click and drag the selected contacts to the group.

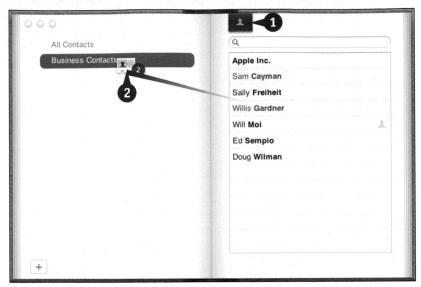

View a Group or Search within It

① Click the group.

Address Book displays the contacts in the group.

② To search within the group, click in the search box and type a search term.

Address Book displays matching contacts.

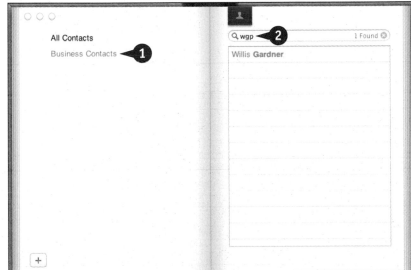

TIPS

How do I remove a contact from a group?

Click the group and then click the contact. Choose **Edit** and **Remove from Group**. Address Book removes the contact from the group but does not delete the contact record.

How do I delete a group?

Click the group, and then choose **Edit** and **Delete Group**.

Address Book displays a confirmation message. Click **Delete**. Deleting a group does not affect the contacts it contains; the contacts remain available through the All Contacts group.

CHAPTER 8

Chatting with iChat and FaceTime

Mac OS X includes iChat for instant messaging and FaceTime for video chat with Mac, iPad, and iPhone users.

Open and Close iChat

To start using iChat, you open the application from Launchpad. If you plan to use iChat frequently, you can add it to the Dock.

The first time you run iChat, you set it up with your instant messaging account. iChat works with Apple's MobileMe service and the iCloud service that is replacing it. iChat also works with the AIM, Jabber, and Google Talk instant messaging services. If you do not already have a suitable account, you can create one during the setup process.

Open and Close iChat

Open iChat

1 Click **Launchpad** (🚀) on the Dock.

The Launchpad screen appears.

2 Click **iChat**.

Note: If you will run iChat frequently, drag the iChat icon from the Launchpad screen to the Dock. You can then launch iChat from the Dock.

The Welcome to iChat dialog opens.

3 Click **Continue**.

The Account Setup dialog opens.

4 Click ⇕ and then choose your account type.

5 Type your account name.

6 Type your password.

7 Click **Continue**.

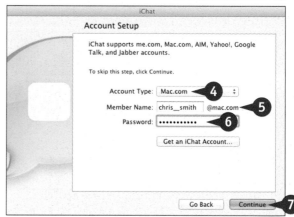

The Conclusion dialog opens.

8 Click **Done**.

The Conclusion dialog closes.

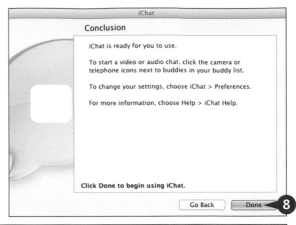

Close iChat

1 When you have finished using iChat, as described on the following pages, click **iChat**.

The iChat menu opens.

2 Click **Quit iChat**.

Where can I get an instant messaging account?
If you have a MobileMe account or iCloud account, you already have an instant messaging account that uses your MobileMe name. Otherwise, the easiest way to get an instant messaging account is to create an iChat account. This is free and takes only a minute. In the Account Setup dialog, choose **mac.com** or **me.com** in the Account Type pop-up menu, and then click **Get an iChat Account**. A Safari window opens to the signup form on the Apple website.

Can I chat without getting an instant messaging account?
You can chat with people on your local network without getting an instant messaging account. In the iChat Buddies window, click the **Bonjour** category to expand its contents, displaying a list of users on your network. Then follow the instructions later in this chapter.

Add Someone to Your Buddy List

After setting up your iChat account, you need to add the people you want to chat with. iChat calls these people *buddies*, and the list to which you add them is your Buddy List. Some other instant messaging services call these people *contacts*.

This task assumes that iChat is already running. If iChat is not running, launch it in one of the ways explained in the previous task.

Add Someone to Your Buddy List

1 Click **Add** (⊞).

The Add menu opens.

2 Click **Add Buddy**.

The Enter the Buddy's Account dialog opens.

3 Type the buddy's account name.

4 Click ⬍ and then click the group you want to add the buddy to: **Buddies**, **Family**, or **Co-Workers**.

5 Type the first name you want to use for your buddy.

6 Type the last name you want to use for your buddy.

7 Click **Add**.

iChat adds the buddy to your Buddy List.

● If your buddy is online, the buddy appears in the group you chose in step **4**.

If your buddy is offline, the buddy appears in the Offline group.

8 Control +click or right-click the buddy.

The shortcut menu appears.

9 Click **Show Info**.

The Info window for the buddy opens.

10 Click **Alerts**.

The Alerts pane opens.

11 Choose any alerts you want for the buddy:

● Click the **Event** ⇕ and choose the event. For example, choose **Buddy Becomes Available** or **Buddy Becomes Unavailable**.

● Click the option you want. For example, click **Play a sound** (☐ changes to ☑), click ⇕ , and then choose the sound.

12 Click ⬤ to close the Info window.

TIPS

How do I remove a buddy from the Buddy List?

Click the buddy in the Buddy List, and then click **Buddies** and **Remove Buddy**. You can also click the buddy and press Delete . A confirmation dialog appears. Click **Remove**. iChat removes the buddy.

How do I change the name iChat displays for a buddy?

Control +click or right-click the buddy, and then click **Show Info** on the shortcut menu. The Info window opens. Click **Address Card**. The Address Card pane opens. Change the name in the First Name field, Last Name field, or Nickname field, and then click ⇕ .

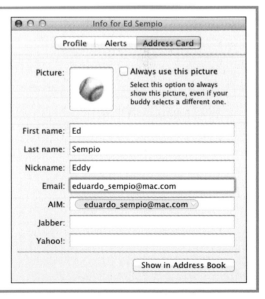

Chat with a Buddy Using Text

The easiest way to start using iChat is by exchanging text messages with one or more buddies who are online and available to chat when you are.

You send an invitation to text chat to your buddy. If your buddy accepts the invitation, iChat opens a chat window. You can then start chatting.

Chat with a Buddy Using Text

1 In iChat, click the buddy in the Buddy List.

2 Click **Start a Text Chat** (🅰).

iChat opens a text chat window.

Note: You can also contact a buddy by sending an instant message or an email message. Click the buddy, click **Buddies,** and then click **Send Instant Message** or **Send Email.**

3 Type a greeting or question.

4 Press (Return).

iChat sends the invitation, which opens on your buddy's computer.

When your buddy accepts the invitation, the response appears in the Chat window.

5 Type a reply.

6 If you want to include an *emoticon* or *smiley*, an expressive icon, click 🙂.

The list of smileys opens.

7 Click the smiley you want to use.

8 Press **Return**.

iChat sends your reply, and the conversation continues.

9 When you have finished chatting, click 🔘.

The Chat window closes.

TIP

How do I prevent people from contacting me?
You can block a buddy from contacting you via instant messaging. When you receive an unwanted invitation from a buddy, click **Block**, and then click **Block** in the confirmation message that opens. With the block in place, the buddy cannot see whether you are online and cannot contact you; similarly, you cannot see or contact the buddy. To unblock a buddy, **Control** +click or right-click the buddy in the Buddy List, and then click **Unblock**.

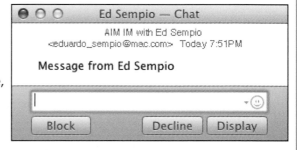

Chat with a Buddy Using Audio and Video

Your iMac includes a built-in microphone and an iSight webcam, so you are fully equipped to chat using audio and video as long as your buddy's computer also has a microphone and webcam.

Chat with a Buddy Using Audio and Video

Start a Video Chat with a Buddy

1. In iChat, click the buddy in the Buddy List.

2. Click **Start a video chat** (◼◂).

   iChat opens a Video Chat window showing your video preview and places a call to your buddy.

3. Adjust your iMac's camera or move so that your preview shows you as you want to appear.

   When your buddy accepts the call, the Video Chat window displays your buddy's picture and shrinks your preview to a picture-in-picture video.

4. Chat with your buddy.

   ● Click **Effects** to open the Effects window, in which you apply visual effects to your video.

   ● Click to use iChat Theater to share a file or pictures from iPhoto.

   ● Click to mute or unmute the audio.

   ● Click to switch to Full-Screen mode.

5. When you have finished chatting, click ◼.

Receiving an Invitation to Video Chat

When your buddy calls, iChat displays a Video Chat invitation window.

1 Position the mouse pointer over the Video Chat invitation window.

The Video Chat invitation window expands to show your preview.

2 Click **Accept** if you want to accept the invitation. Otherwise, click **Decline** to decline it, or click **Text Reply** to send a text reply instead.

If you click Accept, iChat makes the connection and displays your buddy's video.

Note: If you are playing music or a movie in iTunes when you accept the call, iTunes automatically pauses playback.

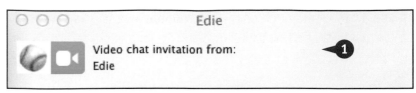

TIP

Can I send video to a buddy whose Mac does not have an iSight webcam?

If your buddy's Mac does not have an iSight or other webcam, you can hold a one-way video chat rather than a two-way chat. Start the chat from your iMac, not from your buddy's Mac. Click your buddy in the Buddy List, and then click **Buddies** and **Invite to One-Way Video Chat**. After accepting the invitation, your buddy sees your video and hears your audio, while you hear your buddy's audio.

Send and Receive Files While You Chat

Text, audio, and video chat are great ways to exchange information, but often you will need to exchange files as well. iChat makes it easy to send files to buddies with whom you are chatting and to receive files from them.

Send and Receive Files While You Chat

Send a File

1 Start a text chat with your buddy as described earlier in this chapter.

2 Click **Finder** (🍎) on the Dock to open a Finder window.

3 Navigate to the folder that contains the file you want to send.

4 Click and drag the file from the Finder window to the Chat window.

iChat adds the file to the Send area.

5 Press **Return** to send the file and any message you have written.

● The file appears in the message, and your buddy receives a prompt to download it.

● The file's name is a link that you can click to open a Finder window to the folder that contains the file.

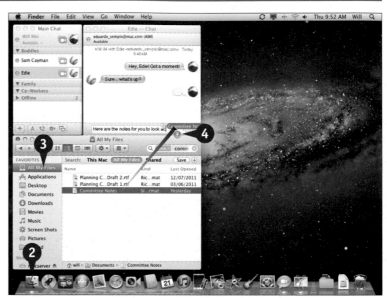

Receive a File

● When your buddy sends you a
file, it appears as a button in
the Chat window.

1 Click 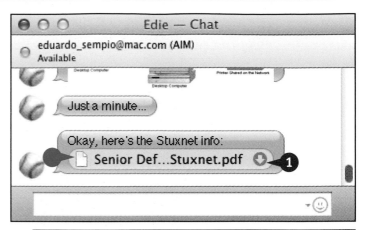 to download the file.

The File Transfers window
opens and transfers the file.

2 Click  to open a Finder
window to the folder that
contains the file.

Open FaceTime, Set It Up, and Close It

FaceTime is Apple's technology for making video calls. At this writing, FaceTime works with all recent Macs, the iPhone 4, the iPad 2, and the fourth-generation iPod touch and later models. Your iMac has a built-in video camera and microphone, so it is ready to use FaceTime right out of the box.

To use FaceTime, you must have an Apple ID. If you have a MobileMe account, or if you have shopped at the iTunes Store or the App Store, you already have an Apple ID. If you do not have an Apple ID, you can create one during the setup process.

Open FaceTime, Set It Up, and Close It

Open and Set Up FaceTime

1 Click **FaceTime** ( ) on the Dock.

Note: If the FaceTime icon does not appear on the Dock, click **Launchpad** ( ) on the Dock, and then click **FaceTime** on the Launchpad screen.

The FaceTime window opens.

2 Type your Apple ID.

Note: If you need to create a new Apple ID, click **Create New Account**, and then follow through the procedure for setting it up.

3 Type your password.

4 Click **Sign In**.

Mac OS X signs you in to FaceTime.

5 Type the email address at which you want people to contact you via FaceTime.

6 Click **Next**.

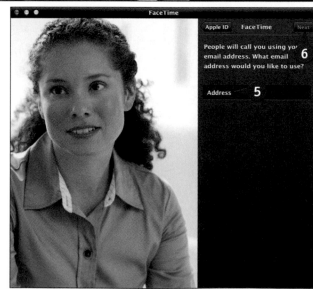

Your contacts list appears.

- Click **Favorites** to display your list of FaceTime favorites.

- Click **Recents** to display a list of recent calls you have made, received, and missed.

- Click **Contacts** to display your main contacts list in Address Book.

You can now make a FaceTime call as explained in the next task.

Close FaceTime

1 When you finish using FaceTime, click **FaceTime**.

The FaceTime menu opens.

2 Click **Quit FaceTime**.

FaceTime closes.

Note: You can also close FaceTime by pressing ⌘+Q.

TIP

How do I change the email address FaceTime is using for me?
To change the email address, click **FaceTime** on the menu bar, and then click **Preferences**. The Preferences pane appears on the right side of the FaceTime window. Click **Add Another Email**, type the email address you want to use, and press Return. Then click the email address you want to remove. On the Email screen that appears, click **Remove This Email**, and then click **Remove Email Address** in the confirmation dialog. Click **Done**.

Make and Receive FaceTime Calls

When you have set up FaceTime with your Apple ID, as described in the previous task, you are ready to make and receive FaceTime calls.

To make a call, you open FaceTime, choose the contact, and then choose the email address or phone number to use for contacting him. To receive a call, you simply answer when FaceTime alerts you to the incoming call.

Make and Receive FaceTime Calls

Make a FaceTime Call

1 Click **FaceTime** ( ) on the Dock.

Note: If no FaceTime icon appears on the Dock, click **Launchpad**, and then click **FaceTime**.

FaceTime opens.

2 In the contacts list, click the contact you want to call.

Note: You can also place a call from the Favorites list or the Recents list.

The contact's record appears.

3 Click the email address or phone number to call.

FaceTime places the call.

4 When your contact answers, smile and chat.

5 When you are ready to finish the call, move the mouse to display the pop-up control bar, and then click **End**.

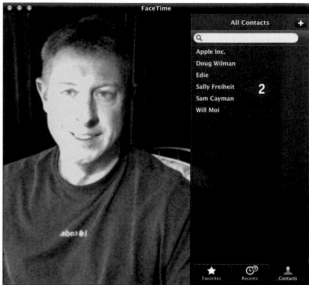

Receive a FaceTime Call

When you receive a FaceTime call, a FaceTime window appears.

1 Click **Accept**.

The call begins.

2 If you want to enlarge the FaceTime window to full screen, move the mouse to display the pop-up control bar, and then click .

3 Smile and chat.

4 When you are ready to finish the call, click **End** on the pop-up control bar.

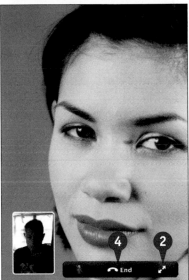

TIP

Do I need to run FaceTime all the time to receive incoming calls?

No. After you set FaceTime up with your Apple ID, FaceTime runs in the background even when the application is not open. When FaceTime detects an incoming call, it displays a window to let you choose whether to accept the call or reject it.

CHAPTER 9

Enjoying Music, Video, and DVDs

Your iMac comes equipped with a full set of applications for enjoying music, video, and DVDs. iTunes enables you to copy songs from CDs, play them back, and watch downloaded videos and movies. DVD Player lets you play back DVDs full screen so that you can enjoy them without distractions.

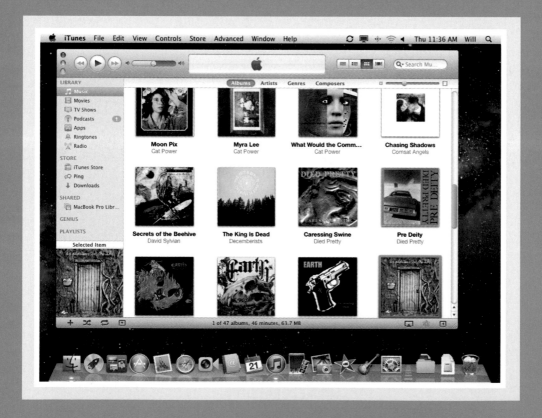

Open and Close iTunes

To use iTunes, you must first open the application. If you listen to music, watch videos extensively, or share your music with others, you may want to leave iTunes running all the time you use your iMac. But if you have finished using iTunes, you can quit the application to close it and allow Mac OS X to take back the memory iTunes was using.

Open and Close iTunes

Open iTunes

1 Click **iTunes** ( ) on the Dock.

Note: If the iTunes icon does not appear on the Dock, click **Launchpad** ( ) on the Dock, and then click **iTunes**.

The iTunes window opens.

Note: The first time you launch iTunes, the application displays a license agreement to which you must agree if you want to use iTunes.

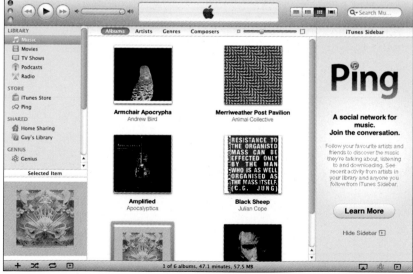

Close iTunes

1 Click **iTunes** on the menu bar.

The iTunes menu opens.

2 Click **Quit iTunes**.

The iTunes window closes.

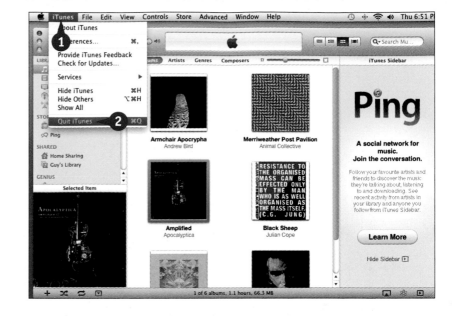

---

iTunes is offering me the Ping sidebar. What is this for, and should I use it?

The Ping sidebar encourages you to sign up for Ping, Apple's social network based on music. Ping is designed to help you follow your favorite artists and the music your friends are listening to.

If you enjoy social networking and do not consider it a threat to your privacy, click **Learn More** (●) to launch the signup process for Ping. If you prefer not to use Ping, click **Hide Sidebar** (●) to hide the sidebar.

Set Up Home Sharing

iTunes includes a feature called Home Sharing that enables you to share songs among your Macs, PCs, iPhones, iPads, and iPod touches. If you have two or more computers — Macs or PCs — on a network, you will probably want to use Home Sharing to share songs easily instead of copying song files manually between your computers. To use Home Sharing, you must have an Apple ID — for example, one you create when setting up an account on Apple's iTunes Store. If you do not already have an Apple ID, you can create one in a couple of minutes.

Set Up Home Sharing

1 If iTunes is not already running, click **iTunes** (⬤) on the Dock.

iTunes launches.

2 In the Source list on the left, click **Home Sharing**.

Note: If the Shared category is collapsed, so that nothing appears under it, position the mouse pointer to the right of the Shared heading. When the Show button appears, click it.

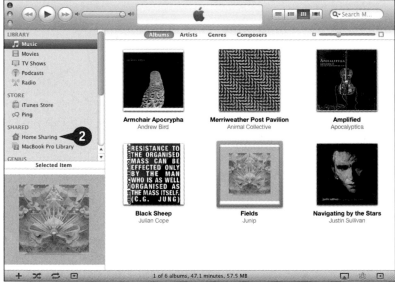

The Home Sharing screen appears.

3 Type your Apple ID.

● If you do not have an Apple ID yet, click the **Need an Apple ID?** link to start the process of getting an Apple ID.

4 Type the password for your Apple ID.

5 Click **Create Home Share**.

The Home Sharing screen appears.

6 Click **Done**.

7 In the Shared category, click one of your computers that is sharing iTunes songs and other items.

The list of shared items appears.

Note: To change the name under which your library appears on another computer, click **iTunes** and **Preferences**. On the General tab, type the name in the Library Name field, and then click **OK**.

8 To import items to your iMac, select them, and then click **Import**.

Note: To select all the items in the shared library, click **Edit** and then **Select All** or press Control + A.

TIP

Can I make iTunes automatically transfer new items to my iMac?
Yes, you can make iTunes automatically transfer new items you purchase to your iMac. Click an item in the Shared category of the Source list to display the Shared screens, and then click **Settings**. In the Home Sharing Settings dialog, click the check box (☐ changes to ☑) for each item you want to transfer automatically. Then click **OK**. You can also share new items automatically among your devices if you sign up for Apple's iCloud service.

Add Your CDs to the iTunes Library

The easiest and least expensive way to add songs to your iTunes music library is to copy the songs from your CDs to iTunes. The copying process is called *ripping*.

iTunes enables you to use different settings to create files using different formats and higher or lower audio quality. The highest-quality files require the most space on your iMac's hard disk.

Add Your CDs to the iTunes Library

1 If iTunes is not already running, click **iTunes** (🎵) on the Dock.

iTunes launches.

2 Insert a CD in your iMac's optical drive.

iTunes recognizes the CD, looks up its title online, and opens a dialog asking if you want to import the CD.

3 Click **No**.

Note: If you want to prevent iTunes from prompting you to import each audio CD you insert, click **Do not ask me again** (☐ changes to ☑) before clicking **No**.

The dialog closes.

4 Control +click or right-click the CD's name in the Devices list.

The shortcut menu opens.

5 Click **Get Info**.

The CD Info dialog opens.

6 Verify that the information is correct. If it is not, correct it.

Note: Many entries for CDs in the online database that iTunes uses contain misspelled or inaccurate information.

7 Click **Compilation CD** (☐ changes to ☑) if the CD is a compilation by various artists.

8 Click **Gapless Album** (☐ changes to ☑) if you want to avoid gaps between songs — for example, on a live album.

9 Click **OK**.

The CD Info dialog closes.

10 Click **Import CD**.

● iTunes imports the songs and adds them to your music library.

11 When iTunes has finished importing, click **Eject** (⏏).

Your iMac ejects the CD.

TIP

How can I create MP3 files rather than AAC files?
iTunes comes set to create files in Apple's preferred Advanced Audio Coding format, or AAC. To create MP3 files, click **Import Settings** from the CD screen. The Import Settings dialog opens. Click the **Import Using** ↕ (●) and choose **MP3 Encoder**. Click the **Setting** ↕ (●) and choose the quality you want; **Higher Quality** is the best choice. Click **Use error correction when reading Audio CDs** (●, ☐ changes to ☑) to ensure you get high-quality files. Click **OK** (●) to close the Import Settings dialog.

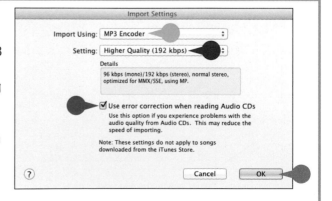

Buy More Songs Online

iTunes is tightly integrated with the iTunes Store, Apple's online store that sells songs, videos, games, and more.

To buy items from the iTunes Store, you must set up an account including either your credit card details or another means of payment, such as an iTunes Gift Card or an allowance account. If you do not already have an account, iTunes prompts you to set one up when you first attempt to buy an item.

Buy More Songs Online

1 Double-click **iTunes Store**.

A new iTunes window opens and loads the home page of the iTunes Store.

Note: You can also browse the iTunes Store in the main iTunes window by clicking **iTunes Store** once. Usually, opening a new window is more convenient because it lets you continue to control your music in the main window.

2 Click **Music**.

The Music pop-up menu opens.

3 Click the type of music you want to browse.

The iTunes Store window displays the kind of music you chose.

④ Click an item to display information on it.

⑤ Highlight a song and click **Play** (▶) next to it to play a sample.

⑥ Click **Buy** to buy the item.

⑦ If the Sign In to Download from the iTunes Store dialog opens, type your username and password, and then click **Buy**.

iTunes downloads the song and adds it to your library.

⑧ Click **Purchased** in the Store category of the Source list to see your purchases.

TIPS

Are there other online stores that sell songs I can play in iTunes?

Many online stores sell songs in the widely used MP3 format, which you can play in iTunes and on iPods and iPhones. Amazon.com (www.amazon.com) sells a wide variety of songs and albums as MP3 files, as does Wal-Mart Stores, Inc.'s Walmart.com (http://mp3.walmart.com/store/home).

How can I restart a download that fails?

If a download stops partway through a song or other item, choose **Store** and **Check for Available Downloads**. You will need to sign in to the iTunes Store if you are not currently signed in. iTunes then automatically restarts any downloads that were not completed.

Play Songs

You can play any song in iTunes by simply double-clicking it and then using the playback controls. First, though, you need to find the songs you want to play. To help you browse your songs, iTunes has four different views — List view, Album List view, Grid view, and Cover Flow view — and a column browser. You can also search for songs.

Play Songs

Play a Song in Grid View

① Click **Grid View** (▦) to see the albums as a grid of covers.

② Double-click the album you want to open.

iTunes opens the album.

③ Double-click a song to play.

iTunes starts playing the song.

④ Use the playback controls as needed:

● Click once to go to the beginning of the song. Click again to go to the previous song.

● Click to pause playback. Click again to restart playback.

● Click to go to the next song.

● Drag to change the volume.

Play a Song in Album List View or List View

1 Click **Album List View** (☷) to see the songs as a list with album covers on the left.

Note: List view is similar to Album List view but does not show the album covers.

2 Double-click a song to play.

iTunes starts playing the song.

Play a Song in Cover Flow View

1 Click **Cover Flow View** (▥).

2 Choose the album you want:

● Click a cover to bring it to the front.

● Click to display the previous cover.

● Click to display the next cover.

● Drag to scroll through the covers.

● Click to switch to full-screen Cover Flow.

The list shows the songs for the selected album.

3 Double-click a song to play.

TIPS

How can I search for songs?
Click in the search box and start typing your search term. iTunes shows matching items as you type. To restrict the search, click the arrow next to the magnifying glass icon and choose **Artist**, **Album**, **Composer**, or **Song** from the pop-up menu. Click ⊗ when you need to clear the search and display all songs.

Can I make iTunes take up less room when it plays?
You can shrink iTunes down to its Mini Player. Click ⊞ or choose **View** and **Switch to Mini Player** or press ⌘+Shift+M. To switch back, press ⊞ again, or choose **View** and **Switch from Mini Player**, or press ⌘+Shift+M again.

Play Videos

Besides playing songs, iTunes also plays videos, including video podcasts. You can buy music videos, TV shows, and movies from the iTunes Store or export files of your own movies from iMovie or other applications.

You can watch video content either within the iTunes window or full screen. You can set iTunes to automatically open particular types of video content full screen if you prefer.

Play Videos

1 In iTunes, click **Movies** under Library.

Note: To watch a TV show, click **TV Shows**. To watch a music video you have purchased, click **Purchased** under Store, or locate the video by the artist's name.

The list of movies appears.

2 Position the mouse pointer over the movie you want to play.

The Play Movie button appears.

3 Click **Play Movie**.

iTunes starts playing the movie.

④ Use the controls on the pop-up bar to control playback.

Note: Optionally, click  to switch to full-screen viewing.

⑤ To stop viewing, click ⊗.

Can I make iTunes always play back movies full screen?

Choose **iTunes** and **Preferences**. The Preferences dialog opens. Click **Playback** (●). Click the **Play Movies and TV Shows** ⬍ (●) and choose **full screen**. If you want to play music videos full screen as well, click the **Play Music Videos** ⬍ (●) and choose **full screen**. Click **OK** (●) to close the Preferences dialog.

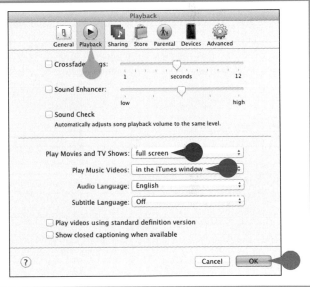

Create Playlists of Songs You Like

The best thing about playing songs on your iMac is that you can play them in any order you want rather than in the order they appear on the CD.

iTunes enables you to create playlists that contain the songs you want in your preferred order. You can listen to a playlist, share it with others, or burn it to a CD for listening on a CD player.

Create Playlists of Songs You Like

1 In iTunes, click **Add** (⊞).

iTunes adds a new playlist to the Playlists section of the Source list and displays an information screen about playlists.

2 Type the name for the playlist and press `Return`.

The playlist takes on the new name.

3 Click **Music**.

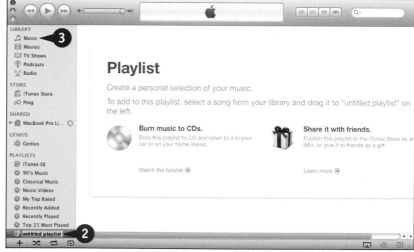

Your songs appear.

4 Click and drag songs to the playlist.

5 Click the playlist's name.

The contents of the playlist appear.

6 Click and drag the songs in the playlist into your preferred order.

Note: To delete a song from a playlist, click it and then press ⟨Delete⟩. The song disappears from the playlist but remains in your iTunes Library.

TIPS

Is there a quick way of creating a playlist?

The quick way of creating a playlist is to select the songs first. Click the first song to include, and then ⌘+click other songs. Choose **File** and **New Playlist from Selection**. iTunes creates a new playlist and displays an edit box around the name. Type the new name and press ⟨Return⟩ to apply it.

How can I keep my playlists organized?

You can organize your playlists into playlist folders. Choose **File** and **New Playlist Folder**. iTunes creates a folder and displays an edit box around the name. Type the name for the folder and press ⟨Return⟩ to apply it. You can then click and drag playlists to the folder. Click ▶ to show the playlists in a folder; click ▼ to hide the playlists.

Have iTunes Create Playlists for You

Instead of creating playlists manually as described on the previous pages, you can have iTunes automatically create playlists for you. These playlists are called *Smart Playlists*.

All you have to do is set up the conditions for the Smart Playlist. iTunes then creates the playlist for you and automatically updates it when you add songs to your library or remove songs.

Have iTunes Create Playlists for You

1 In iTunes, press and hold Option and click **Add** (⊞).

Note: ⊞ changes to ⚙ when you press Option.

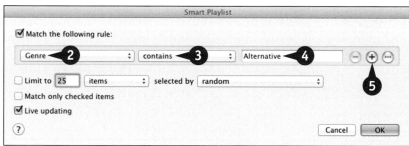

The Smart Playlist dialog opens.

2 Click the first ⬍ and select the item for the first condition — for example, **Genre**.

3 Click the second ⬍ and select the comparison for the first condition — for example, **contains**.

4 Click the text field and type the text for the comparison — for example, **Alternative**, making the condition "Genre contains Alternative."

5 To add another condition, click **Add** (⊕).

The Smart Playlist dialog adds another line of controls.

6 Click ↕ and choose **any** to match any of the rules or **all** to match all the rules.

7 Set up the second condition by repeating steps **2** to **4**.

Note: You can add as many conditions as you need to define the playlist.

8 If you want to limit the playlist, click **Limit to** (☐ changes to ☑). Use the controls on that line to set the limit.

9 Make sure that **Live updating** is checked (☑).

10 Click **OK**.

iTunes creates the Smart Playlist and adds it to the Playlists section of the Source list.

11 If you want to change the name iTunes gives the playlist, click the name.

An edit box appears around the name.

12 Type the name for the Smart Playlist, and then press Return.

TIPS

How do I produce a playlist the right length for a CD?

To create a playlist the right length for a CD, check **Limit to** (☐ changes to ☑). Click the left ↕ and choose **minutes**, and set the number before it to **74** or **80**, depending on the capacity of the CD.

What does the Match Only Checked Items option do?

If you check **Match only checked items** (☐ changes to ☑), your Smart Playlist contains only songs whose check boxes are selected. This means you can uncheck the check box for a song to prevent it from appearing in your Smart Playlists.

Create a Custom CD of Your Songs

After creating a custom playlist, you can copy it to a CD so that you can play it in any CD player. Creating a CD like this is called *burning* a CD.

You will need a blank recordable CD, or CD-R.

Create a Custom CD of Your Songs

1 In iTunes, click the playlist from which you want to create the CD.

The songs in the playlist appear.

2 Click **File**.

The File menu opens.

3 Click **Burn Playlist to Disc**.

The Burn Settings dialog opens.

④ Make sure that **Maximum Possible** is selected in the Preferred Speed pop-up menu.

Note: If the audio CDs you burn skip or click during playback on some CD players, reduce the Preferred Speed setting.

⑤ Verify that **Audio CD** is selected (◉).

⑥ Click the **Gap Between Songs** ⬍ and choose the gap: **none**, **1 second**, **2 seconds**, **3 seconds**, **4 seconds**, or **5 seconds**. 2 seconds is typical.

⑦ Click **Use Sound Check** (☐ changes to ☑) if you want iTunes to standardize the audio volume of the songs on the CD.

⑧ Click **Burn**.

iTunes prompts you to insert a CD.

⑨ Insert a CD in your iMac's optical drive.

iTunes checks the disc and burns the CD.

● The display shows the progress of the burn.

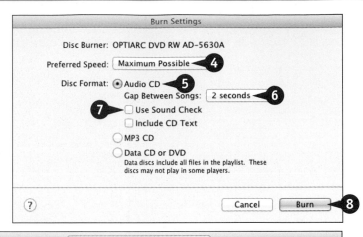

TIPS

Is it a good idea to use Sound Check?
Whether to use Sound Check is entirely up to you. Without Sound Check, songs originally recorded at different levels play at different volumes from the CD. This can be awkward. Sound Check makes the overall volume more consistent but can rob songs of their dynamic range and power.

Can I burn songs to a DVD?
You can burn a playlist to a DVD as backup to guard against hardware failure. You can also burn an MP3 DVD, which many set-top DVD players can play. But you cannot create an audio DVD in the same way that you can create an audio CD.

Listen to Radio Stations over the Internet

iTunes enables you to listen to a wide variety of online radio stations that broadcast across the Internet. You listen to the stations in real time as they broadcast, and you cannot pause playback.

If a station does not appear in iTunes' list of stations, you can open it manually.

Listen to Radio Stations over the Internet

1 In the iTunes Source list, click **Radio**.

A list of radio categories appears in the main window.

2 Click ▶ next to the category you want to display (▶ changes to ▼).

The category expands to show the stations it contains.

3 Double-click the radio station you want to listen to.

Note: If the radio station has two or more entries, try playing the one with the highest bit rate first if you have a broadband Internet connection. The higher the bit rate, the higher the audio quality. Control +click or right-click the **Comments** column heading, and then click **Bit Rate** to display the Bit Rate column.

The radio station starts playing.

4 Click **Stop** (■) when you want to stop the radio playing.

TIPS

How can I listen to a radio station that does not appear on iTunes' list?

If the station does not appear in iTunes' list, find out the URL of the station's audio stream by consulting the station's website. In iTunes, choose **Advanced** and **Open Stream** to display the Open Stream dialog. Type or paste the URL and click **OK**. iTunes starts playing the radio station's audio stream.

How can I record a song from the radio in iTunes?

iTunes does not provide a feature for recording radio. This is because recording a radio station can be a violation of copyright. To record, you need third-party software such as RadioLover from Bitcartel Software (http://bitcartel.com/radiolover/). Before you record, you should understand your country's copyright laws about recording.

Enjoy Podcasts

A *podcast* is an audio or video file that you can download from the Internet and play on your iMac or a digital player like the iPhone, iPad, or iPod.

The iTunes Store makes a wide variety of podcasts available. You can either simply download a podcast or subscribe to a podcast so that iTunes automatically downloads new episodes for you.

Enjoy Podcasts

1 In iTunes, double-click **iTunes Store**.

iTunes opens a new window showing the home page of the iTunes Store.

2 Click **Podcasts**.

The Podcasts menu opens, showing the different categories of podcasts.

3 Click the category of podcasts you want to see.

The window shows the category you chose.

④ Click the podcast you are interested in.

⑤ Click **Subscribe** if you want to subscribe to the podcast.

A dialog opens to confirm the subscription.

⑥ Click **Subscribe**.

iTunes subscribes you to the podcast and downloads the available episodes.

TIP

How do I watch the podcasts I have downloaded?

In the main iTunes window, click **Podcasts** under Library in the Source list. The list of podcasts appears. Double-click a podcast to see the available episodes, and then double-click the episode you want to listen to or watch. iTunes starts playing the podcast and displays a bar of pop-up controls for handling playback.

Watch a DVD on Your iMac

M ac OS X includes a full-feature DVD player, called simply DVD Player, for enjoying movies.

Watch a DVD on Your iMac

1 Insert the DVD in your iMac's optical drive.

DVD Player automatically launches and starts playing the DVD full screen.

2 Move the mouse pointer to the bottom of the screen.

DVD Player displays the control bar for controlling playback.

3 After you use the controls as needed, move the mouse pointer away.

DVD Player hides the control bar again.

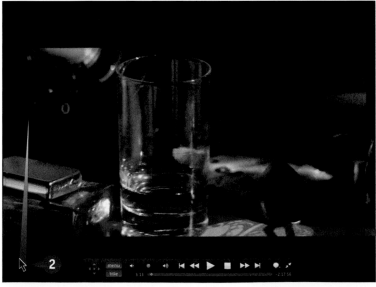

④ Move the mouse pointer to near the top of the screen.

DVD Player displays a navigation bar that at first shows the chapters in the DVD.

⑤ Click the chapter to which you want to jump.

DVD Player starts playing that chapter.

⑥ When you have finished watching the DVD, move the mouse pointer to the top of the screen.

The Mac OS X menu bar appears.

⑦ Click **DVD Player**.

The DVD Player menu opens.

⑧ Click **Quit DVD Player**.

DVD Player quits.

TIP

Why does the You Need to Select the Region for Your DVD Drive dialog appear?

To create separate markets, DVDs use eight different region codes: Region 1 is North America, Region 2 is Europe, Region 3 is Southeast Asia, and so on. Most DVDs are tied to one specific region and can play only on players built for that region. This dialog appears when you insert a disc from a different region than your iMac's DVD drive is set to play. You can change the drive's region up to five times; after that, it remains locked to the last region you used. To change region, click the **Change drive region to** ⬍ (●), choose the region, and then click **Set Drive Region** (●).

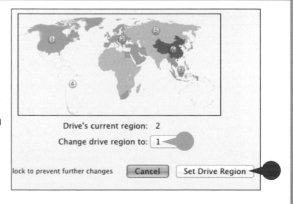

CHAPTER 10

Making the Most of Your Photos

Each new iMac comes with iPhoto, a powerful but easy-to-use application for managing, improving, and enjoying your photos. You can import photos from your digital camera; crop them, straighten them, and improve their colors; and turn them into albums, slideshows, or email messages.

Open and Close iPhoto

To get started with iPhoto, you must first open the application. When you finish using iPhoto, you can leave the application running if you plan to use it again soon, or you can quit the application to close it and make the memory it was using available for other applications to use.

Open and Close iPhoto

Open iPhoto

1 Click **iPhoto** (🖼) on the Dock.

Note: If the iPhoto icon does not appear on the Dock, click **Launchpad** (🚀) on the Dock. On the Launchpad screen, click **iPhoto**.

The iPhoto window opens.

Close iPhoto

1 Click **iPhoto** on the menu bar.

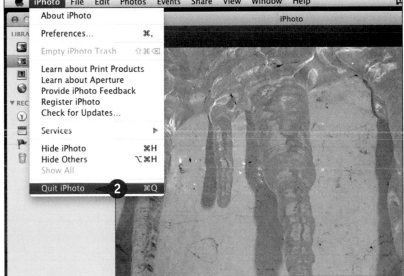

The iPhoto menu opens.

2 Click **Quit iPhoto**.

The iPhoto window closes.

TIP

When I launch iPhoto, a dialog asks me if I want to use iPhoto when I connect my digital camera. Should I click Yes or No?

If iPhoto displays the Do You Want to Use iPhoto When You Connect Your Digital Camera? dialog, normally it is a good idea to click **Yes**. The exception

is if you plan to use another application, such as Mac OS X's Image Capture or a third-party application supplied by the camera's maker or another software manufacturer, to import your digital photos.

Import Photos from Your Digital Camera

iPhoto enables you to import photos directly from your digital camera's memory or from a memory card. iPhoto can work with a wide variety of types of digital cameras, and normally recognizes a camera automatically when you connect it to your iMac and switch it on.

You can use this technique to import photos from an iPhone, an iPad, or an iPod touch.

Import Photos from Your Digital Camera

1 Connect your digital camera to your iMac with a USB cable.

2 Turn on the digital camera.

Note: Some digital cameras turn on automatically when you connect them to a powered USB port, but most cameras need to be turned on manually.

Your iMac launches iPhoto if it is not running, or brings it to the front if it is running.

● The digital camera appears in the Devices category in the Source list.

● iPhoto displays thumbnails of the camera's photos in the viewing area.

3 If you want to import all the photos, you need not select any. To import just some photos, click the first, and then ⌘+click the others.

4 Click **Hide Photos Already Imported** (☐ changes to ☑) if the camera contains photos you have already imported.

iPhoto hides the photos you have already imported.

5 Type a name for the photos.

6 Click **Split Events** (☑ changes to ☐) if you want to prevent iPhoto from putting photos in different Events based on their dates and times.

7 Click **Import All**.

Note: If you selected photos in step **3**, click **Import Selected** rather than Import All.

iPhoto copies the photos from the digital camera to your iMac.

The Delete Photos on Your Camera? dialog opens.

8 Click **Delete Photos** if you want to delete the photos. To keep the photos, click **Keep Photos**.

9 Click ⏏ next to the camera's entry in the Source list.

iPhoto ejects the camera, and you can safely disconnect it. You can now browse your photos as explained in the next task.

TIPS

How can I connect my digital camera to my iMac if I do not have the right kind of connector cable?

If you do not have the right cable to connect your digital camera directly to your iMac, remove the digital camera's memory card and insert it in a memory card reader connected to the iMac. The iMac then recognizes the memory card as a digital camera, and you can import the photos from it as described in this task.

What is an Event, and what names should I give my Events?

An Event is a way of grouping photos in iPhoto. When you import photos, you assign them to an Event, and you can then browse and organize them through the Event. An Event can be a period of time from a few hours to a week or more, but you can also create Events based on ideas or themes as needed.

Browse through Your Photos

After adding your photos to iPhoto, you can browse through them in several ways. Usually, the best way to start is by viewing the Last Import category, which contains the photos you most recently imported. You can view the photos either within the iPhoto window or full screen for greater effect.

Browse through Your Photos

1 In iPhoto, click ▣ next to Recent if the Recent category is collapsed.

The contents of the Recent category appear.

2 Click **Last Import**.

The last batch of photos you imported into iPhoto appears.

Note: Normally, the Last Import item shows photos from your digital camera. But if you last added photo files from a folder, email, webpage, or scanner, those photos appear in Last Import.

3 Scroll through your pictures as needed.

4 Double-click the photo you want to view.

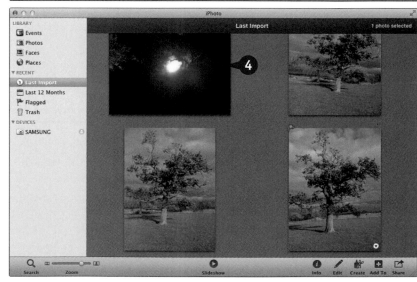

iPhoto displays the photo you clicked, expanded to fit the window.

5 Click ➡ or press ➡ to display the next photo, or click ⬅ or press ⬅ to display the previous photo.

6 To jump to another photo, position the mouse pointer over the thumbnail bar, and then click the picture you want.

7 Click ⬈.

iPhoto expands to fill the entire screen.

8 Click ➡ or press ➡ to display the next photo, or click ⬅ or press ⬅ to display the previous photo.

9 To jump to another photo, position the mouse pointer over the thumbnail bar, and then click the picture you want.

iPhoto displays the full-screen control bar, which contains tools for editing photos.

10 Click **Last Import** to return to viewing thumbnails of the photos.

Note: Press Esc or move the mouse pointer to the top of the screen and click ⬛ when you want to return iPhoto from full screen to a window.

TIP

What are Events, Photos, Faces, and Places in the iPhoto sidebar?
Click **Events** to browse photos by the Events you and iPhoto have created. Double-click an Event to display its photos. Click **Photos** to see all the photos in your iPhoto Library. Click ▶ to expand a collapsed group of photos or ▼ to collapse an expanded group. Click **Faces** to open the Faces feature for using facial recognition to identify the people in photos. Click **Places** to use the Places feature for sorting photos by their GPS location or locations you add manually.

Crop a Photo to the Right Size

To improve a photo's composition and emphasize its subject, you can crop off the parts you do not want to keep. iPhoto enables you to crop to any rectangular area within a photo, so you can choose exactly the part of the photo that you need.

Crop a Photo to the Right Size

1 Click the photo you want to crop.

2 Click **Edit** (✎).

iPhoto opens the photo for editing and displays the editing tools.

3 Click **Quick Fixes**.

The Quick Fixes pane appears.

4 Click **Crop** (▣).

iPhoto displays the cropping tools.

5 If you want to crop to specific proportions or dimensions, click **Constrain** (☐ changes to ☑).

6 Click ⬍ and choose the size or proportions — for example, **Square** or **3 × 5**.

7 Click in the cropping rectangle and drag it so that the center square covers the middle of the area you want.

8 Click and drag a corner handle to crop to the area you want.

9 Click **Done**.

iPhoto crops the picture to the area you chose.

10 Click **Edit**.

iPhoto hides the editing tools again.

TIP

I cropped off the wrong part of the photo. How can I get back the missing part?

You can undo an edit by choosing **Edit** and **Undo** or pressing ⌘+Z, but you can also return to a photo's original state. To do so, choose **Photos** and **Revert to Original**. You can click this command to go back to the original version of the photo. A dialog opens to make sure that you want to revert to the original. Click **Revert**.

Rotate or Straighten a Photo

If you take a photo with the camera sideways or the wrong way up, you can easily rotate the photo by 90 or 180 degrees in iPhoto to fix the problem.

iPhoto also enables you to straighten a photo by rotating it up to 10 degrees, automatically cropping off the parts that no longer fit.

Rotate or Straighten a Photo

Rotate a Photo

1. **Control**+click or right-click the photo you want to rotate.

   The pop-up control panel appears.

2. Click **Rotate** (⟲).

   iPhoto rotates the photo 90 degrees counterclockwise.

   Note: If you have a Magic Trackpad, you can rotate a photo by placing two fingers on the trackpad and then rotating them clockwise or counterclockwise.

3. If you need to rotate the photo further, click **Rotate** (⟲) again.

Straighten a Photo

1. Click the photo you want to straighten.

2. Click **Edit** (✎).

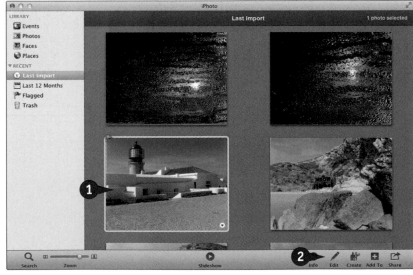

iPhoto opens the photo for editing and displays the editing tools.

3 Click **Quick Fixes**.

The Quick Fixes pane appears.

4 Click **Straighten** (🔲).

● iPhoto displays the straightening tools.

5 Click and drag the **Angle** slider to straighten the photo.

Note: Use the major and minor gridlines in the straightening grid to judge when lines in the picture have reached the horizontal or the vertical.

6 Click **Done**.

iPhoto applies the straightening.

7 Click **Edit** (✏️).

iPhoto hides the editing tools again.

TIP

How can I rotate a photo clockwise rather than counterclockwise?

To quickly rotate a photo clockwise, **Option**+click **Rotate** (🔄) on the pop-up panel. If you usually need to rotate clockwise rather than counterclockwise, choose **iPhoto** and **Preferences**. The Preferences window opens. Click **General** on the toolbar. The General preferences pane opens. Click the clockwise **Rotate** option (○ changes to ●), and then click 🔲.

Remove Red-Eye from a Photo

A camera's flash can make all the difference when taking photos in dark or dull conditions, but flash often gives people *red-eye* — glaring red spots in the eyes. iPhoto's Red-Eye tool enables you to remove red-eye from your photos, making your subjects look normal again.

Remove Red-Eye from a Photo

1 Click the photo you want to remove red-eye from.

2 Click **Edit**.

iPhoto opens the photo for editing and displays the editing tools.

3 Click **Quick Fixes**.

The Quick Fixes pane appears.

4 Click and drag the slider to zoom in.

5 Click and drag the highlight in the Navigation window so that the red-eye is visible.

6 Click **Fix Red-Eye** (⊗).

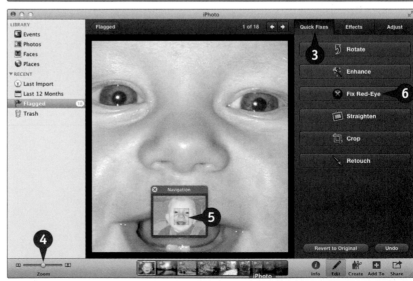

● iPhoto displays the red-eye tools.

● By default, the Auto-Fix Red-Eye check box is selected, and iPhoto attempts to remove the red-eye.

7 If you need to remove red-eye manually, drag the **Size** slider until the circle is the right size to cover the pupil of the eye in the photo.

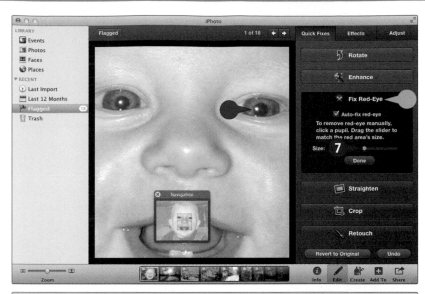

8 Click the red-eye.

iPhoto removes the red-eye from the eye.

9 Click **Done**.

iPhoto applies the changes to the photo.

10 Click **Edit** (✏).

iPhoto hides the editing tools again.

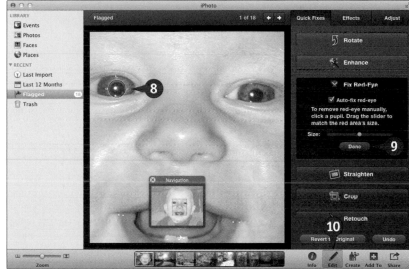

TIP

Should I use the Auto-Fix Red-Eye tool or fix red-eye manually?
This is up to you. The Auto-Fix Red-Eye tool should be the quickest way to remove red-eye from a photo, and in many photos it successfully identifies and removes red-eye. But where the tool cannot remove red-eye, drag the **Size** slider to the right size for the red-eye you need to remove, and then click each affected eye in turn.

Improve the Colors in a Photo

iPhoto includes powerful tools for improving the colors in your photos. If a photo is too light, too dark, or the colors look wrong, you can use these tools to make it look better. You can also use the Enhance tool to give flat colors in a photo a fast and easy boost while muting overly bright colors.

Improve the Colors in a Photo

Quickly Enhance the Colors in a Photo

1. Click the photo you want to enhance.

2. Click **Edit**.

   iPhoto opens the photo for editing and displays the editing tools.

3. Click **Quick Fixes** to display the Quick Fixes pane.

4. Click **Enhance** (⬛).

   iPhoto adjusts the exposure and enhances the colors.

5. Click **Edit** again.

Improve the Colors with the Adjust Window

1. Click the photo you want to adjust.

2. Click **Edit**.

   iPhoto opens the photo for editing and displays the editing tools.

3. Click **Adjust** to open the Adjust pane.

4. To add dark tones to the photo, click and drag the **Black Point** slider to the right.

5. To add light tones to the photo, click and drag the **White Point** slider to the left.

6. To adjust the gray balance, click and drag the **Midtones** slider to the left or right.

7. If white in the picture appears gray or pink, click the eyedropper (⬛) and then click the color that should be white.

8 Click and drag **Exposure** right to make the photo lighter or left to make it darker.

9 Click and drag **Contrast** right to increase the contrast or left to decrease it.

10 Click and drag **Saturation** right to increase the color saturation or left to decrease it.

11 Click and drag **Definition** to increase the overall clarity of the photo.

12 Click and drag **Highlights** to recover lost detail in the lighter areas of the photo.

13 Click and drag **Shadows** to bring out detail in the darker areas of the photo.

14 Click **Edit** (✎).

TIPS

What do the Sharpness and De-noise sliders in the Adjust dialog do?
Sharpness tries to make the photo look sharper by increasing the contrast between neighboring pixels that have different colors. Adjust the Sharpness slider gradually because big adjustments can give an unnatural look. De-noise attempts to remove incorrect colors and artifacts from the photo. Again, make changes gradually to achieve a better look.

How can I make the same change to several photos?
After making changes to one photo, click **Edit** and **Copy Adjustments**. Click the first photo you want to paste the adjustments onto, and then click **Edit** and **Paste Adjustments**. Repeat the Paste Adjustments operation as needed for other photos that need the same adjustments.

Add an Effect to a Photo

To add life and interest to a photo, you can apply one of iPhoto's effects to it. For example, you can turn a photo black and white or sepia, boost or fade the color, or turn the subject into a vignette in a blacked-out oval.

Add an Effect to a Photo

1 Click the photo to which you want to apply the effect.

2 Click **Edit** (✏️).

iPhoto opens the photo for editing and displays the editing tools.

3 Click **Effects**.

The Effects pane appears.

4 Click the effect you want to apply.

The photo takes on the effect.

5 If the effect shows a number in the Effects window, click the right arrow to increase the effect or the left arrow to decrease it.

iPhoto adjusts the effect correspondingly.

6 Click **Edit** (✏).

iPhoto hides the editing tools again.

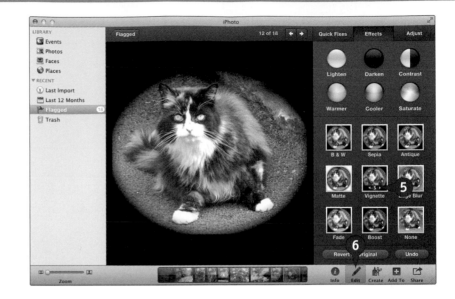

TIPS

How can I remove the effects from a photo?
To remove the effects you have applied to a photo, click **None** (⬤) at the bottom of the Effects tab.

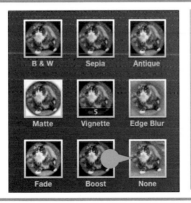

Can I apply multiple effects to a photo?
You can apply two or more effects to a photo at the same time. Some of the effects are mutually exclusive — for example, you cannot apply both B & W and Sepia to a photo at the same time. But you can apply other combinations of effects, such as applying both Sepia and Vignette to a photo.

Sort Your Photos into Events

Photo automatically creates Events when you import photos, but you can move photos from one Event to another as needed to keep your photos organized. You can also split one Event into two Events, or merge two or more existing Events into a single Event.

Sort Your Photos into Events

Move Photos from One Event to Another

1 In iPhoto, click **Events** in the Source list.

● The list of Events appears.

Note: Each Event appears as a stack of photos with a key photo on top. Move the mouse around over the key photo to see other photos in the Event.

2 Click the Event that contains the photos you want to move.

3 ⌘+click the Event to which you want to move the photos.

4 Press **Return**.

iPhoto opens the Events.

5 In one Event, select the photos you want to move.

6 Click and drag the photos to the other Event.

Note: If you want to put all the photos from one Event in another Event, you do not need to open the Events as described here. Instead, on the Events screen, drag one Event on top of the other Event.

7 Click **All Events** to return to the Events list.

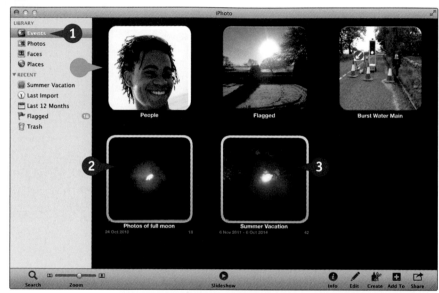

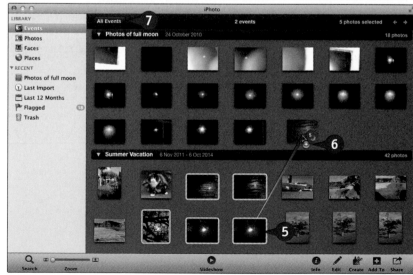

Split an Event into Two Events

1 Click **Events** in the Source list.

The list of Events appears.

2 Double-click the Event you want to open.

3 Click the photo before which you want to split the Event off to a new Event.

4 Click **Events**.

The Events menu opens.

5 Click **Split Event**.

iPhoto creates a new Event named Untitled Event, starting with the photo you selected.

6 Click the Event name.

7 Type the name you want to give the Event.

8 Press Return.

The Event takes on the new name.

TIP

Can I change how iPhoto creates Events?

You can set iPhoto to create an Event for every two hours, every eight hours, every day, or every week. iPhoto uses the times and dates in the photos you import, not your iMac's clock. Choose **iPhoto** and **Preferences**. The Preferences window opens. Click **Events** to open the Events preferences pane. Click **Autosplit into Events** and choose **Two-hour gaps**, **Eight-hour gaps**, **One event per day**, or **One event per week**, as needed. Click 🔘 to close the Preferences window.

Create Albums of Your Photos

When you want to assemble a custom collection of photos, create a new album. You can then add to it exactly the photos you want and arrange them into your preferred order.

iPhoto can also create *Smart Albums* that automatically include all photos that meet the criteria you choose.

Create Albums of Your Photos

1 Click **Create** (![icon]).

The Create pane opens.

2 Click **Album** (![icon]).

Note: If the Event or other item you are viewing contains photos you want to add to the new album, select those photos before clicking **Create** and **Album**. iPhoto includes those photos in the new album.

- The new album appears in the Albums list in the Source list. iPhoto selects the default name, Untitled Album.

3 Type the name for the album and press **Return**.

iPhoto applies the name to the album.

4 Click **Photos** in the sidebar.

Note: You can also add photos to the album from Events, from Last Import, or from any of the other items in the sidebar. This example uses Photos.

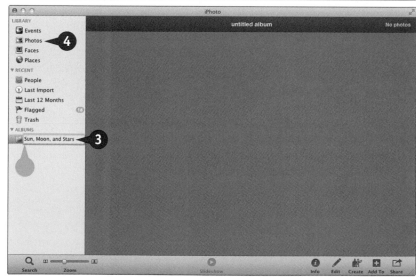

236

The list of photos appears.

5 Select the photos you want to add to the album.

6 Click in the selection and drag the photos to the new album.

iPhoto adds the photos to the album.

7 Click the album in the Source list.

The photos in the album appear.

8 To change the order of the photos, click a photo and drag it to where you want it.

iPhoto arranges the photos.

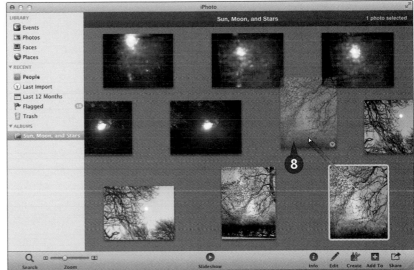

TIP

What is a Smart Album, and how do I create one?

A Smart Album is an album based on criteria you choose. For example, you can create a Smart Album of photos with the keyword "family" and a rating of four stars or better. iPhoto then automatically adds each photo that matches those criteria to the Smart Album. To create a new Smart Album, choose **File** and **New** and **Smart Album**, and then set your criteria in the New dialog. Click ⊞ to add another row of criteria to the Smart Album.

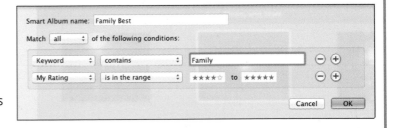

Create a Slideshow of Your Photos

One of the best ways to enjoy your photos and share them with others is to create a slideshow. You can either create a simple, silent slideshow or one that includes effects and transitions and is accompanied by music.

Create a Slideshow of Your Photos

1 Click **Create** (🏃).

Note: If the Event or other item you are viewing contains photos you want to add to the new slideshow, select those photos before clicking **Create** and **Slideshow**. iPhoto includes those photos in the new slideshow.

2 Click **Slideshow** (▣).

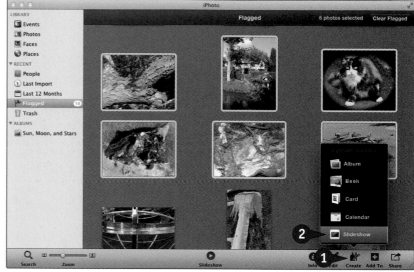

The new slideshow appears in the Slideshows category in the Source list. iPhoto puts an edit box around the default name.

3 Type the name for the slideshow, and then press Return.

The slideshow takes on the name.

4 Click **Photos** in the sidebar.

Note: You can also add photos to the slideshow from Events, from Last Import, or from any of the other items in the sidebar. This example uses Photos.

The list of photos appears.

5 Select the photos you want to use in the slideshow.

6 Click in the selection and drag the photos to the new slideshow.

iPhoto adds the photos to the slideshow.

7 Click the slideshow in the sidebar.

The photos in the slideshow appear.

8 Click and drag the photos into the order in which you want them to appear in the slideshow.

9 Click **Themes** (⊞).

TIP

How do I create a custom title slide for my slideshow?
Click the first slide in the slideshow, and then click **Text Slide** (⊞) on the toolbar. iPhoto adds a text slide before the first slide. Type the text for the title slide on the placeholder. iPhoto then displays this text superimposed on the first slide. You can use this method to place text on any slide as needed.

continued ▶

To make a slideshow look the way you want it to, you can give the slideshow one of iPhoto's themes. The themes include animated transitions between slides that give slideshow a particular look.

During the slideshow, you can play a particular song or an existing playlist, or you can create a custom playlist to accompany the slideshow. You can also choose whether to play each slide for a minimum length of time or to fit the slideshow to the music you provide for it.

Create a Slideshow of Your Photos (continued)

The Choose a Slideshow Theme dialog appears.

⑩ Click the theme you want to use.

⑪ Click **Choose**.

The Choose a Slideshow Theme dialog closes, and iPhoto applies the theme to the slideshow.

⑫ Click **Music** (♫).

The Music Settings dialog appears.

⑬ Choose the music to play with the slideshow.

Note: For a silent slideshow, click **Play music during slideshow** (☑ changes to ☐).

⑭ Click **Choose**.

⑮ Click **Settings** (✿).

The Slideshow Settings dialog appears.

16 Choose how long to play each slide (○ changes to ●).

17 Choose whether to play transitions between slides (☐ changes to ☑).

18 Click ⊗.

19 Click **Play** (▶).

The slideshow starts playing.

20 Use the controls on the control bar to move from slide to slide or stop the slideshow.

Coastal Scenes

TIP

How do I create a custom playlist for a slideshow?
Click **Music** (♫) on the toolbar to display the Music Settings dialog. Click **Custom Playlist for Slideshow** (☐ changes to ☑). A box appears for creating the playlist. Drag songs into the box (●), and then drag them into the order you want. Click **Choose**.

Identify Faces in Your Photos

iPhoto's Faces feature enables you to use facial recognition to automatically identify the people in your photos. First, you identify a face and teach iPhoto the name for it. Second, iPhoto scans your other photos for other instances of the same face. Third, you check through the photos iPhoto has found, confirm the matches, and reject the misses.

After identifying faces, you can browse your photos by them, or use them to create albums, slideshows, or other collections.

Identify Faces in Your Photos

Identify a Face

1 Double-click the photo that contains the face.

iPhoto enlarges the photo to fill the window.

2 Click **Info** (*i*).

The Info pane appears.

3 Move the mouse pointer over the face in the photo.

A white outline appears around the face.

Note: If the white outline is not around the face, click ⊗. Then click **Add a face** in the Info pane and drag the new outline to where the face actually is.

4 Click the **click to name** prompt, type the name, and press Return.

iPhoto learns the name for the face.

Browse the Faces in Your iPhoto Library

1 In iPhoto's Source list, click **Faces**.

The Faces screen appears.

2 Double-click the face whose pictures you want to see.

The pictures for the face appear.

You can now work with the photos as normal. For example, double-click a photo to expand it, or click **Edit** (✐) to open it for editing.

3 Click **All Faces** when you want to return to the Faces screen.

TIP

What does the Confirm Additional Faces button do?
If the Confirm Additional Faces button is available, click it to display a screen showing other faces that iPhoto has identified as being similar to this face. You can then confirm each match or reject each mismatch.

Send a Photo via Email

From iPhoto, you can quickly create an email message containing one or more photos. You can choose among various graphical designs, and you can either include the full version of the photo or create a smaller version of it that will transfer more quickly.

Send a Photo via Email

1 In iPhoto, click the photo you want to send via email.

2 Click **Share** ( ).

The Share panel opens.

3 Click **Email** ( ).

Note: The first time you give the Email command, you must follow through a procedure to set up iPhoto with your email account.

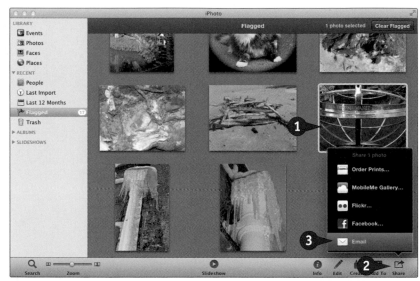

iPhoto creates a message containing the photo.

4 Click the stationery template you want to use.

5 Type the recipient's address.

6 Type the subject of the message.

7 Type any message text needed to explain why you are sending the photo.

8 Click the **Photo Size** ⬍ .

The Photo Size pop-up menu opens.

9 Click the size of photo to send — for example, **Large (Higher Quality)**. See the tip for recommendations.

10 Click **Send**.

iPhoto sends the message.

Which size should I use for sending a photo?

In the Photo Size pop-up menu, choose **Small (Faster Downloading)** if the recipient needs only to view the photos at a small size in the message. Choose **Medium** to let the recipient view more detail in the photos in the message. Choose **Large (Higher Quality)** to send versions of the photos that the recipient can save and use in albums or web pages. Choose **Actual Size (Full Quality)** to send the photos unchanged, so that the recipient can enjoy, edit, and use them at full resolution.

Take Photos or Videos of Yourself

Your iMac includes a built-in iSight camera that is great not only for video chats with iChat and FaceTime but also for taking photos and videos of yourself using the Photo Booth application. You can use Photo Booth's special effects to enliven the photos or videos.

Take Photos or Videos of Yourself

1 Click **Photo Booth** (■) on the Dock.

Note: If Photo Booth does not appear on the Dock, click **Launchpad** (●) on the Dock. On the Launchpad screen, click **Photo Booth**.

Photo Booth opens.

2 If your face appears off center, tilt your iMac's screen or move yourself so that your face is correctly positioned.

3 Choose the type of picture to take:

● For four pictures, click **Take four quick pictures** (▦).

● For a single still, click **Take a still picture** (□).

● For a video, click **Take a movie clip** (▣).

4 To add effects to the photo or video, click **Effects**.

246

The Photo Booth window shows various effects applied to the preview.

Note: To see more effects, click ▶. The center effect on each screen is Normal. Use this effect to remove any other effect.

5 Click the effect you want to use.

6 Click **Take Photo** (◉) or **Take Movie** (◉).

Photo Booth counts down from three and then takes the photo or photos, or starts recording the movie.

If you are taking a movie, click ● when you are ready to stop.

● Photo Booth adds the photo or movie to the photo well.

TIP

How can I use the photos and video I take in Photo Booth?
After taking a photo or video, click it in the photo well, and then click **Share**. Photo Booth displays a panel with buttons for sharing the photo or video. Click **Email** to send it in a message. Click **iPhoto** to add it to iPhoto. Click **Set Account Picture** to use it as your account picture. Click **Set Buddy Picture** to make it your buddy picture in iChat.

CHAPTER 11

Creating Your Own Movies

Your iMac includes all the software you need to make professional-quality movies from your own video footage. You can import video from a DV tape camcorder, a digital camcorder or iPhone, or a digital camera; edit the footage; add titles and credits; and give the movie a soundtrack. You can then share the movie with other applications, export the movie to a file, or post it on YouTube.

Open and Close iMovie

iMovie is a powerful but easy-to-use application for importing video from camcorders, editing the video, and creating movies from it.

To work with iMovie, you must first open the application, either from the Dock or from Launchpad. After you have finished using iMovie, close the application to free up your iMac's hardware resources again.

Open and Close iMovie

Open iMovie

1 Click **iMovie** ( ) on the Dock.

Note: If iMovie does not appear on the Dock, click **Launchpad** ( ) on the Dock. On the Launchpad screen, click **iMovie**.

The iMovie window opens.

If this is the first time you have run iMovie, the application creates a new movie project named My First Project.

If you have already run iMovie and created other projects, iMovie displays your most recently accessed project.

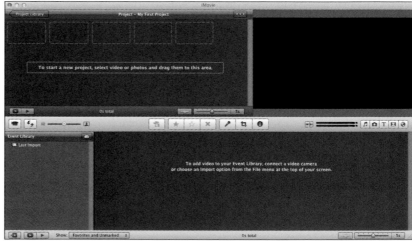

Close iMovie

① Click **iMovie**.

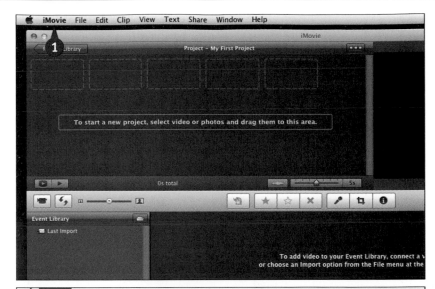

The iMovie menu opens.

② Click **Quit iMovie**.

iMovie closes.

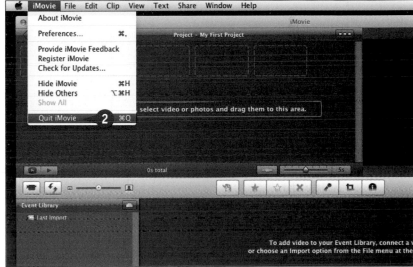

Where do I create my movies in iMovie?

To enable you to make movies as easily as possible, the iMovie window has the Project Library and the Project pane share the same space. From the Project Library, double-click a project to open it in the Project pane so that you can work in it. From the Project pane, click the **Project Library** button to close the project and display the Project Library again.

How do I save changes to a movie project in iMovie?

After you create a movie project, iMovie automatically saves changes to the project for you. This means that you do not need to save changes manually as you have to do in many applications.

Import Video from a DV Tape Camcorder

I f you have video footage on a camcorder that records on to digital video tape such as miniDV, you can connect the camcorder to your iMac with a FireWire cable and import the video. You can either import all of the footage at once or select the parts of it to import, using your iMac to control the camera's playback.

You can also record video directly from the iSight camera built into your iMac. The iSight is good for making instructional videos or political speeches.

Import Video from a DV Tape Camcorder

Import All the Footage from the Tape

① Connect the camcorder to your iMac using a FireWire cable.

Note: Check the FireWire ports on your iMac and the camcorder. You may need to get an adapter cable — for example, from a 4-pin port on the camcorder to a 9-pin port on the iMac.

② Switch the camcorder to Play mode or VCR mode. Your iMac may recognize the camcorder and activate iMovie. If not, click **File** and **Import from Camera** in iMovie.

③ In the Import From window, make sure the switch is set to Automatic.

④ Click **Import**.

⑤ In the import options dialog, click ♦ and choose the hard disk and folder to save the video to.

⑥ Click **Create new Event** (○ changes to ⊙).

⑦ Type the name for the Event.

⑧ Click **Split days into new Events** (☑ changes to ☐) if you do not want to make each day a separate Event.

252

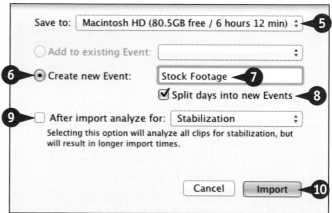

⑨ Click **After import analyze for** (☐ changes to ☑) and click **Stabilization** to apply stabilization automatically.

⑩ Click **Import**, and iMovie winds the tape back to the beginning and imports the video footage.

Import Chosen Footage from the Tape

1 Repeat steps **1** and **2**.

2 In the Import From window, click **Manual**; iMovie displays playback controls.

3 Wind the tape to where you want to start importing:

● Click ▶ to start playback.

● Click ▶▶ to speed up playback forward.

● Click ◀◀ to reverse playback at speed.

4 Click **Import**.

5 In the import options dialog, click **Create new Event** (○ changes to ◉).

6 Type the name for the Event.

7 Click **Split days into new Events** (☑ changes to ☐) if you do not want to make each day a separate Event.

8 Click **After import analyze for** (☐ changes to ☑) and click **Stabilization** to apply stabilization automatically.

9 Click **Import**.

10 Click **Stop** (■) at the end of the video you want to import.

11 Click **Done**.

TIPS

Which hard disk should I save the video footage on?

When you are starting to use iMovie, save the video to your iMac's hard disk, which is normally called Macintosh HD unless you have renamed it. But if you have connected a high-speed external hard disk that you can devote to iMovie files, choose that disk instead.

What is an Event, and how do I use Events?

An Event is a way of dividing up your video clips by the date and time you took them or by their theme. When you import video, you can choose between putting it in an existing Event or creating a new Event. You can create further Events later as needed and move video clips to them.

Import Video from a Digital Camcorder or iPhone

If you have video footage on a camcorder that records on to internal memory, a memory card, or a hard disk, you can connect the camcorder to your iMac with a USB cable and import the video. Because the video clips are stored as separate files, you can choose which clips to import, or simply import all of them at once.

You use this method to import video from an iPhone, iPad, or iPod touch capable of taking video. This example uses an iPhone.

Import Video from a Digital Camcorder or iPhone

1 Connect the camcorder or iPhone to your iMac with a USB cable.

Note: Connect the USB cable to a USB port on the iMac, not to a port on the keyboard.

2 Switch the camcorder on and put it in Play mode or VCR mode.

Your iMac may recognize the camcorder and activate iMovie automatically. If not, click **File** and **Import from Camera** in iMovie.

The Import From window opens.

Note: If you want to import all the clips, go to step **5**.

3 Click **Manual**.

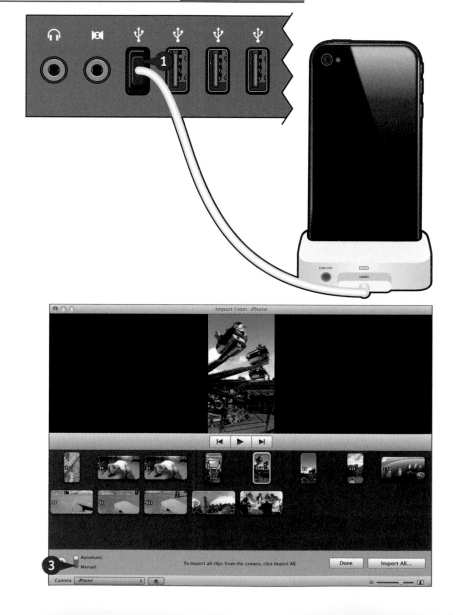

④ Click ☑ for each clip you do not want to import (☑ changes to ▣).

Note: Click **Uncheck All** if you need to uncheck all the boxes quickly.

⑤ Click **Import All** or **Import Checked**, as appropriate.

A dialog of import options opens.

⑥ Click **Create new Event** (◯ changes to ◉).

⑦ Type the name for the Event.

⑧ Click **Split days into new Events** (☑ changes to ▣) if you do not want to make each day a separate Event.

⑨ Click **After import analyze for** (▣ changes to ☑) and click **Stabilization** to apply stabilization automatically.

⑩ Select **Optimize video** (▣ changes to ☑) and choose the size in the pop-up menu.

⑪ Click **Import**.

iMovie imports the movie clips.

⑫ Click **Done**.

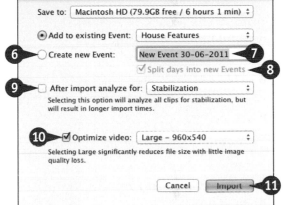

Should I analyze my clips for stabilization when importing video?

iMovie's video stabilization has two steps. First, you have iMovie analyze the video to decide which parts need stabilization; you can do this either when you import video, or later. Second, you apply the stabilization. Generally, it is better to analyze video for stabilization after importing it, for two reasons. First, the analysis makes the video importing take longer. Second, you may want to discard footage without analyzing it for stabilization, and analyze only the footage you want to use. iMovie can also analyze clips for people, trying to pick out footage that contains faces. Analyzing for people after import rather than during import is usually best.

Import Video from a Digital Camera

If your digital camera takes videos as well as still photos, you can bring the videos into iMovie and use them in your movies.

To import videos from a digital camera, you must normally use iPhoto rather than iMovie. You can then access the videos through iMovie's iPhoto Videos collection. To tell which application to use, see which application becomes active when you connect your digital camera.

Import Video from a Digital Camera

1 Connect the digital camera to your iMac with a USB cable.

2 Switch the camera on.

iPhoto automatically launches and displays the contents of the camera.

Note: If iMovie launches when you connect your digital camera, import the video as described in the previous task.

Note: If the digital camera contains both photos and videos, iPhoto displays both. Each video has the ▣ icon.

3 Type the name you want to give the Event.

Note: To import just some videos, select those you want and then click **Import Selected**.

4 Click **Import All**.

iPhoto imports the videos.

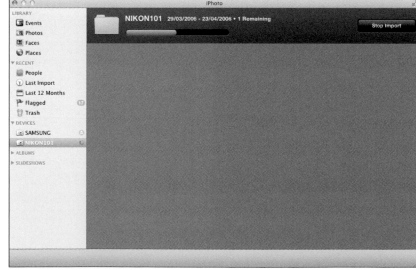

The Delete Photos on Your Camera? dialog opens.

5 Click **Keep Photos**.

Note: The Delete Photos on Your Camera? dialog always mentions photos even if you have imported videos. Keeping the photos or videos on the camera until you have checked what you imported is best.

The dialog closes, and the videos appear in the Last Import list in iPhoto.

6 In iMovie, click **iPhoto Videos** in the Event Library.

● The iPhoto videos appear, and you can use them in your movies as described later in this chapter.

Can I play a video in iPhoto?
In iPhoto, double-click the video to start it playing. You can then control playback by using the on-screen control bar that appears (●).

Import Video Files from Your iMac

I f you have video files stored on your iMac, you can import them into iMovie so that you can use them in your movies.

You can also use this technique to import video files from a digital camera whose memory card you can remove from the camera and connect to your iMac.

Import Video Files from Your iMac

1 In iMovie, click **File**.

The File menu opens.

2 Click **Import**.

The Import submenu opens.

3 Click **Movies**.

4 In the Import dialog, click the folder that contains the video files.

5 Click the file, or select multiple files.

6 Click the **Save to** ⇕ , and click the drive on which you want to store the files.

7 Click **Create new Event** (◯ changes to ◉).

8 Type the name for the Event.

Note: If you want to add the video files to an existing Event, click **Add to existing Event**, click ⇕ , and then click the Event.

9 Make sure **Optimize video** is checked (☑).

10 Make sure **Full – Original Size** appears in the pop-up menu.

11 Click **Copy files** (◯ changes to ◉).

12 Click **Import**.

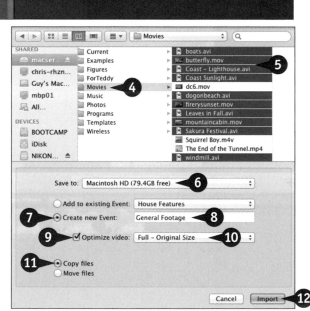

iMovie imports and optimizes the video or videos.

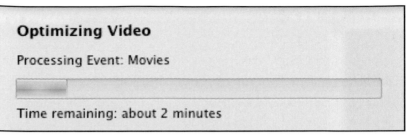

● The video clips appear in the Last Import area.

TIP

Why should I choose Full – Original Size when importing video?
iMovie can import high-definition video either at full quality or at reduced quality, which iMovie describes as Large. Use full quality unless your iMac is severely short of disk space. It is better to retain video quality so that your video footage is as good as possible. After making your movie, you can export it at a lower resolution if you want, while retaining a full-quality version on your iMac.

Create a Movie Project

To make a movie, you first create a *movie project*, a file that contains the details of the movie. You then add video clips to the movie project, arrange and edit them, and add transitions and titles.

iMovie automatically creates a new movie project named My First Project when you first launch the application. You can rename this project or delete it and start a new project from scratch.

Create a Movie Project

1 Click **New Project** (⊞).

Note: If the Project Library shows you two or more hard disks, first click the disk on which you want to create the project — for example, Macintosh HD, or an external hard disk you dedicate to video. Then click **New Project**.

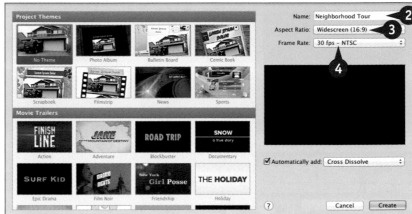

The New Project dialog opens.

2 Type the name for the project.

3 Click the **Aspect Ratio** ⇕ and choose the aspect ratio for the movie: **Widescreen (16:9)**, **Standard (4:3)**, or **iPhone (3:2)**.

4 Click the **Frame Rate** ⇕ and choose the frame rate for the movie. If you are in the U.S.A. or Canada, 30 fps – NTSC is the best choice.

5 If you want to apply a theme, click it in the Theme area.

Note: A theme is a predefined set of screen transitions, titles, and other effects for a movie.

6 If you chose a theme, make sure **Automatically add transitions and titles** is checked (☑).

Note: If you are not using a theme, you can check **Automatically add** (☐ changes to ☑) to automatically add transitions between clips. Click ⬍ and choose the transition type — for example, **Cross Dissolve**.

7 Click **Create**.

● iMovie creates the project, adds it to the Project Library, and opens it in the Project pane.

How do I rename a movie project?

To rename a movie project, double-click its name (●) in the Project Library. iMovie displays an edit box around the name. Type the new name and press Return.

How do I delete a movie project?

To delete a movie project, you move it to the Trash. Control+click or right-click the project in the Project Library, and then click **Move Project to Trash** on the shortcut menu. Deleting a movie project deletes only the details of the items it contains. The video clips remain in your Event Library, where you can use them in other projects.

Select the Video Footage You Want to Use

After importing video from your camcorder or your iMac, you have one or more Events in iMovie containing *video clips* — short sections of video.

Next, identify the video footage you want to use in your projects. To do so, you play back the clips and select the parts you want to use. You can mark a clip as a Favorite or as a reject for easy sorting.

Select the Video Footage You Want to Use

View a Clip

1. In the Event Library, click the Event that contains the clip you want to view.

2. Position the mouse pointer over a clip.

   The playhead appears as a vertical red line across the clip.

   ● The viewer displays the frame under the playhead.

3. Press **Spacebar**, and iMovie plays the clip in the viewer.

4. Press **Spacebar** again to stop playback.

Select Part of a Clip

1. In the Event Library, click the Event that contains the clip you want to view.

2. Position the mouse pointer over the clip.

3. Click the clip.

   iMovie selects a four-second section from where you clicked.

Note: See the tip for instructions on changing what iMovie selects when you click.

4. Click and drag a selection handle left or right to change the length of the selection.

Note: To move a selection without changing its length, click the yellow line at the top of the selection and then drag left or right.

Mark a Selection as a Favorite or a Reject

1 Select part of a clip.

2 Click **Mark Selection as Favorite** (★).

● iMovie puts a green bar across the top of the selection, indicating it is a favorite.

3 Select part of another clip.

4 Click **Reject Selection** (✕).

● iMovie puts a red bar across the top of the selection, indicating it is a reject.

5 Click **Unmark Selection** (☆), and iMovie removes the marking from the selection.

View Only Your Favorites

1 Click the **Show** ⇕, and then click **Favorites Only**.

iMovie displays only the footage you have marked as favorites.

Note: You can choose **Favorites and Unmarked** to view favorites and footage you have not marked as rejected.

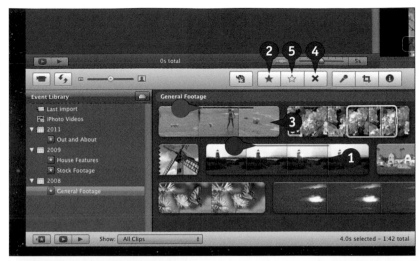

TIP

Can I change the amount of video iMovie selects when I click a clip?
Choose **iMovie** and **Preferences** to open the Preferences window, and then click the **Browser** tab (●). Click and drag the **Clicking in Event Browser selects** slider (●) to choose the number of seconds a click selects. You can also click **Clicking in Event Browser selects entire clip** (●, ○ changes to ●) if you prefer. You can also set what a double-click does by clicking **Edit** or **Play** in the Double-Click To area (●, ○ changes to ●). Click 🔘 to close the Preferences window.

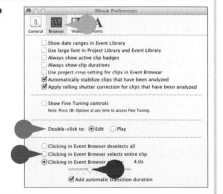

After grading your clips, you can quickly add your favorites to the movie project to build the movie. You can then arrange the clips into the order in which you want them to play.

Build the Movie Project from Clips

1 In the Project Library, double-click the project.

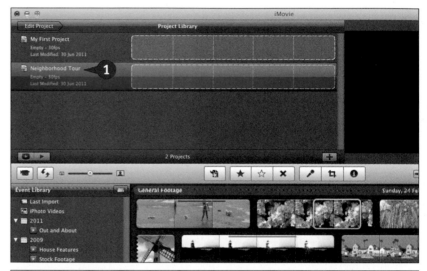

iMovie opens the project in the Project pane.

2 Select the clip or partial clip you want to add to the project.

Note: Use the selection methods explained in the previous task to select part of a clip. Option+click to select an entire clip.

3 Click the clip and drag it to the Project pane.

iMovie adds the clip to the project.

Note: If you chose to have iMovie add transitions to your movie automatically, a transition icon such as ⊠ appears before and after each clip.

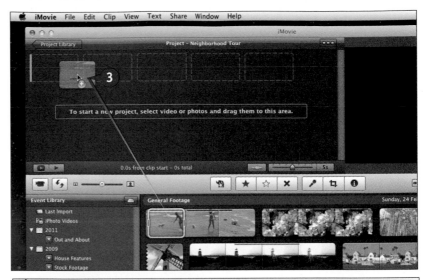

4 To rearrange the clips in the movie, click a clip and drag it to where you want it.

● The vertical green bar shows where the clip will land.

Note: To remove a clip from a project, click the clip in the Project pane and then press Delete.

TIP

Why does iMovie break up my video footage into separate clips?
When you import video footage from a tape camcorder, iMovie automatically creates clips from different sections of the tape by using the time code stamped on the frames: Where the time code contains a gap, iMovie creates a new clip. A camcorder that stores digital files in memory, on a hard disk, or on DVD automatically creates its own clips as you record, and iMovie preserves these clips.

Add Transitions between Video Clips

To make one clip flow better into the next, you can apply an effect called a *transition* between the clips. For example, the widely used Cross Dissolve transition gradually replaces the end of the first clip with the beginning of the second clip.

iMovie can apply transitions automatically, but you can retain greater control by applying them manually.

Add Transitions between Video Clips

1 Click **Transitions** (▣).

● The Transitions browser pane opens.

2 Click the transition you want to apply.

Note: Position the mouse pointer over a transition to see a preview of its effect.

3 Drag the transition to the Project pane and drop it between the clips.

iMovie adds an icon representing the transition.

Note: Each transition has a different icon. With practice, you can identify transitions by their icons.

④ Position the mouse pointer over the transition icon.

● The viewer shows a preview of the transition.

⑤ Double-click the transition icon.

● An Inspector dialog opens.

⑥ Type the duration of the transition.

⑦ Make sure **Applies to all transitions** is unchecked (☐).

⑧ Click **Done**.

The Inspector dialog closes.

TIPS

How can I change to a different transition?
After applying a transition between two video clips, you can switch to another transition by clicking and dragging it from the Transitions browser and dropping it on the existing transition. The replacement transition picks up the duration of the existing transition. You do not need to delete the existing transition first.

Should I add transitions to my movie automatically?
When using a theme to create a movie, set iMovie to add transitions automatically because doing so gives you the best effect from the theme. When creating a movie without a theme, apply transitions manually, adding them only where the clips actually need them. For clips that flow easily from one to the next, leave a *straight cut* with no transition.

Add a Still Photo to the Movie Project

As well as video clips, you can use still photos in your movie projects. This capability lets you enrich your movies with your iPhoto library.

You can crop a photo to show exactly the right part, and you can bring life and movement to it by adding a Ken Burns effect, panning and zooming across the photo.

Add a Still Photo to the Movie Project

1 Click **Photos** (🔲).

● The Photo browser pane opens.

2 Click a photo, drag it to the Project pane, and drop it where you want it to appear.

3 Double-click the photo in the Project pane.

● An Inspector dialog opens.

4 Set the number of seconds you want the photo to play.

5 Make sure that **Applies to all stills** is unchecked (🔲).

6 Click **Done**.

The Inspector dialog closes.

7 Click the photo.

Control buttons appear on the photo.

8 Click **Action** (⚙▾).

The Action menu opens.

9 Click **Cropping, Ken Burns & Rotation**.

The viewer displays the cropping tools.

10 Click **Ken Burns**.

The Ken Burns tools appear.

11 Click and drag the green rectangle to cover the area where you want the Ken Burns effect to start.

12 Click and drag the red rectangle to cover the area where you want the effect to end.

● To switch the green and red rectangles, click [icon].

13 Click **Play Clip** ([icon]).

iMovie plays a preview of the effect.

14 Click **Done**.

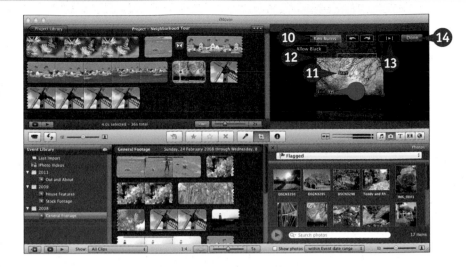

How do I crop or rotate a photo?

Click the photo in the Project pane, click **Action** ([icon]), and then click **Cropping, Ken Burns & Rotation**. Click **Crop** to display the cropping tools. Click and drag a corner handle to specify the cropping. Click [icon] to rotate 90 degrees counterclockwise, or click [icon] to rotate 90 degrees clockwise. Click **Allow Black** to allow black borders on the photo, or click **Disallow Black** to prevent black borders from appearing. Click **Done** when you have finished cropping and rotating.

Create a Soundtrack for the Movie

Your movie includes any audio you recorded along with your video clips, but you can also create a soundtrack for a movie by adding a song or playlist that plays in the background.

You can also add a sound effect at a particular point in a movie, or add narration to any footage that needs it.

Create a Soundtrack for the Movie

Add a Background Track

1 Click **Music and Sound Effects** (🎵).

● The Music and Sound Effects browser pane opens.

2 Click ⇕ and choose the source of music — for example, **iTunes**.

3 Click a song and drag it to the Project pane.

Note: Make sure the Project pane shows a green background when you drop the song. This means the song becomes a background track for the first part of the movie.

4 Click **Play Project from Beginning** (▶).

iMovie plays the movie with the soundtrack.

Add a Sound Effect to a Video Clip

1 Click **Music and Sound Effects** (♫).

● The Music and Sound Effects browser pane opens.

2 Click ↕ and choose the source of sound effects — for example, **iLife Sound Effects**.

3 Click a sound effect and drag it to the Project pane.

4 Move the mouse pointer across a clip to the frame at which you want the sound effect to start playing.

5 Drop the sound effect.

iMovie attaches the sound effect to the clip.

Set the Sound Level

1 Double-click the audio clip or background in the Project pane.

An Inspector dialog opens.

2 Click **Audio**.

The audio controls appear.

3 Click and drag the **Volume** slider.

4 Click **Done**.

The Inspector dialog closes.

 TIP

How do I add narration to a movie?

Click **Voiceover** (🎙) to open the Voiceover dialog. Click the **Record From** ↕ (●) and choose the microphone. Speak sample text and click and drag the **Input Volume** slider (●) to set the input volume. Position the mouse pointer over a clip to position the playhead where you want narration to start, and then click to start recording. When you have finished recording, click again. Click ⊗ or 🎙 to close the Voiceover dialog.

Add Titles and Credits

To give your movie an identity and a professional look, add a title, subtitle, and credits. iMovie provides a wide variety of title types suitable for different kinds of movies.

You can also add title screens to other parts of the movie that need them — for example, to make a change of scene explicit to the audience.

Add Titles and Credits

Add a Title

1 Click **Titles** (T̄).

● The Titles browser pane opens.

2 Click a title and drag it to the beginning of the movie. Drop the title before the first clip.

● iMovie adds the title and displays the Choose Background dialog.

3 Click the background you want.

iMovie closes the Choose Background dialog and applies the background.

4 Click each placeholder and type your text in its place.

Note: If you do not need one of the placeholders, select it, and then press Delete to delete it.

5 Click **Done**.

iMovie applies the text to the title.

Add Credits

1 Click **Titles** (⊤).

● The Titles browser pane opens.

2 Click the Scrolling Credits title and drag it to the end of the movie. Drop the title after the last clip.

● iMovie adds the title to the movie and displays the Choose Background dialog.

3 Click the background you want.

iMovie applies the background.

4 Click each placeholder and type your text in its place.

Note: If you do not need one of the placeholders, select it, and then press **Delete** to delete it.

5 Click **Done**.

iMovie applies the text to the title.

6 Click **Titles** (⊤).

The Titles browser pane closes.

Can I superimpose a title or credits on a screen?

Yes. Click the title in the Titles browser and drag it to the Project pane. Position the mouse pointer over a clip until the playhead is at the frame where you want the title to start playing, and then drop the title. You can then edit the title text

(●) in the viewer. When you superimpose a title like this, iMovie does not display the Choose Background dialog because the title uses the clip as its background.

Share the Movie on YouTube

To share a movie with everybody on the Internet, you can post it to the YouTube video-sharing site. iMovie includes a built-in command for creating movies in the format that YouTube requires and for posting movies to the site.

Before you can post movies on YouTube, you must create a YouTube account.

Share the Movie on YouTube

1 In the Project Library, Control +click or right-click the project.

2 Click **Publish to YouTube**.

Note: The first time you open the Publish Your Project to YouTube dialog, click **Add**. The Add Account dialog opens. Type your YouTube account name, and then click **Done**.

3 Make sure the Account pop-up menu is showing the right account.

4 Type your YouTube password.

5 Click ⬍ and choose the category to assign to the movie.

6 Type a title.

7 Type a description.

8 Type tags for the movie. See the second tip.

9 Click the size you want to publish (○ changes to ◉). Usually, **Medium** is the best choice.

10 Click **Make this movie personal** (☑ changes to ☐) if you want the movie to be available to everyone on YouTube.

11 Click **Next**.

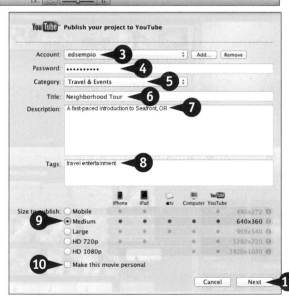

The YouTube Terms of Service screen opens.

⑫ Read the terms.

⑬ Click **Publish**.

iMovie publishes the project to YouTube.

A dialog opens.

⑭ Click **Tell a Friend** if you want to start an email message to friends telling them the movie is available.

⑮ Click **View** if you want to check that the movie has transferred properly.

⑯ Click **OK** to close the dialog.

TIPS

How do I get an account on YouTube?
Click **Safari** (　) on the Dock to open a browser window. Triple-click in the Address field, type **youtube.com**, and press ⟨Return⟩. Safari displays the YouTube home page. Click the **Create Account** link, and then follow the instructions on the web page that appears. Be sure to review the Google Terms of Service and YouTube Terms of Service before accepting the agreement.

What are tags and why should I use them?
A *tag* is a text term that helps explain concisely what a movie is about. YouTube uses tag information in searches, so the tags help people find movies they are interested in. By adding suitable tags to your movie, you can make your movie easier to find and increase its audience.

CHAPTER 12

Customizing Your iMac

Mac OS X is easy to use straight out of the box, but you can customize it to suit your needs. For example, you can apply a screen saver, change the icons on the Dock, give yourself more screen space, and make the keyboard and mouse easier to use. You can also give your iMac commands with your voice, run applications each time you log in, or put your iMac to sleep when you are not using it.

Change Your Desktop Background

The easiest way to make your iMac look different is to change the desktop background. Mac OS X includes various backgrounds, but you can also use your own photos to add a personal touch.

You can choose between displaying a single picture on the desktop and displaying a series of images that change automatically.

Change Your Desktop Background

① **Control**+click or right-click the desktop.

The shortcut menu opens.

② Click **Change Desktop Background**.

The Desktop pane of Desktop & Screen Saver preferences opens.

③ Click the category of image you want to see.

Note: The Apple section of the categories list contains the built-in desktop backgrounds. The iPhoto section contains your iPhoto library. If you add folders, as described in the tip, they appear in the Folders section.

The images in the category appear in the right-hand pane.

④ Click the image you want to apply to the desktop.

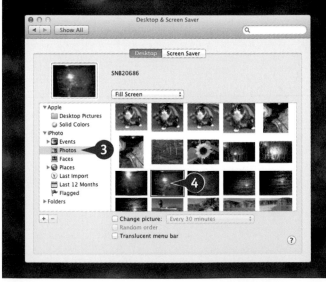

The image appears on the desktop.

5 If you chose a photo or picture of your own, click ⬍ and choose how to fit the image to the screen. See the tip for details.

6 If you want to set a series of background images, click the category.

7 Click **Change picture** (☐ changes to ☑).

8 Click the **Change Picture** ⬍ and choose the interval — for example, **When logging in** or **Every 30 minutes**.

9 Click **Random order** (☐ changes to ☑) if you want the images to appear in random order.

10 Click **Translucent menu bar** (☑ changes to ☐) if you want the menu bar to appear solid gray rather than translucent.

11 Click the **System Preferences** menu and click **Quit System Preferences** to close System Preferences.

TIPS

Which option should I choose for fitting the image to the screen?
In the Desktop & Screen Saver preferences, choose **Fit to Screen** to match the image's height or width — whichever is nearest — to the screen. Choose **Fill Screen** to make an image fill the screen without distortion but cropping off parts that do not fit. Choose **Stretch to Fill Screen** to stretch the image to fit the screen exactly, distorting it as needed. Choose **Tile** to cover the desktop with multiple copies of the image. Choose **Center** to display the image at full size in the middle of the desktop.

I have a folder of pictures I want to use as desktop backgrounds. Can I add them to the Desktop tab?
Click **Add** (⊞) below the categories box. A dialog opens. Click the folder, and then click **Choose**. The folder appears in the Folders section of the categories list. Click the folder, and then click the picture you want.

Set Up a Screen Saver

A *screen saver* is an image, a sequence of images, or a moving pattern that Mac OS X displays to hide what your screen is showing when you leave your iMac idle. You can choose what screen saver to use and how soon to start it. If you prefer, you can use no screen saver at all.

Mac OS X comes with a variety of attractive screen savers. You can download other screen savers from websites.

Set Up a Screen Saver

1 Control +click or right-click the desktop.

The shortcut menu opens.

2 Click **Change Desktop Background**.

The Desktop pane of Desktop & Screen Saver preferences opens.

3 Click **Screen Saver**.

The Screen Savers pane appears.

4 Click a screen saver in the list on the left.

Note: The Apple category of screen savers contains the screen savers supplied with Mac OS X. The Pictures category enables you to create screen savers from your photos or from pictures included with Mac OS X.

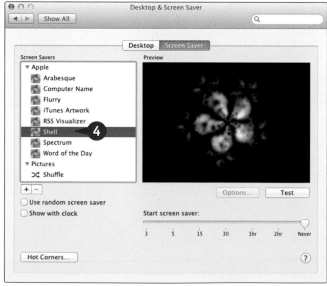

The screen saver you clicked starts playing in the Preview area.

⑤ Click and drag **Start screen saver** to set the length of time before the screen saver starts.

Note: To turn the screen saver off, click and drag **Start screen saver** to Never, all the way to the right.

⑥ Click **Test** if you want to see the full screen saver.

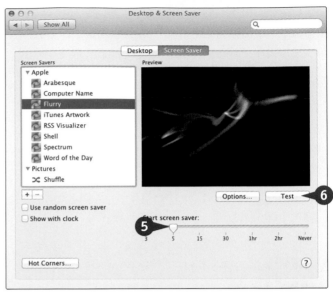

The screen saver plays full screen.

⑦ Click anywhere on the screen saver when you want to stop the preview.

The Screen Saver pane of the Desktop & Screen Saver preferences appears again.

⑧ Click the **System Preferences** menu and click **Quit System Preferences** to close System Preferences.

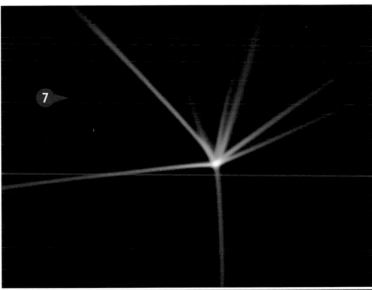

TIPS

Must I use a screen saver to protect my iMac's screen from damage?
Screen savers originally protected cathode ray tube (CRT) displays from having static images "burned in" to their screens. LCD screens, such as that on your iMac, do not suffer from this problem, so you need not use a screen saver. Nowadays you can use a screen saver to protect the information on-screen or to provide visual entertainment.

What are the Display Style buttons that appear when I click a screen saver in the Pictures category?
After selecting a Pictures screen saver, you can click **Slideshow** (▣) to make a slideshow of the pictures. Click **Collage** (◈) to make each picture spiral down to form a collage on a background. Click **Mosaic** (▦) to display miniature versions of the pictures tiled in a mosaic.

Make the Dock Show the Icons You Need

The Dock is your control center for the applications you run on your iMac, so it is well worth spending a few minutes customizing the Dock to contain the icons you need. You can add applications, files, or folders to the Dock or remove most existing items.

Make the Dock Show the Icons You Need

Add an Application to the Dock

1 Click **Launchpad** (🚀) on the Dock.

The Launchpad screen of applications appears.

Note: If necessary, scroll left or right to reach the Launchpad screen that contains the application you are looking for.

2 In the list of applications, click and drag the application you want to the left side of the Dock.

An icon for the application appears on the Dock.

Note: After you open an application from Launchpad, you can `Control`+click or right-click its icon on the Dock, highlight or click **Options**, and then click **Keep in Dock**.

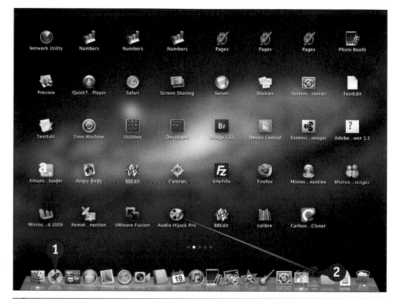

Add a File or Folder to the Dock

1 Click **Finder** (😀) on the Dock.

2 In the Finder window, navigate to the file or folder you want to add to the Dock.

3 Click and drag the file or folder to the right side of the Dock.

An icon for the file or folder appears on the Dock.

Remove an Item from the Dock

1 Click and drag the icon from the Dock to the desktop.

The icon vanishes in a puff of smoke.

Resize the Dock

1 Click the Dock divider bar and drag it up to make the Dock bigger or down to make the Dock smaller.

The Dock icons grow or shrink so that they occupy all the space on the Dock.

TIP

Can I customize the Dock further?

You can position the Dock on the left or right side of the screen rather than at the bottom. You can hide the Dock so that it appears only when you move the mouse pointer to the bottom or side of the screen. You can also turn on magnification, which makes the Dock icons grow for easy identification when you position the mouse pointer over them. To reach these options, **Control**+click or right-click the Dock divider bar (●) and use the shortcut menu. You can also find all these options in the Dock preference pane in System Preferences.

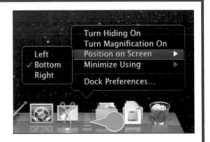

Create and Remove Extra Desktop Spaces

To spread out your documents and applications so that you can see exactly what you need to work with, you can create as many extra desktop spaces as required. You can then position applications as needed on these desktop spaces.

When you have finished using a desktop space, you can close it in moments.

Create and Remove Extra Desktop Spaces

Create a Desktop Space and Add Applications to It

1 Click **Mission Control** (🗗) on the Dock.

The Mission Control screen appears.

2 Move the mouse pointer to the upper-right corner of the screen.

A panel showing a + sign appears.

3 Click the + panel.

● Mac OS X adds another desktop space.

④ Optionally, click a window and drag it to the desktop space you want it to appear in.

⑤ Click the desktop space you want to display.

The desktop space appears.

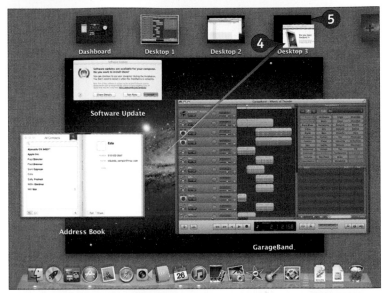

Remove a Desktop Space

① Click **Mission Control** (⬛) on the Dock.

The Mission Control screen appears.

② Move the mouse pointer over the desktop space you want to close.

The ⊗ button appears.

③ Click the ⊗ button.

The desktop space closes.

④ Click the desktop space you want to display.

Mission Control displays that desktop space.

TIP

How can I assign an application to a particular desktop?
Use Mission Control to activate the desktop you want to assign the application to. Then Control +click or right-click the application's Dock icon (●), click **Options**, and click **This Desktop**. To use the application on all desktops, click **All Desktops** in the Assign To section of the Options menu.

Create Hot Corners to Run Mission Control Easily

As discussed in Chapter 3, Mission Control lets you see all your open windows and pick the one you need.

To run Mission Control with the mouse, set up a *hot corner*, a screen corner that automatically triggers Mission Control when you position the mouse pointer there. You can also set up hot corners for starting and stopping the screen saver or putting the display to sleep.

Create Hot Corners to Run Mission Control Easily

Set Up a Hot Corner

1 Click .

The Apple menu opens.

2 Click **System Preferences**.

The System Preferences window opens.

3 Click **Mission Control**.

The Mission Control preferences pane opens.

4 Click **Hot Corners**.

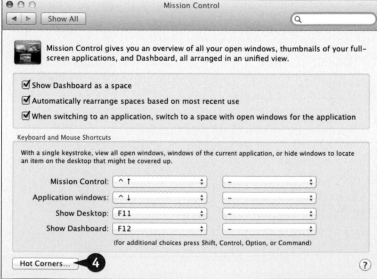

The Hot Corners dialog opens.

5 Click 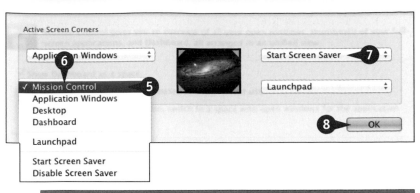 for the hot corner you want to set.

The pop-up menu opens.

6 Click the action you want. For example, click **Mission Control** to make the hot corner show Mission Control.

7 Choose other hot corner actions as needed.

Note: You can set up two or more hot corners for the same feature if you want.

8 Click **OK**.

The Hot Corners dialog closes.

9 Click the **System Preferences** menu and click **Quit System Preferences** to close System Preferences.

Use a Hot Corner to Run Mission Control

1 Move the mouse pointer to the hot corner you allocated to Mission Control.

Mission Control resizes and moves the windows so that you can see them all.

2 Click the window you want to display.

TIP

Are there other ways I can run Mission Control using the Magic Mouse or Magic Trackpad?

As well as using a hot corner, you can use the mouse's secondary button or a gesture, or another button or gesture, to run Mission Control. In the Keyboard and Mouse Shortcuts section in Mission Control preferences, click the **Mission Control** ⬍ and choose the mouse button or gesture. Press and hold ⌘, Alt, Control, Shift, or a combination of the four keys to add them to the keystroke. Use the same technique for the Application Windows pop-up menu, the Show Desktop pop-up menu, and the Show Dashboard pop-up menu.

Add a Second Display So You Can See More

Your iMac has a bright and beautiful screen built in, but you can also add an external display to give yourself more space for your work. For a digital screen, you need a Mini DisplayPort-to-DVI connector. For a CRT display or analog LCD screen, you need a Mini DisplayPort–to-VGA connector. If your iMac has one or more Thunderbolt ports, you can add the Apple Thunderbolt Display using the cable that comes with the display.

Add a Second Display So You Can See More

1 Plug the Mini DisplayPort connector at the end of the connector cable into the Mini DisplayPort or Thunderbolt port on the back of the iMac.

2 Plug the display's cable into the DVI port or VGA port on the other end of the connector cable.

3 Connect the display's power supply.

4 Turn the display on.

5 Click ![Apple menu].

The Apple menu opens.

6 Click **System Preferences**.

The System Preferences window opens.

7 Click **Displays**.

Note: Your iMac may automatically open the Displays pane of System Preferences after you connect the display and turn it on.

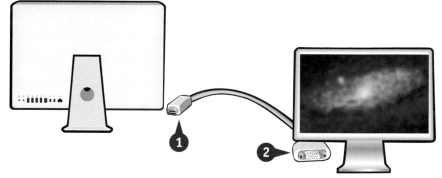

The Displays preferences open on each display.

8 In the external display's Displays pane, click **Display** if it is not already highlighted.

9 Click the resolution you want.

10 If the Brightness slider is available, drag it to adjust the display's brightness.

11 If the Colors pop-up menu appears, make sure it shows Millions.

12 For a CRT, click the **Refresh Rate** $\updownarrow$, and then click the highest refresh rate available.

13 In the iMac's Displays pane, click **Arrangement**.

14 In the Arrangement pane, click and drag either monitor icon to match the monitors' physical locations.

15 To move the menu bar and Dock, click and drag the menu bar from the iMac's icon to the external display's icon.

16 Close System Preferences.

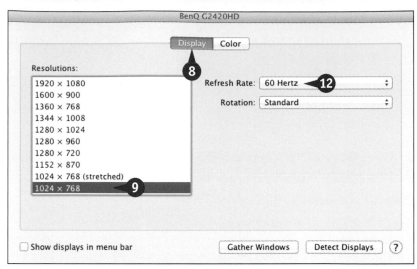

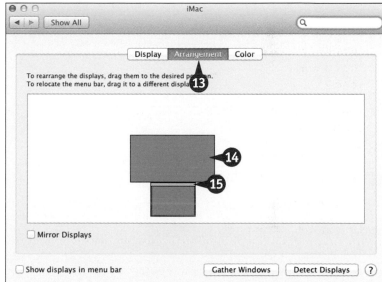

TIPS

How big of an external monitor can I connect to my iMac?

Current iMacs can drive an external screen as large as Apple's 27-inch Thunderbolt Display or LED Cinema Display, which have a resolution of 2560 x 1440 pixels. For this, you need a Mini DisplayPort to Dual-Link DVI Adapter cable. Older iMacs can drive external LCDs at resolutions of up to 1920 x 1200 pixels.

Can I use my iMac as a display for my MacBook?

If your iMac supports Target Display mode, as 27-inch iMac models do, you can use it as a display. With the iMac running, connect a male-to-male Mini DisplayPort cable to each Mac's Mini DisplayPort. The iMac enters Target Display mode automatically, and the other Mac's screen appears. You can press ⌘+F2 to toggle between Target Display mode and the iMac's own output.

Make the Keyboard and Mouse or Trackpad Easier to Use

Your iMac's keyboard and Magic Mouse or Magic Trackpad come with default settings that work well for many people, but you may need to change the settings to make the devices easier and more comfortable for you to use.

Make the Keyboard and Mouse or Trackpad Easier to Use

Control the Keyboard's Repeat Rate

1 Click **⌘**, **System Preferences**, and then **Keyboard**.

2 In the Keyboard pane, click **Keyboard** if it is not already highlighted.

3 Click and drag the **Key Repeat** slider to control how quickly a key repeats when you hold it down.

4 Click and drag the **Delay Until Repeat** slider to set the length of time Mac OS X waits before repeating a key you hold down.

5 Click **Show All** to see the full set of System Preferences.

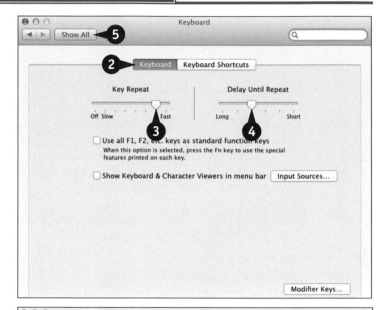

Make the Mouse or Trackpad Easier to Use

6 Click **Mouse** or **Trackpad**. This example uses Mouse.

7 Click **Point & Click**.

8 Click and drag the **Tracking** slider to control how fast the pointer moves.

9 Choose other scroll, tap, and double-tap options.

10 Click **Show All**.

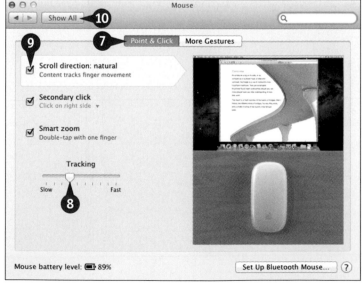

The full set of System Preferences appears.

11 Click **Universal Access**.

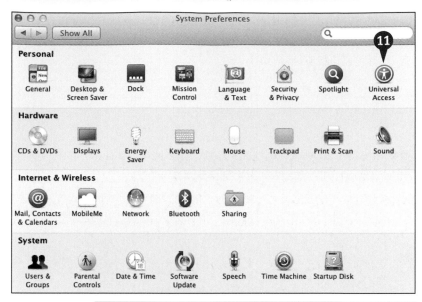

The Universal Access pane opens.

12 Click **Mouse & Trackpad**.

The Mouse & Trackpad options appear.

13 To make the pointer respond more slowly, drag the **Initial Delay** slider to the right.

14 To slow down the pointer's movements, drag the **Maximum Speed** slider to the right.

15 To make the pointer easier to see, drag the **Cursor Size** slider to the right.

16 Click the **System Preferences** menu and click **Quit System Preferences** to close System Preferences.

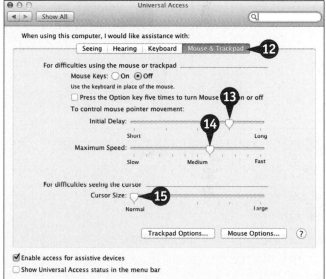

TIP

What are the options on the Scroll & Zoom tab and More Gestures tab in Mouse preferences or Trackpad preferences?

The Scroll & Zoom tab in Trackpad preferences lets you choose options for scrolling, zooming, and rotating using the trackpad. The More Gestures tab in Mouse preferences and Trackpad preferences lets you choose extra gestures. Select a check box (☐ changes to ☑) to turn a gesture on. If it has a ▼, click to display options you can choose — for example, the number of fingers to use for swiping left or right.

Make the Screen Easier to See

If you have trouble seeing the screen on your iMac, you can use the Universal Access preferences to make it easier to see.

Make the Screen Easier to See

1 Click ![Apple].

The Apple menu opens.

2 Click **System Preferences**.

The System Preferences window opens.

3 Click **Universal Access**.

The Universal Access pane opens.

4 Click **Seeing**.

5 To make items on-screen larger, click **On** (⚪ changes to ⚫) under Zoom.

6 Click **Options**.

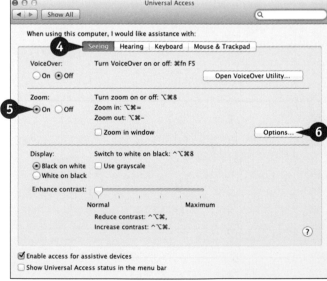

The Options dialog for zooming opens.

7 Click and drag the **Maximum Zoom** slider to set the maximum zoom.

8 Click and drag the **Minimum Zoom** slider to set the minimum zoom.

9 Click **Done**.

The Options dialog for zooming closes.

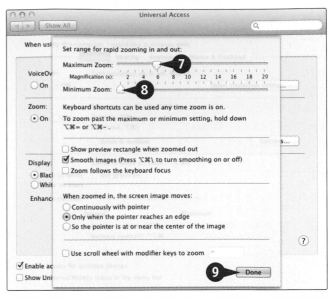

10 Click **White on black** (⚪ changes to ⚫) if you want to reverse the video to make the screen easier to see. The effect is like viewing a photographic negative, with each color inverted.

11 Click and drag the **Enhance contrast** slider if you want to increase the contrast.

12 Click the **System Preferences** menu and click **Quit System Preferences** to close System Preferences.

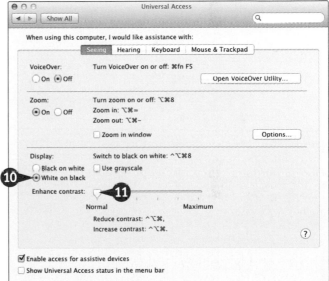

TIP

What is the quickest way to turn on the Universal Access features for seeing the screen?
To turn on the Universal Access features for seeing the screen, use keyboard shortcuts. Press ⌘+Option+8 to toggle zoom on or off. Press ⌘+Option+= to zoom in or ⌘+Option+− to zoom out. Press ⌘+Option+Control+8 to toggle White on Black on or off.

Tell Spotlight Which Folders to Search

Mac OS X's Spotlight feature is great for locating the files and folders you need. But if Spotlight finds irrelevant results, or if it does not find the results you are looking for, you can change the folders that Spotlight searches. This change is easy to make, but it makes a huge difference to the search results you get.

Tell Spotlight Which Folders to Search

1 Click 🔍.

The Spotlight search field opens.

2 Type a few letters in the search field.

The list of search results appears.

3 Click **Spotlight Preferences**.

The System Preferences window opens with the Spotlight pane at the front.

4 Click **Search Results** if it is not already highlighted.

5 Click ☑ next to any item for which you do not want to see search results (☑ changes to ☐).

6 If you want to change the order of search result categories, click and drag a category up or down the list.

● The horizontal blue line shows where it will land.

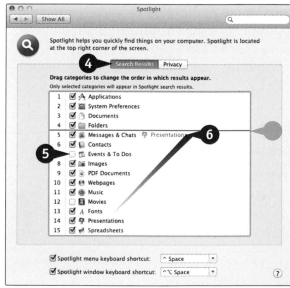

7 Click **Privacy**.

The Privacy pane of Spotlight preferences opens.

8 Click **Add** (⊞).

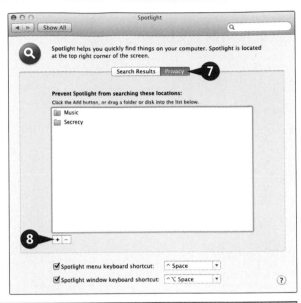

A dialog opens.

9 Click the folder you want to add.

Note: You can select two or more folders by clicking the first and then ⌘+clicking each of the others.

10 Click **Choose**.

The dialog closes, and the folder appears in the list.

11 Click the **System Preferences** menu and click **Quit System Preferences** to close System Preferences.

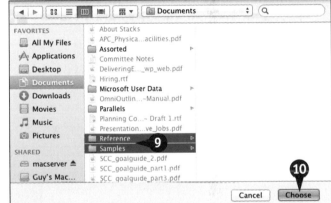

TIP

Is there another way to add folders to the Privacy list?
Instead of using the dialog to build the list of folders you do not want Spotlight to search, you can work from a Finder window. Click **Finder** (🙂) on the Dock to open a Finder window, and position it so that you can see both it and the Spotlight preferences pane. Click and drag from the Finder window to the Spotlight preferences pane the folders you want to protect to add them to the list. You can select multiple folders at once to save time.

Control Your iMac with Your Voice

To save wear and tear on your fingers and wrists, Mac OS X enables you to control your iMac by speaking commands into a microphone.

For best results, you need to connect an external microphone to your iMac rather than use the built-in microphone. The best kind is a headset microphone that keeps the microphone positioned near to your mouth.

Control Your iMac with Your Voice

1 Click .

The Apple menu opens.

2 Click **System Preferences**.

● The System Preferences window opens.

3 Click **Speech**.

The Speech preferences pane opens.

4 Click **Speech Recognition** if it is not already highlighted.

5 Next to Speakable Items, click **On** (○ changes to ⊙).

6 Click **Settings** if it is not already highlighted.

7 Click the **Microphone** ⏷ and choose the microphone you want to use.

8 Click **Calibrate**.

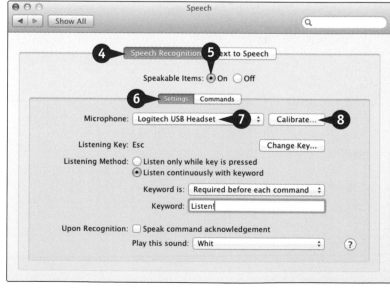

The Microphone Calibration dialog opens.

9 Speak into the microphone, and click and drag the **input volume** slider until the volume meter registers up to the right end of the green bars but not into the red bars.

10 Click **Done** to close the Microphone Calibration dialog.

11 Click **Commands**.

The Commands sub-tab opens.

12 Select the check box for each set of commands you want to use.

13 To choose settings for a command set such as Global Speakable Items, click the set and click **Configure**.

A configuration dialog opens.

14 Choose settings for the commands.

Note: Different sets of commands have different options. Some sets have no options.

15 Click **OK**.

16 Click the **System Preferences** menu and click **Quit System Preferences** to close System Preferences.

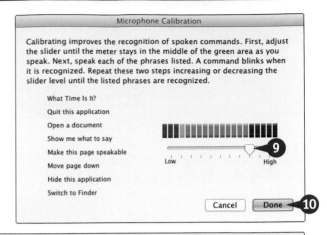

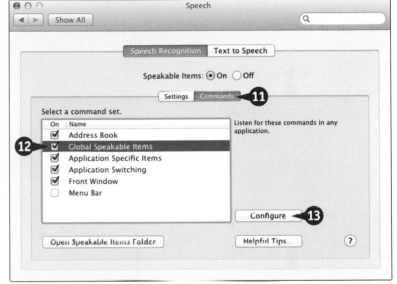

TIP

Should I choose Listen Only While Key Is Pressed or Listen Continuously with Keyword?

This depends on how much you will use spoken commands. Click **Listen only while key is pressed** (○ changes to ●) if you will use speech recognition only seldom and you do not want to waste the iMac's computing power listening to commands that do not come. Click **Listen continuously with keyword** (○ changes to ●) if you will use speech recognition frequently and you are prepared to say the keyword each time you need the computer's attention. Type the word you want to use in the Keyword field.

Save Time by Running Applications Each Time You Log In

Of the many applications installed on your iMac, you most likely run some every day, others less frequently, and the rest hardly ever. You can save time by setting Mac OS X to open your most-used applications automatically each time you log in to your iMac. You can set this up either from the Dock or from System Preferences.

Save Time by Running Applications Each Time You Log In

Use the Dock to Set an Application to Run at Login

1 If the application does not have an icon on the Dock, open the application as usual.

2 **Control**+click or right-click the application's icon.

The shortcut menu opens.

3 Click or highlight **Options**.

The Options submenu opens.

4 Click **Open at Login**.

Mac OS X places a check mark next to Open at Login.

Use System Preferences to Set an Application to Run at Login

1 Click .

The Apple menu opens.

2 Click **System Preferences**.

The System Preferences window opens.

3 Click **Users & Groups**.

The Users & Groups preferences pane opens showing your user account.

4 Click **Login Items**.

The list of login items appears.

Note: You can click ☐ in the application's Hide column (☐ changes to ☑) to hide the application when it launches. This setting is useful for applications that run in the background but not for applications you need to see.

5 Click **Add** (⊞).

A dialog opens showing a list of the applications in the Applications folder.

Note: You can also add documents to the list for automatic opening. Just navigate to the document, select it, and click **Add**.

6 Click the application you want to run automatically at login.

Note: To select multiple applications, click the first, and then ⌘+click each of the others.

7 Click **Add**.

The dialog closes, and the application appears in the list on the Login Items pane.

8 Click the **System Preferences** menu and click **Quit System Preferences** to close System Preferences.

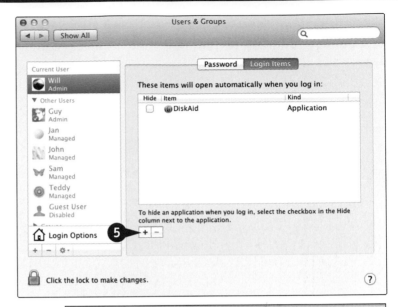

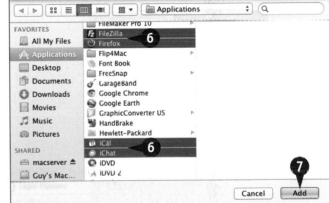

TIPS

Is there another way to add an application to the Login Items pane of Accounts preferences?
Instead of clicking **Add** (⊞) and using the dialog to pick the applications, you can click and drag the applications from a Finder window. Click **Finder** (🙂) on the Dock to open a Finder window, and then click **Applications** in the sidebar. Click the application you want, and then drag it across to the Login Items pane of Account preferences.

Is there a disadvantage to running applications at login?
The more applications you run at login, the longer the login process takes. Normally, it is best to run only a handful of applications at login — those you use in every computing session. Run other applications from the Dock or Launchpad when you need them instead of launching them at login in case you need them later.

Save Power by Putting Your iMac to Sleep

When you are not using your iMac, you can put it to sleep to save electricity. When you know you will be away from your iMac for a while, you can put it to sleep manually, but you can also set the Energy Saver feature to put your iMac to sleep after a period of inactivity.

Save Power by Putting Your iMac to Sleep

1 Click .

The Apple menu opens.

2 Click **System Preferences**.

The System Preferences window opens.

3 Click **Energy Saver**.

The Energy Saver pane appears.

4 Click and drag the **Computer sleep** slider to set the length of time to wait before putting the iMac to sleep.

5 Click and drag the **Display sleep** slider to set the amount of time to wait before blanking the display.

Note: Set Display Sleep to a shorter time than Computer Sleep.

6 If you want to have your iMac go to sleep or wake up on a schedule, click **Schedule**.

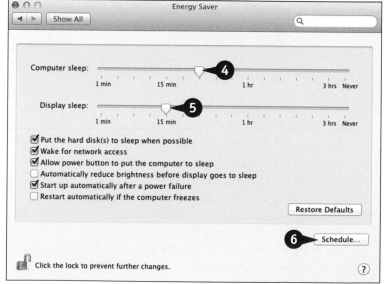

The Schedule dialog opens.

7 To set a wake-up time, click **Start up or wake** (☐ changes to ☑).

8 Click ↕ and choose the frequency: **Weekends**, **Weekdays**, **Every Day**, or a particular day of the week.

9 Click ⟐ to set the wake-up time.

10 To set a sleep or shutdown time, click ☐ on the second row.

11 Click ↕ and choose **Sleep** or **Shut Down**.

Note: You can also set the iMac to restart on schedule. Generally, this setting is less useful than sleep or shutdown.

12 Click ↕ and choose the frequency.

13 Click ⟐ to set the time.

14 Click **OK**.

15 Click the **System Preferences** menu and click **Quit System Preferences** to close System Preferences.

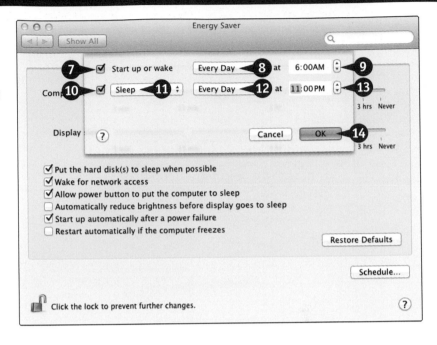

TIPS

Which button do I press to wake my iMac from sleep?
You can press any key on the keyboard to wake the iMac. If you are not certain whether the iMac is asleep or preparing to run a screen saver, press Shift or ⌘. These keys do not type a character if the iMac turns out to be awake rather than asleep.

Is it a good idea to select the Automatically Reduce Brightness Before Display Goes to Sleep check box?
Dimming the screen saves some power, but having the screen dim when you are taking a moment to compose your thoughts can be distracting. You may find it more helpful to set a shorter Display sleep time and clear the Automatically Reduce Brightness Before Display Goes to Sleep check box.

Choose When to Check for Software Updates

To keep your iMac running smoothly and protect it from both online and offline threats, you should apply the software updates that Apple releases for Mac OS X and for Apple applications.

Usually, having the Software Update utility check for updates automatically is easiest, but you can check manually instead if you prefer.

Choose When to Check for Software Updates

1 Click ⬛.

The Apple menu opens.

2 Click **System Preferences**.

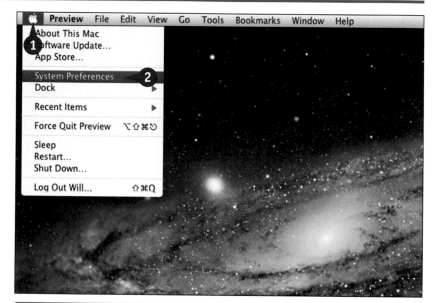

The System Preferences window opens.

3 Click **Software Update**.

The Software Update pane opens.

4 Click the **Scheduled Check** tab.

5 Make sure **Check for updates** is selected (☑).

6 Click ⬍ and click **Daily**, **Weekly**, or **Monthly**, as appropriate. See the first tip for advice.

7 Make sure **Download updates automatically** is selected (☑).

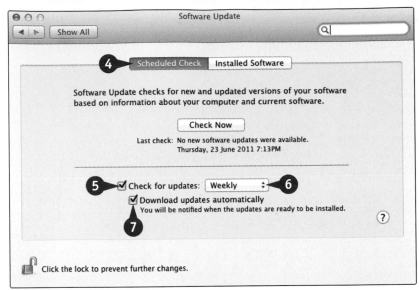

8 Click **System Preferences**.

The System Preferences menu opens.

9 Click **Quit System Preferences**.

The System Preferences window closes.

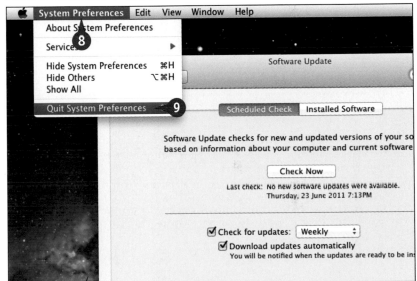

TIPS

How frequently should I check for software updates?
If you have an always-on Internet connection, set Software Update to check for updates daily in step **6**. This ensures you receive the updates as soon as possible, so that your iMac remains up to date and protected against the latest threats. Use the Weekly setting if you find the updates frequent enough to interrupt your work. Avoid the Monthly setting because it may leave your iMac unprotected for several weeks.

Will I need to restart my iMac after installing updates?
Some updates to Mac OS X require you to restart your iMac, whereas most updates to Apple applications do not need a restart. Software Update always warns you when an update requires a restart, so you can delay applying the update if the timing is not convenient.

CHAPTER 13

Using Your iMac on a Network

This chapter shows you how to use iMac's networking capabilities, including AirDrop file sharing, printer sharing, and remote control.

Transfer Files Using AirDrop

When you need to transfer files quickly between your iMac and another Mac on your network, you can use Mac OS X's AirDrop feature. With AirDrop, you display a screen that shows the Macs using AirDrop on your network, and then drag the file to the Mac to which you want to send it. When the recipient accepts the file, the transfer begins. Similarly, your colleagues can send files to you via AirDrop.

Transfer Files Using AirDrop

Send a File via AirDrop

1 Click **Finder** (⬛) on the Dock.

A Finder window opens.

2 Click **AirDrop**.

The AirDrop screen appears.

Note: To use AirDrop, both your iMac and the other Mac must be running Mac OS X 10.7, Lion. Earlier versions of Mac OS X do not have the AirDrop feature.

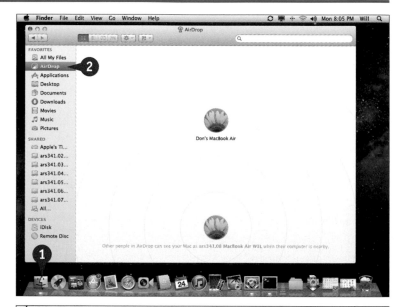

3 Click and drag the file to the icon for the Mac you want to send it to.

Note: If necessary, open another Finder window by clicking **File** and **New Finder Window**, and then navigate to the folder that contains the file you want to send.

A confirmation dialog appears.

4 Click **Send**.

The Finder sends the file to the recipient.

Receive a File via AirDrop

When someone sends you a file via AirDrop, a dialog appears on-screen.

1 Click the appropriate button:

● Click **Save and Open** to save the file and open it for viewing.

● Click **Decline** to decline the transfer.

● Click **Save** to save the file so you can use it later.

If you chose to accept the file, your iMac receives the file.

If you chose to save and open the file, your iMac opens the file in the default application for that file type, if it has a default application. You can then work with the file.

TIPS

Why is there no AirDrop icon in the Finder sidebar?

First, make sure Wi-Fi is on. If still no AirDrop icon appears in the Finder sidebar, it means that your iMac cannot use AirDrop. Use a shared folder or a Public folder, as discussed in the next task.

Should I use AirDrop or a shared folder on the network to transfer files?

If your iMac connects to a network with shared folders, use those folders instead of AirDrop. By storing a file in a shared folder, you and your colleagues can work on it directly without transferring copies back and forth. AirDrop is useful for sharing on networks that do not have shared folders or for sharing files with Macs to which your iMac does not normally connect.

Connect to a Shared Folder

Sharing files is one of the most popular uses of a network, either at home or at work. To access files that someone else is sharing, you need to connect to the shared folder.

Connect to a Shared Folder

1 Click **Finder** (🙂) on the Dock.

A Finder window opens.

2 If the Shared category is collapsed, position the mouse pointer over it, and then click **Show** to expand it.

3 Click the computer that is sharing the folder.

4 Click **Connect As**.

Note: If you do not have a user account on the computer sharing the folder, use Guest access to the shared folder. Do not click Connect As; instead, go to step **8**.

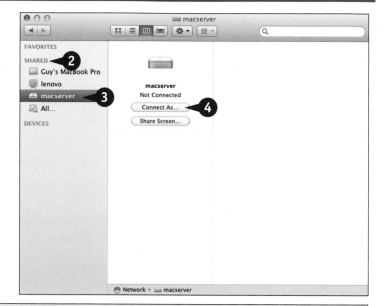

The Connect As dialog opens.

5 Type your username for the computer you are accessing.

6 Type your password for that computer.

Note: Click **Remember this password in my keychain** (☐ changes to ☑) if you want to store your password for future use.

7 Click **Connect**.

● The full list of shared folders appears.

Note: The shared folders you see are the folders you have permission to access. Different folders may be shared with other users than are shared with you.

⑧ Click the folder whose contents you want to see.

⑨ Work with files as usual. For example, open a file to work on it, or copy it to your iMac.

⑩ When you finish using the shared folder, click ⏏ next to the computer's name in the Shared list.

Your iMac disconnects the shared folder.

Note: If the Finder window is in Column view, you can click **Disconnect** in the first column to disconnect the shared folder.

TIP

How can I connect to a shared folder that does not appear in the Shared list in the Finder window?
If the shared folder does not appear in the Shared list, find out the name or IP address of the computer sharing the folder. Open the **Go** menu and choose **Connect to Server**. The Connect to Server dialog opens. In the Server Address field (●), type or paste the computer's name or IP address, and then click **Connect**. To reconnect to a server you have used before, click **Choose a Recent Server** (⊙▾) in the Connect to Server dialog.

Share a Folder on the Network

Just as you can connect to folders that other people are sharing on the network, you can share one or more of your iMac's folders on the network.

To share a folder on the network, you need to set up the File Sharing service and decide who you will allow to access the folder.

Share a Folder on the Network

1 Click .

The Apple menu opens.

2 Click **System Preferences**.

The System Preferences window opens.

3 Click **Sharing**.

The Sharing preferences pane opens.

4 Click **File Sharing** (☐ changes to ☑).

Mac OS X turns on file sharing.

5 Click **Add** (⊞) under the Shared Folders box.

A dialog for choosing a folder opens.

6 Click the folder you want to share.

7 Click **Add**.

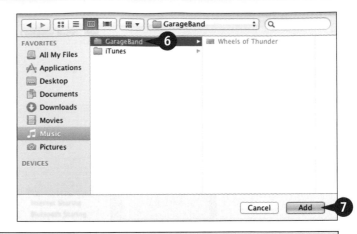

The dialog closes, and the folder appears in the Shared Folders list.

8 Click the folder.

9 Click **Everyone**.

10 Click the Permissions pop-up menu and choose **Read Only** if you want other people to be able only to open or copy files in the folder.

Note: If you want other people to be able to create and change files in the folder, choose **Read & Write**. If you need to create a drop box folder that people cannot view but can add files to, choose **Write Only (Drop Box)**.

11 Click the **System Preferences** menu and click **Quit System Preferences** to close System Preferences.

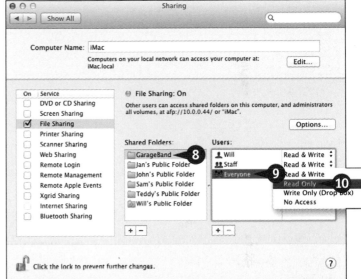

TIPS

How do I share files with Windows users?

To share files with Windows users, click **Options** in Sharing preferences. In the dialog that opens, click **Share files and folders using SMB (Windows)** (☐ turns to ☑). In the list box, click the username (●), enter the user's password, and then click **Done**.

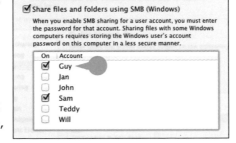

Can I share files without setting up the File Sharing service?

Yes, you can. In Finder, click **Go** and **Home**, and then click **Public** to open your Public folder. Place the files you want to share in this folder. Other Macs on the network can then view the files and copy them; they cannot change the files on your iMac. They can copy files to the Drop Box folder in your Public folder, but they cannot see its contents.

Connect to a Shared Printer

Sharing one or more printers on a network is a great way of keeping costs down while enabling each computer to print different types of documents as needed.

This task shows you how to connect to a shared printer. The following task shows you how to share your iMac's printer.

Connect to a Shared Printer

Open Print & Scan Preferences

1 Click and then **System Preferences**.

The System Preferences window opens.

2 Click **Print & Scan**.

The Print & Scan preferences pane opens.

Add a Printer Shared by a Mac

1 Click **Add** (⊞) and **Add Other Printer or Scanner**.

The Add Printer dialog opens.

2 Click **Default** to open the Default pane.

3 In the Printer Name list box, click the printer.

● You can change the printer's name and location.

4 Click **Add**.

Mac OS X adds the printer. The printer appears in the Print & Scan preferences pane.

5 Click the **System Preferences** menu and click **Quit System Preferences** to close System Preferences.

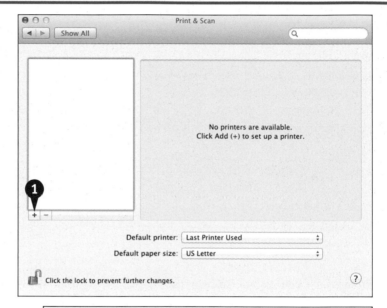

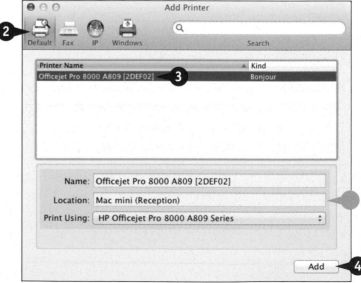

Add a Printer Shared by a Windows PC

1 In the Print & Scan preferences pane, click **Add** (⊞).

2 In the Add Printer dialog, click **Windows** to open the Windows pane.

3 Click the name of the network or workgroup that contains the printer.

A list appears of the computers sharing printers.

4 Click the computer sharing the printer.

5 If you have a username and password for the computer, type them in the dialog that opens. Otherwise, click **Guest** (○ changes to ◉).

6 Click **Connect**.

The list of printers appears in the Add Printer dialog.

7 Click the printer.

● You can change the printer's name and location.

8 Click **Add**.

The printer appears in the Print & Fax preferences pane.

9 Close System Preferences.

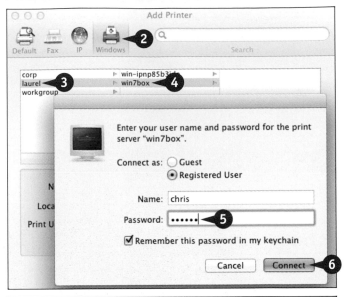

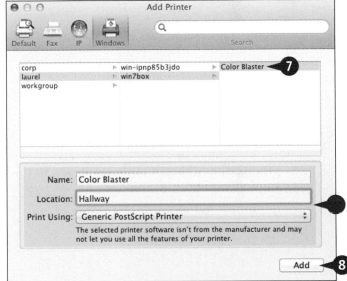

TIP

What should I do when the Print Using pop-up menu says "Choose a Driver or Printer Model"?

This message appears when Mac OS X cannot identify the driver software needed for the printer. Click the **Print Using** ⬍ and then click **Select Printer Software**. The Printer Software dialog opens. Type a distinctive part of the name in the search box to see a list of matching items, and then click the driver for the printer model (●). Click **OK**.

Share Your iMac's Printer on the Network

If you have a printer connected to your iMac, you can share it with other computers on the network. To do so, you turn on the Printer Sharing feature in System Preferences, and then choose which printer or printers to share.

Share Your iMac's Printer on the Network

1 Click ![].

The Apple menu opens.

2 Click **System Preferences**.

The System Preferences window opens.

3 Click **Sharing**.

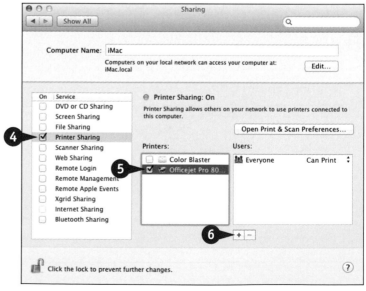

The Sharing preferences pane opens.

4 Click **Printer Sharing** (☐ changes to ☑).

Mac OS X turns on Printer Sharing and displays the Printer Sharing preferences.

5 Click each printer you want to share (☐ changes to ☑).

6 If you want to control who can use the printer, click **Add** (⊞).

A dialog for selecting users opens.

7 Click the user you want to add.

Note: To select multiple users, click the first, and then ⌘+click each of the others.

8 Click **Select**.

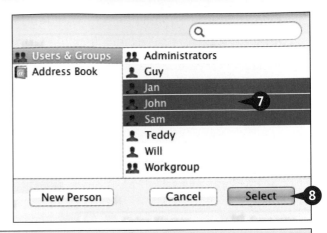

● Each user appears in the Users list.

● Mac OS X automatically changes the Everyone item from **Can Print** to **No Access**.

9 Click the **System Preferences** menu and click **Quit System Preferences** to close System Preferences.

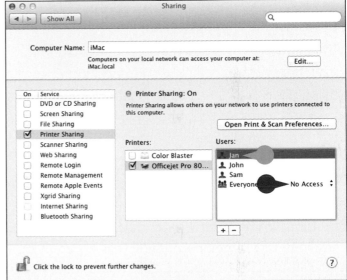

TIP

Can Windows users share my iMac's printer?
Users of PCs running Windows need to install Apple's Bonjour for Windows to access shared printers. Bonjour for Windows is available free from http://support.apple.com/downloads/Bonjour_for_Windows. After installing Bonjour for Windows, the user runs the Bonjour Printer Wizard and chooses the printer she wants to install (●).

Connect Remotely to Your iMac via Back to My Mac

To connect remotely to your iMac across the Internet, use the Back to My Mac feature. This feature lets you view your iMac's screen and control the iMac via an Internet connection. You must first turn on the Back to My Mac feature and Screen Sharing in System Preferences.

Back to My Mac works through Apple's iCloud service, so you must have an iCloud ID to use Back to My Mac.

Connect Remotely to Your iMac via Back to My Mac

Turn On Screen Sharing

1 Click and then **System Preferences**.

The System Preferences window opens.

2 Click **Sharing**.

The Sharing preferences pane opens.

3 Click **Screen Sharing** (☐ changes to ☑).

4 Change the name in the Computer Name field to make it easily recognizable.

5 In the Allow Access For area, click **Only these users** (○ changes to ⦿).

6 Click **Add** (⊞).

A dialog appears.

7 Click your username.

8 Click **Select**.

● The dialog closes, and your name appears in the box.

9 Click **Administrators**.

10 Click **Remove** (⊟).

Administrators disappears from the box.

11 Click **Computer Settings**.

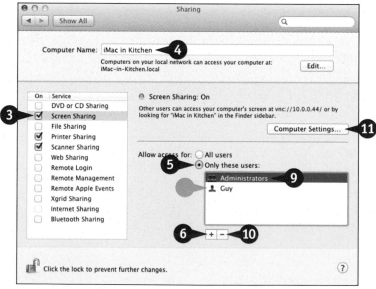

The Computer Settings dialog opens.

⑫ Click **Anyone may request permission to control screen** (☑ changes to ☐).

⑬ Click **OK**.

⑭ Click **Show All**.

Turn On Back to My Mac

① In the System Preferences window, click **Mail, Contacts & Calendars**.

The Mail, Contacts & Calendars preferences pane opens.

② In the left pane, click your primary iCloud account.

Note: Your primary iCloud account does not have a specific indication that it is the primary account. But your other iCloud accounts show the message "This is not your primary iCloud account."

The controls for your iCloud account appear.

③ Click **Back to My Mac** (☐ changes to ☑).

④ On the Mac from which you will connect, click and then **System Preferences**, and then repeat steps **1** to **3** to make the other Mac connect to Back to My Mac.

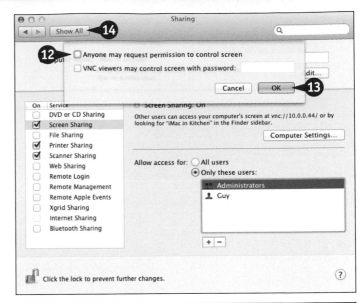

TIPS

Why does Back to My Mac fail to connect and give a message about NAT-PMP?

Back to My Mac establishes a two-way path through your Internet router to the iCloud servers using either the Network Address Translation Port Mapping Protocol, NAT-PMP, or Universal Plug and Play, UPnP. If Back to My Mac cannot connect, turn on NAT-PMP or UPnP on your router. Most routers support one, the other, or both.

What else may be preventing Back to My Mac from connecting to the MobileMe servers?

If you use the Mac OS X firewall to protect your iMac from dangerous Internet traffic, you must allow File Sharing connections and Screen Sharing connections for Back to My Mac to work. If you use the Block All Incoming Connections feature of the firewall, Back to My Mac cannot work.

continued ▶ 317

After connecting your iMac to the Back to My Mac service, you are ready to connect to it from a remote Mac across the Internet.

After you connect, your iMac's desktop appears in a Screen Sharing window on the remote Mac. You can control the screen with the mouse and keyboard, enabling you to work on your iMac much as if you were sitting at it. The main difference is that screen updates appear more slowly because of the remote connection, so you may need to work slowly and patiently.

Connect Remotely to Your iMac via Back to My Mac (continued)

Use Screen Sharing via Back to My Mac

1. Click **Finder** ( ) on the Dock to open a Finder window.

2. If the Shared category is collapsed, position the mouse pointer over it and click **Show** to expand it.

3. Click your iMac.

4. Click **Share Screen**.

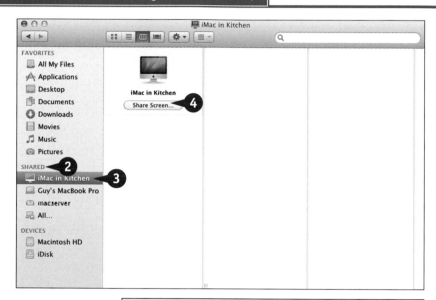

The Screen Sharing dialog opens.

5. In the Connect area, click **As a registered user** (○ changes to ⊙).

6. Type your account name and password for your iMac.

7. Click **Remember this password in my keychain** (☐ changes to ☑) if you want to store the password.

8. Click **Connect**.

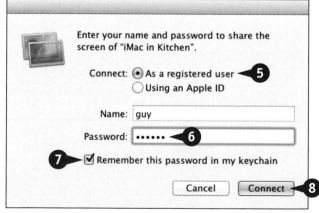

The Screen Sharing window opens.

Work on the iMac as you would work on the Mac you are using.

● Click **Fit screen in window** (⊞) if the remote screen is too big for the window you are using.

● Click **Get the remote clipboard contents** (▣) to copy the iMac's clipboard contents to the clipboard on the Mac you are using.

● Click **Send clipboard contents to remote clipboard** (▣) to put this Mac's clipboard contents on the iMac's clipboard.

● Click ▨ to view your iMac's screen full screen.

End Your Screen Sharing Session

1 Click **Screen Sharing**.

2 Click **Quit Screen Sharing**.

The Screen Sharing window closes.

TIP

If Screen Sharing is too slow, can I connect to my iMac a faster way?
Instead of connecting to your iMac via Screen Sharing and sending large amounts of screen data across the Internet, you can connect via File Sharing. This enables you to transfer files to and from your iMac and work with them on whichever Mac you are using. To connect to your user account, which is what you normally want, you do not need to turn on the File Sharing service as discussed earlier in this chapter, but simply connect with your username and password. On the remote Mac, open a Finder window. Click your iMac in the sidebar, and then click **Connect As**. Type your username and password, and then click **Connect**.

CHAPTER 14

Keeping Your iMac and Data Safe

To keep your iMac and your data safe, you must understand Internet threats, install and use antivirus software, and recognize phishing attacks.

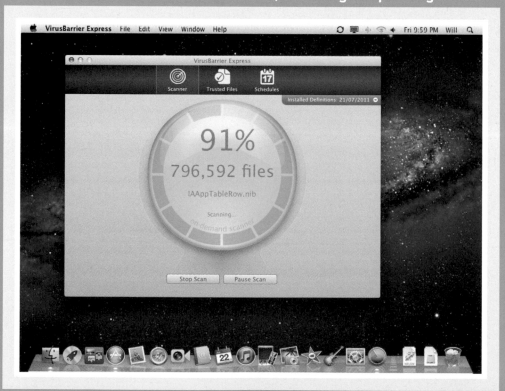

Understanding Threats to Your iMac and Your Data

To keep your iMac and your data safe, you should understand the main threats they face. These threats range from malevolent software to people accessing your iMac without permission, from deliberate attacks to accidental data corruption or hard-disk failure.

Viruses and Malevolent Software

Just as you expose yourself to viruses and bacteria in public, you expose your iMac to computer viruses and other malevolent software when you use the Internet or share files. Viruses and other malevolent software can delete your data or corrupt your iMac's operating system or applications, so you must protect the iMac with antivirus software.

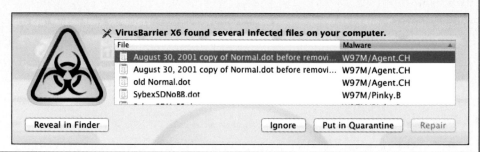

Unauthorized People Accessing Your iMac

Anyone who can log in to your iMac in person or across the Internet can attack your data. For example, an intruder can copy your files, steal them, or simply delete them. To ensure that each user must log in to the iMac, always lock your iMac when you have finished using it. You can do this by logging out, displaying the login window when Fast User Switching is on, or putting the iMac to sleep when you have set it to require a password on waking. You must also turn off automatic login.

Internet Attacks

When your iMac is connected to a network or the Internet, it needs protection from possible attacks from other computers. Mac OS X includes a powerful firewall that can protect your iMac against many threats, but you may need to turn it on and change its configuration to enjoy full protection.

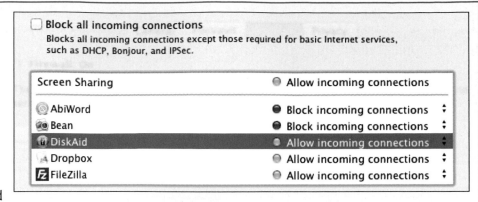

Phishing and Pharming Attacks

Be on your guard against phishing attacks — attacks in which a phisher attempts to make you divulge valuable information such as bank account information, login names, passwords, or credit card numbers. Most phishing takes place via email, but phishers also use instant messaging and telephones to persuade people to give up information against their interests.

Also watch out for pharming attacks — ones in which a malefactor redirects a legitimate site to a fake site that tries to grab your details.

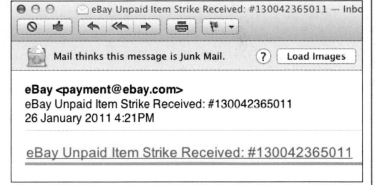

Power Outages and Hardware Failures

To protect your iMac from power outages or electric surges, give it power through an uninterruptible power supply (UPS) or a surge suppressor instead of directly from a socket. A UPS uses a battery to provide steady, conditioned power to your iMac and enable you to save files and shut down when a power outage occurs. To protect your data against hardware failure, back up your data as explained in Chapter 15.

Install Antivirus Software

Malevolent hackers on the Internet target Macs as well as Windows PCs, so you must protect your iMac by installing and running antivirus software. This task shows you how to install VirusBarrier Express, a widely used antivirus package, and keep it updated.

You can buy and download antivirus software from the App Store, buy the software on a CD or DVD from a physical store or by mail order, or download antivirus software from a website. After installing the antivirus software, you may need to restart your iMac.

Install Antivirus Software

Install Antivirus Software

1 Click **App Store** (●) on the Dock.

● The App Store window opens.

Note: If you prefer to use another antivirus application than VirusBarrier Express, buy it online or from a physical store. Buying your antivirus software online is safest because you get the latest version.

2 Click in the Search box and type **virusbarrier**.

The search results appear.

3 Click **Free**.

The Install App button appears.

4 Click **Install App**.

5 In the Sign In to Download from the App Store dialog, type your Apple ID.

6 Type your password.

7 Click **Sign In**.

The App Store signs you in, and then displays the Launchpad screen while it downloads and installs the application.

8 When the VirusBarrier Express icon appears on the Launchpad screen, click it.

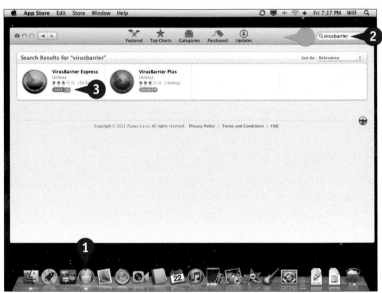

VirusBarrier Express opens.

Keep Your Antivirus Software Up to Date

1 Click **VirusBarrier Express** on the menu bar.

The VirusBarrier Express menu opens.

2 Click **Update Malware Definitions**.

VirusBarrier Express downloads and installs the latest malware definition files, and then displays the Malware Definitions Updates dialog.

3 Click **Scan** if you want to scan your iMac for malware now; see the next task for details. Click **Do Nothing** if you do not want to scan now.

TIPS

Which antivirus software shall I get for my iMac?
For basic protection, try the free VirusBarrier Express from Intego. For more protection, including real-time scanning of files, try VirusBarrier X6 from Intego and Norton Antivirus for Mac or Norton Internet Security for Mac from Symantec. If you prefer not to pay and are prepared to put a little more effort into setup, look at ClamXav 2 (http://clamxav.com).

What features should I look for in antivirus software?
The main feature to look for is protection against malevolent software. This includes viruses, Trojan-horse programs that hide harm in a program that seems helpful, and rootkits, which try to build secret entry points into your computer. Protection against spyware programs, phishing messages, and infected websites are useful too.

Scan Your iMac for Viruses

After installing antivirus software as described in the previous task, you should run a full scan of your iMac. This task shows you how to run a scan using VirusBarrier Express from Intego.

Scanning your iMac for viruses can take several hours. Exactly how long depends on the number of files your iMac contains, the speed of its processor, and how much RAM it has. It is best to set aside plenty of time to run the scan.

Scan Your iMac for Viruses

1 Click **Launchpad** ( ) on the Dock.

2 Click **VirusBarrier Express**.

The VirusBarrier Express window opens.

3 Click **Full Scan**.

VirusBarrier counts the files and then scans them.

● The green light indicates all is well so far.

The light turns red when VirusBarrier finds an infected file.

When the scan finishes, a VirusBarrier dialog opens showing a list of infected files.

④ Click the file.

⑤ Click the button for the action you want to take:

● Click **Ignore** to ignore the infected file.

● Click **Repair** to try to repair the file, removing the infection so that you can use the file.

After you click a button, VirusBarrier removes the file from the list.

When you have dealt with all the infected files, the dialog closes.

⑥ Click the **VirusBarrier Express** menu and then click **Quit VirusBarrier Express**.

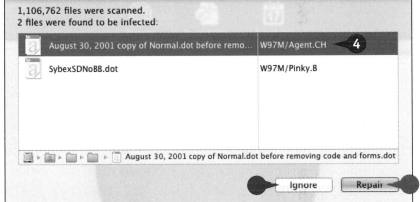

When should I ignore an infected file?
Normally, you should not ignore an infected file. Unless you are certain that a file is harmless, and that your antivirus application has falsely accused it of harboring malware, you should repair the file. Some antivirus applications also give you the option of placing a file in quarantine, putting it in a secure area so that you can review it later. Quarantine prevents the infected file from damaging your iMac but does not remove the infection.

Turn Off Automatic Login

When you install Mac OS X from scratch, Installer may set up your iMac with automatic login for the Administrator account you first create. If so, when you create another user account, Mac OS X prompts you to turn automatic login off, but you can continue to use it if you want.

Automatic login is convenient when you are the only person who uses your iMac, but you can make your iMac more secure by turning off automatic login so each user must log in.

Turn Off Automatic Login

1 Click ⌘.

The Apple menu opens.

2 Click **System Preferences**.

The System Preferences window opens.

3 Click **Security & Privacy**.

The Security & Privacy preferences pane opens.

4 Click **General**.

The General pane appears.

5 Click 🔒.

The Authenticate dialog opens.

6 Type your password.

7 Click **Unlock**.

The Authenticate dialog closes.

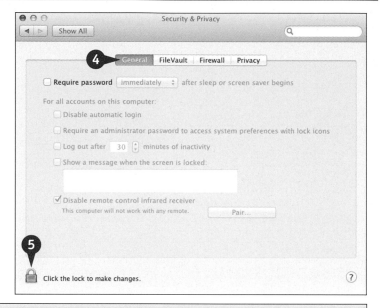

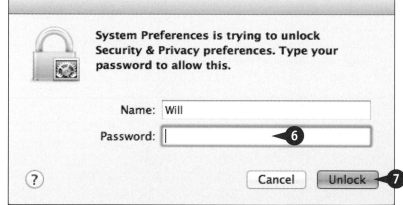

Mac OS X enables the preferences (🔒 changes to 🔓).

8 Click **Disable automatic login** (☐ changes to ☑).

9 For greater security, click **Require password _N_ seconds after sleep or screen saver begins** (☐ changes to ☑).

10 Click ↕ and choose **immediately** or a short time: 5 seconds, 1 minute, or 5 minutes.

11 Click **Log out after _N_ minutes of inactivity** (☐ changes to ☑).

12 Click ↕ to choose a short time, such as 5 minutes or 10 minutes.

13 Click **Disable remote control infrared receiver** (☐ changes to ☑) if you want to prevent the iMac from responding to a remote control.

14 Click 🔓 (🔓 changes to 🔒).

15 Click **System Preferences** and then **Quit System Preferences** to close the System Preferences window.

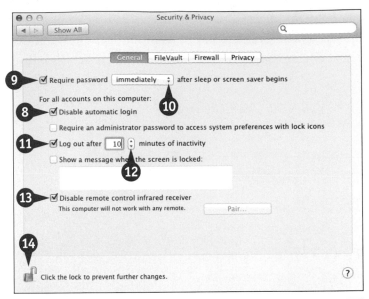

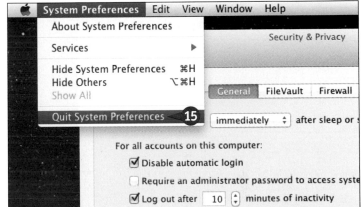

TIP

Are there other options for tightening my iMac's security?
In Users & Groups preferences, click **Login Options**. You can then click **Name and password** (○ changes to ●) to hide the list of usernames so that anyone logging on must type a username as well as a password. Click **Show the Sleep and Shut Down buttons** (☑ changes to ☐) to remove these buttons from the login screen, so that nobody can shut down the iMac without logging in unless he turns off the iMac's power. Click **Show password hints** (☑ changes to ☐) if you want to prevent password hints from appearing.

Increase the Security of the Mac OS X Firewall

A firewall protects your iMac from unauthorized access by other computers on your network or on the Internet. Your Internet router likely has its own firewall to keep Internet threats out of your network, but Mac OS X also includes a built-in firewall to give your iMac even greater protection.

Increase the Security of the Mac OS X Firewall

1 Click .

The Apple menu opens.

2 Click **System Preferences**.

The System Preferences window opens.

3 Click **Security & Privacy**.

The Security & Privacy preferences pane opens.

4 Click **Firewall**.

The Firewall pane appears.

5 Click .

The Authenticate dialog opens.

6 Type your password.

7 Click **Unlock**.

The Authenticate dialog closes.

● changes to .

8 If "Firewall: Off" appears, click **Start**.

The firewall starts, and "Firewall: On" appears.

9 Click **Advanced**.

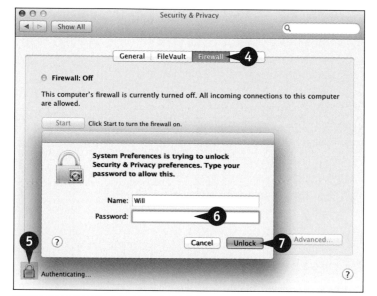

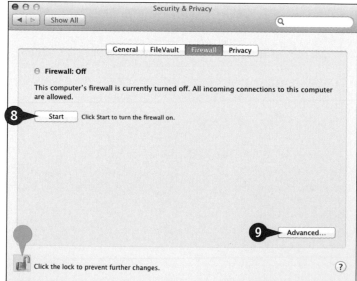

10 In the Advanced dialog, click **Automatically allow signed software to receive incoming connections** (☑ changes to ☐) if you want to prevent your iMac from accepting connections automatically across the network.

11 Click **Enable stealth mode** (☐ changes to ☑) if you want to prevent your iMac from responding to network test applications.

12 To allow incoming connections to a particular application, click **Add** (⊞).

13 In the Add dialog, click the application.

14 Click **Add**.

Mac OS X adds the application to the list.

15 Click **OK** to close the Advanced dialog.

16 In the Security preferences pane, click 🔓 (🔓 changes to 🔒).

17 Click the **System Preferences** menu.

18 Click **Quit System Preferences**.

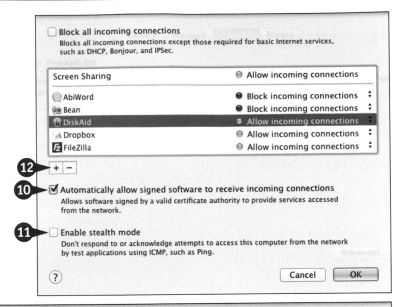

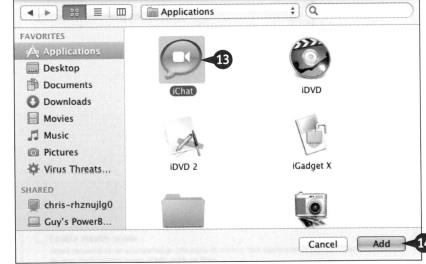

TIPS

When should I use the Block All Incoming Connections option?

Click **Block all incoming connections** when you need to tighten security as much as possible. The usual reason for blocking all connections is connecting your iMac to a network that you cannot trust, such as a public wireless network. This option is more widely used with MacBooks than with desktop Macs.

Can I block incoming connections only to a specific application?

To block incoming connections only to a specific application, add that application to the list in the Advanced dialog as described in this task. Then click the application's **Allow incoming connections** button in the list and click **Block incoming connections**.

Recognize and Avoid Phishing Attacks

Phishing is an attack in which someone tries to make you provide valuable information such as bank account numbers, login names, passwords, or credit card numbers. After acquiring this information, the phisher either uses it directly — for example, withdrawing money from your bank account — or sells it to criminals.

Recognize and Avoid Phishing Attacks

Recognize a Phishing Email Message

1 In Mail, open the message.

2 Look for signs of phishing:

- Mail has detected suspicious signs in the message.

- The message does not show your name as the recipient.

- The message has a generic greeting, such as Dear Customer, or no greeting at all.

- The message claims you need to take action, such as clearing a security lockout or reenabling your account.

- The message contains links it encourages you to click.

Note: Phishers frequently target eBay customers. Genuine eBay messages always address you by your member name and include the actual name you have given eBay, and never ask for personal information.

3 Position the mouse pointer over a link but do not click.

- A ScreenTip appears showing the address to which the link leads.

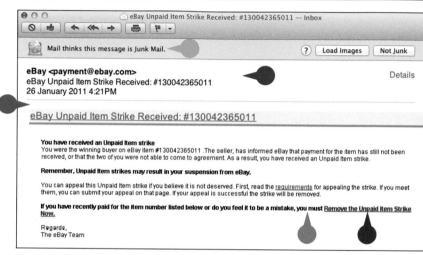

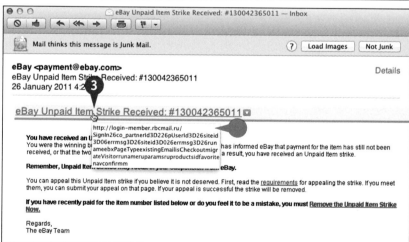

Connect Securely to a Website

① Click **Safari** (●) on the Dock.

A Safari window opens.

② Click the address box.

③ Type the address of the website and press `Return`.

Safari opens the website.

④ Click the padlock icon (🔒).

Note: Safari displays the padlock icon when you have connected securely to a website. The address of a secure connection starts with https:// rather than http://.

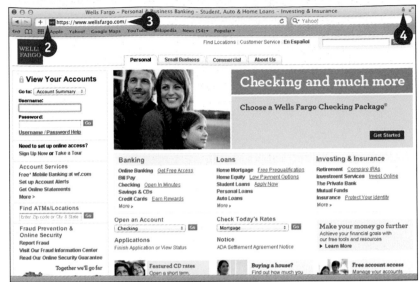

A dialog opens showing the details of the digital certificate that identifies the website.

⑤ Click ▶ (▶ changes to ▼) to expand the dialog.

⑥ Verify that the certificate is valid.

⑦ Click **OK** to close the dialog.

⑧ If you are convinced that the website is genuine, log in to it.

Is it possible to make a secure connection to a dangerous website?

Yes. The padlock icon means only that the connection between your iMac and the website server is secure and cannot be read in transmission. The website may be safe or it may be dangerous; it is up to you to establish which.

Is a message definitely genuine if it includes my name?

Even if a message includes your name, be alert for other signs of phishing. Some phishers send customized phishing messages in the hope of ensnaring particular high-value victims. This technique is called *spear-phishing*. Evaluate the message's content for sense and likelihood, and remember that anything too good to be true is usually not true.

CHAPTER 15

Troubleshooting Your iMac

Apple has built your iMac and Mac OS X to keep running as smoothly as possible, but you will need to perform basic maintenance, such as emptying the Trash, updating your iMac with the latest fixes, and backing up your files. If things go wrong, you will also need to troubleshoot your iMac — for example, solving problems with corrupt preference files, fixing disk permission errors, or repairing the hard disk.

Reclaim Space by Emptying the Trash

When you throw a file from one of your iMac's drives in the Trash, it remains there in case you change your mind and decide to recover it. But when you need to reclaim space on your iMac's hard disk, you can empty the Trash and get rid of all the files and folders in it permanently.

If you find the Trash contains items you still need, you can put them back in their previous folders or move them to other folders.

Reclaim Space by Emptying the Trash

Empty the Trash

1 Click **Trash** (🗑) on the Dock.

A Finder window opens showing the contents of the Trash folder.

2 Double-check the files and folders in the Trash to make sure it contains nothing you want to keep.

To quickly view the contents of a file, use Quick Look. Click the file, and then press `Spacebar`.

Note: You cannot open a file while it is in the Trash. If you want to open a file, you must remove it from the Trash.

3 Click **Empty**.

A dialog opens to confirm that you want to permanently erase the items in the Trash.

④ Click **Empty Trash**.

Mac OS X empties the Trash and then closes the Finder window.

Restore a File or Folder to Its Previous Location

① In the Trash folder, click a file or folder.

② Click ⚙ ▾.

The Action pop-up menu opens.

③ Click **Put Back**.

Mac OS X restores the file or folder to its previous location.

Note: To move a file from the Trash to another folder, drag the file to that folder. For example, you can drag a file to the desktop.

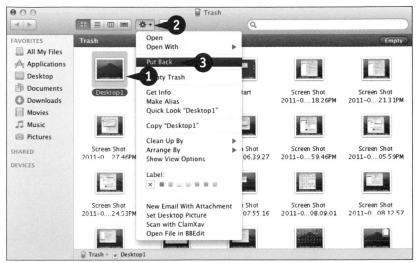

TIPS

Is there a quicker way to empty the Trash?

If you are sure that the Trash contains no files or folders you need, Control+click or right-click **Trash** (🗑) on the Dock. The Dock menu opens. Click **Empty Trash**. A confirmation dialog opens. Click **Empty Trash**. To turn off this warning, click **Finder** and **Preferences**, click **Advanced**, and click **Show warning before emptying the Trash** (☑ changes to ☐).

What does the Secure Empty Trash command do, and when should I use it?

When you need to get rid of files and folders and make sure no one can recover them, use the Secure Empty Trash command. Click the desktop, and then choose **Finder** and **Secure Empty Trash**. A confirmation dialog opens. Click **Secure Empty Trash**. Mac OS X overwrites the files and folders beyond recovery.

Keep Your iMac Current with the Latest Updates

To keep your iMac running smoothly, use the Software Update feature to install the latest updates and fixes that Apple provides for Mac OS X and Apple's applications.

Your iMac must be connected to the Internet in order to check for and download the updates. You can install the updates when your iMac is either online or offline.

Keep Your iMac Current with the Latest Updates

1 Click .

The Apple menu opens.

2 Click **Software Update**.

The Software Update window opens, and Software Update automatically checks for updates.

If updates are available, the New Software Is Available for Your Computer dialog opens.

Note: If Software Update displays the message "Your software is up to date," click **Quit**. Software Update then quits.

3 If you do not want to install any of the updates, click ☑ next to them (☑ changes to ☐).

Note: Normally, installing all available updates is best unless you have heard that a specific update may cause problems with your iMac.

4 Click **Install *N* Items**, where *N* is the number of items.

Note: If one or more License Agreement dialogs open, read each license, and then click **Agree** if you accept the agreement.

Software Update downloads the updates and then installs those that do not require restarting the iMac.

⑤ If Software Update prompts you to restart your iMac, save any unsaved work, and then click **Restart**.

Mac OS X logs you out, installs the updates that require the restart, and then restarts.

Note: If you are too busy to restart your iMac when Software Update prompts you, click **Not Now**. You can then restart your iMac whenever it suits you. During the restart, Software Update installs the updates.

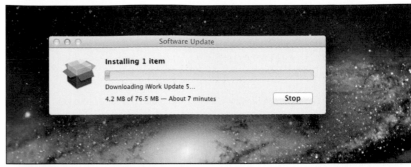

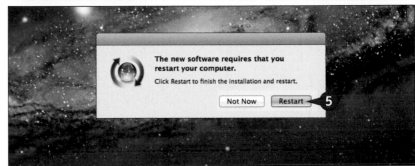

TIP

Why does Software Update sometimes prompt me to install updates?
In Mac OS X, Software Update comes set to check for updates automatically; when it finds updates, it prompts you to install them. You can change the frequency of these checks, choose whether to download important updates automatically, or turn off automatic checks. See Chapter 12 for instructions.

Back Up Your Files with Time Machine

To help keep your valuable files safe, Mac OS X includes an automatic backup application called Time Machine. Time Machine automatically saves copies of your files to an external hard disk connected to your iMac. You can choose which drive to use, how frequently to back up your files, and which folders to include.

To protect your data, you must use one form of backup or another. Time Machine is the best choice because it takes only a few minutes to set up and thereafter runs automatically.

Back Up Your Files with Time Machine

1 Connect an external hard disk to your iMac.

Note: When you connect an external hard disk to your iMac for the first time, a dialog may open asking if you want to use the disk for Time Machine. If you do, click **Use as Backup Disk**; if not, click **Cancel**.

2 Click [Apple] and then **System Preferences**.

The System Preferences window opens.

3 Click **Time Machine**.

The Time Machine preferences pane opens.

4 Click **Select Disk**.

Note: If you have already selected your backup disk, go to step **8**.

The Select Disk dialog opens.

5 Click the disk you want to use.

6 Click **Use Backup Disk**.

The Select Disk dialog closes.

The disk appears in the Time Machine pane, with the Time Machine switch turned on.

7 Make sure Show Time Machine Status in Menu Bar is checked. If not, click it (☐ changes to ☑).

8 Click **Options**.

The Exclude These Items from Backups dialog opens.

9 Click **Add** (⊞).

A dialog opens.

10 Select each drive or folder you want to exclude from backup.

11 Click **Exclude**.

The dialog closes, and Time Machine adds the items to the Exclude These Items from Backups dialog.

12 Click **Save** to close the Exclude These Items from Backup dialog.

13 Click the **System Preferences** menu and click **Quit System Preferences** to close System Preferences.

TIPS

What kind of disk should I use for Time Machine?
You can connect an external hard disk to your iMac by using Thunderbolt, USB, or FireWire 400 on an older iMac that has a FireWire 400 port, or FireWire 800. Thunderbolt gives by far the best performance but tends to be expensive. Either version of FireWire or USB is fine. Buy a high-capacity disk — for example, one or two terabytes (TB) so that you have plenty of space for backups.

How often does Time Machine back up my files?
Time Machine backs up all your files two minutes after you set it up. After that, it creates an hourly backup of files that have changed since the last backup. Time Machine consolidates the hourly backups into daily backups, which it consolidates into weekly backups.

Recover Your Files from a Time Machine Backup

When you find that you have deleted, damaged, or lost a vital file, you can recover it from a Time Machine backup. Normally, you will want to recover the most recent undamaged version of the file because this contains the latest changes, but you can also recover older versions if you need to.

Recover Your Files from a Time Machine Backup

1 Click the **Time Machine** status icon (⊙) on the menu bar.

The Time Machine menu opens.

2 Click **Enter Time Machine**.

Note: If the Time Machine status icon does not appear on the menu bar, click **Launchpad** (🚀) on the Dock, and then click **Time Machine** on the Launchpad screen.

Time Machine launches and takes over the entire desktop, including the Dock area.

● The front window shows your iMac's drive or drives in their current state. You can navigate to any folder as usual.

● Backups of the selected drive or folder appear in the windows behind it, from newest to oldest.

● The timeline on the right shows how far back in time the available backups go.

3 In the timeline, click the date or time to which you want to go back.

Note: You can also click one of the Finder windows behind the front Finder window to display its contents.

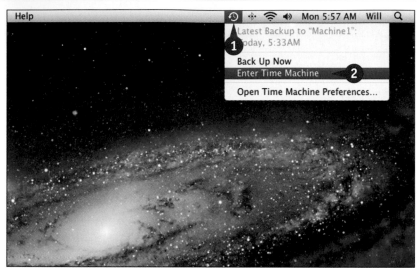

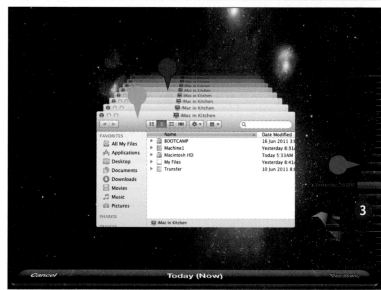

Time Machine brings the backup you chose to the front.

4 Select the item or items you want to restore.

5 Click **Restore**.

Time Machine disappears, and you see your desktop and the Dock again.

If restoring a file will overwrite a file in the current version of the folder, the Copy dialog opens.

6 Choose how to handle the file conflict:

● Click **Replace** if you want to replace the current file with the older file.

● Click **Keep Original** if you want to keep the current file and not restore the file from Time Machine.

● Click **Keep Both** if you want to keep both versions of the file. Time Machine adds "(Original)" to the name of the current version of the file so that you can distinguish the two.

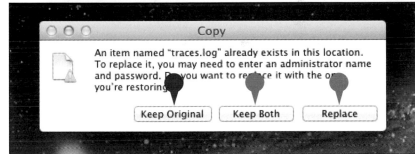

TIPS

What are the arrow buttons above the Restore button for?

The two arrow buttons are for navigating among the available backups. Click the upward arrow to move to the previous backup, further in the past. Click the downward arrow to move to the next backup, nearer to the present.

Can I create Time Machine backups manually?

You can create a Time Machine backup any time you want. Click the **Time Machine status** icon (⊙) on the menu bar, and then click **Back Up Now**. The menu also enables you to quickly access Time Machine and Time Machine preferences.

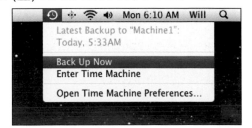

Remove Applications You No Longer Need

If you install applications frequently, you will probably end up with many applications that you no longer need. These useless applications take up disk space and may cause your iMac to run more slowly, so removing them is a good idea.

You can remove some applications by placing them in the Trash. Other applications include uninstall utilities.

Remove Applications You No Longer Need

Remove an Application by Moving It to the Trash

1 Click open space on the desktop.

The Finder becomes active.

2 Click **Go**.

The Go menu opens.

3 Click **Applications**.

A Finder window opens showing your Applications folder.

4 Click the application you want to remove.

5 Click ✱▾.

The Action pop-up menu opens.

6 Click **Move to Trash**.

Mac OS X moves the application to the Trash.

7 Click ⬤.

The Finder window closes.

Note: You can also drag an application to the Trash from Launchpad. Click **Launchpad** (⬤) on the Dock, click the application, and then drag it to the Trash (🗑) on the Dock.

Remove an Application by Using an Uninstall Utility

1 Click open space on the desktop.

The Finder becomes active.

2 Click **Go**.

The Go menu opens.

3 Click **Applications**.

A Finder window opens showing your Applications folder.

4 Press and hold Option while double-clicking the uninstall utility. See the tip for instructions on where to find the utility.

The uninstall utility opens, and the Finder window closes.

5 Follow through the steps of the uninstall utility. For example, click **Continue**.

6 When the uninstall utility has finished running, close it.

TIP

Where do I find the uninstall utility for an application?

If the application has a folder within the Applications folder, look inside that folder for an uninstall utility. If there is no folder, open the CD, DVD, or disk image file from which you installed the application and look for an uninstall utility there. Some applications use an installer for both installing the application and uninstalling it, so if you do not find an uninstall utility, try running the installer and see if it contains an uninstall option.

See Which Application Is Causing Your iMac Problems

Sometimes you may find that your iMac starts to respond slowly to your commands, even though no application has stopped working. When this occurs, you can use the Activity Monitor utility to see which application is consuming more of the processor's cycles than it should. To resolve the problem, you can quit that application and then restart it.

If you cannot quit the application normally, you can force quit it. You can force quit it either from Activity Monitor or by using the Force Quit Applications dialog, as discussed in the following task.

See Which Application Is Causing Your iMac Problems

1 Click **Finder** (🙂) on the Dock.

A Finder window opens to your default folder or view — for example, All My Files.

2 Click **Go**.

The Go menu opens.

3 Click **Utilities**.

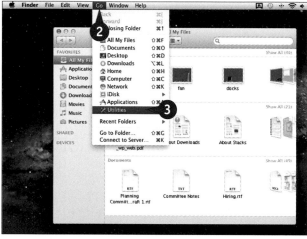

The Finder window shows the items in the Utilities folder.

4 Press and hold Option and double-click **Activity Monitor**.

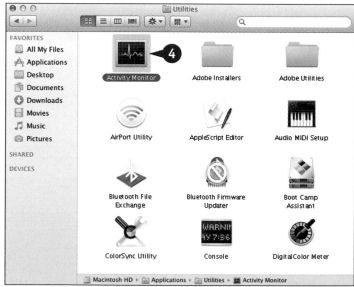

The Activity Monitor window opens, listing all your running applications and utilities.

5 Click **CPU**.

The details of your iMac's central processing units, or CPUs, appear.

Note: Most iMacs have dual-core processors that appear in Activity Monitor as two separate CPUs. If your iMac has a quad-core processor, you will see four separate CPUs in Activity Monitor.

6 Click **% CPU** once or twice to display ▼.

Activity Monitor sorts the applications and items by CPU activity so that you see which is using the most processor cycles.

7 Identify the application that is using the most processor cycles.

8 Click that application's Dock icon.

The application appears.

9 Save your work in the application, and then quit it.

10 Click the Activity Monitor window.

11 Click the **Activity Monitor** menu and click **Quit Activity Monitor** to close Activity Monitor.

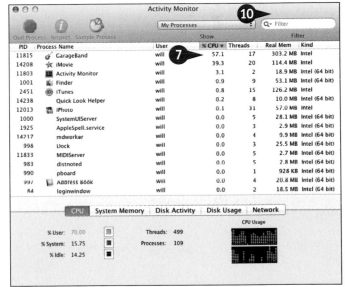

What should I do if I cannot quit or force quit the problem application?

If you cannot force quit the application from the Dock or the Force Quit Applications dialog, try force quitting from Activity Monitor. In Activity Monitor, click the application's process name, and then click **Quit Process** on the toolbar. A confirmation dialog opens. Click **Force Quit**.

How do I see whether my iMac is running short of memory?

In Activity Monitor, click **System Memory**. The details of memory usage appear. Free shows unused RAM. Wired shows used RAM that cannot currently be released. Active shows RAM currently using information actively. Inactive shows RAM holding data but not using it actively. The four totals add up to your iMac's amount of RAM.

Force a Crashed Application to Quit

Sometimes an application may stop responding to the keyboard or mouse, so that you cannot quit it as usual. The application may freeze, so that the window does not change, or it may display the spinning beach ball that indicates that the application is busy. When this happens, you usually need to force quit the application so that you can resume work.

Force a Crashed Application to Quit

Force Quit an Application from the Dock

① Pressing and holding Option, click the application's icon on the Dock. Keep holding down the mouse button until the Dock menu appears.

② Click **Force Quit**.

Mac OS X forces the application to quit.

Force Quit an Application from the Force Quit Applications Dialog

① Click .

The Apple menu opens.

② Click **Force Quit**.

Note: You can open the Force Quit Applications dialog from the keyboard by pressing ⌘+Option+Esc.

The Force Quit Applications dialog opens.

3 Click the application you want to force quit.

4 Click **Force Quit**.

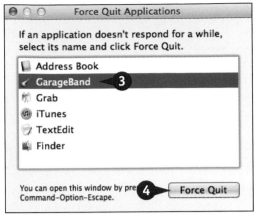

A dialog opens to confirm that you want to force quit the application.

5 Click **Force Quit**.

Mac OS X forces the application to quit.

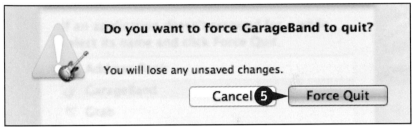

6 Click .

The Force Quit Applications dialog closes.

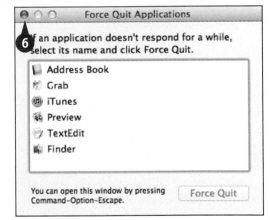

TIP

How do I recover the unsaved changes in a document after force quitting the application?

When you force quit an application, you normally lose all unsaved changes in the documents you were using in the application. However, some applications automatically store unsaved changes in special files called *recovery files*. Such applications then open any recovery files when you relaunch them after force quitting. For other applications, if the unsaved changes are visible on-screen before you force quit the application, press ⌘+Shift+3 to capture a picture of your desktop to a file on the desktop so that you can see the changes you will need to make again. For some applications, you may also be able to return to an earlier version of the document, as discussed in the following task.

Go Back to an Earlier Version of a Document

M ac OS X Lion includes a feature called *versions* that enables applications to save different versions of the same document in the same file. You can display the different versions of the document at the same time and go back to an earlier version if necessary.

Only applications written to work with Mac OS X Lion can use the versions feature. This example uses TextEdit, the text editor and word processor included with Mac OS X.

Go Back to an Earlier Version of a Document

1 In the appropriate application, open the document. For example, open a word processing document in TextEdit.

2 Click the document's name in the title bar.

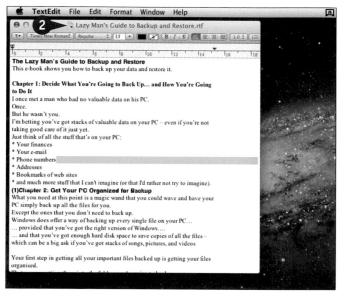

A pop-up menu appears.

3 Click **Browse All Versions**.

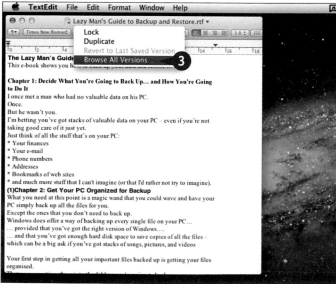

● Mac OS X displays earlier versions of the document on the right, newer versions at the front, and older versions at the back.

● The current version appears on the left.

4 Position the mouse over the time bars, and then click the version you want.

The version comes to the front.

5 Click **Restore**.

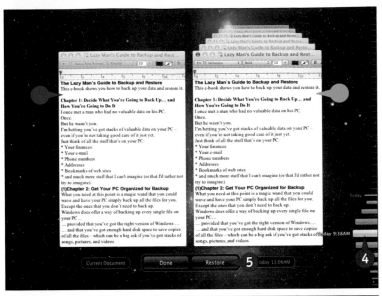

Mac OS X restores the version, and it opens so that you can work with it.

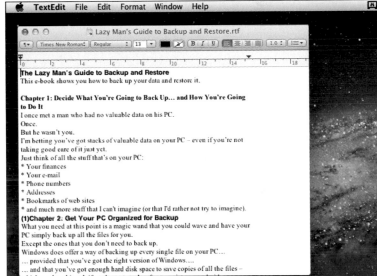

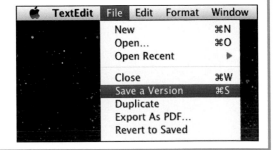

Recover When Mac OS X Crashes

Normally, Mac OS X runs stably and smoothly for days or weeks on end, but sometimes the operating system may suffer a crash.

Your iMac may detect that the crash has occurred and display an informational message, but in other cases the iMac's screen may simply freeze and continue displaying the same information.

Recover When Mac OS X Crashes

Recover from the Screen Freezing

1 If the mouse pointer shows the "wait" cursor that looks like a spinning beach ball, wait a couple of minutes to see if Mac OS X can recover from the problem. If the mouse pointer has disappeared, go straight to step **2**.

2 To verify that your iMac is not responding, press keys on the keyboard or move the mouse.

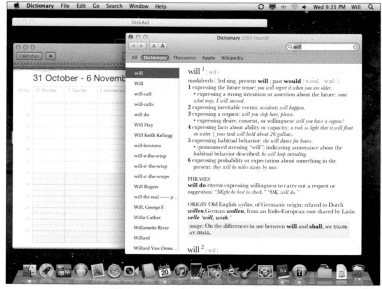

3 Press and hold ⌘+Control and press the iMac's power button.

4 If the iMac does not respond to that key combination, press and hold the iMac's power button for about four seconds.

The iMac turns off.

5 Wait eight seconds, and then press the power button once to restart the iMac.

Recover from a Detected Crash

When your iMac detects a Mac OS X crash, it dims the screen and displays a message in the center.

1 Read the message for information.

2 Press and hold the iMac's power button for about four seconds.

The iMac turns off.

3 Wait eight seconds, and then press the power button once to restart the iMac.

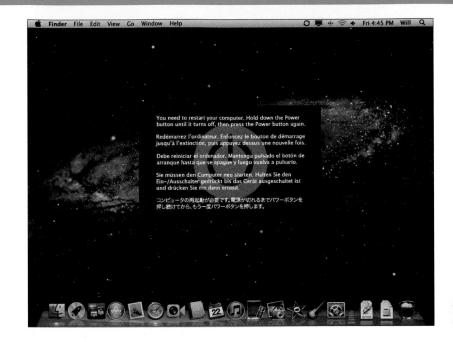

What causes Mac OS X to crash, and how can I avoid crashes?

Crashes can occur because of power fluctuations or bad memory modules, because your iMac is running too many applications, because an application is corrupted, or because of problems with disk permissions.

- Limit the number of applications you run at once. When you finish using an application, close it.

- Make sure your iMac has hard disk space free. Click **Finder** (🙂) on the Dock to open a Finder window, click your iMac's hard disk in the Devices area, and then look at the status bar readout of space available. Try to keep at least 50GB free; more is better.

- If you notice that running a particular application causes your iMac to crash, uninstall that application, and then reinstall it.

- You may also need to repair disk permissions, as discussed later in this chapter.

Solve Problems with Corrupt Preference Files

Each application stores details of its configuration in a special file called a *preference file*. Sometimes a preference file becomes corrupted, leading to the application not running properly or even crashing.

To fix the problem, you delete the preference file. This forces the application to create a new preference file from scratch, resetting the preferences to their default settings. When the application is running properly again, you must choose your custom settings again.

Solve Problems with Corrupt Preference Files

1 Quit the problem application if it is running.

Note: If you cannot quit the application by using its Quit command, force quit it as described earlier in this chapter.

2 Click open space on the desktop.

The Finder becomes active.

3 Click **Go**.

The Go menu opens.

4 Press and hold Option.

The Library item appears on the Go menu.

Note: Mac OS X hides the Library item on the Go menu until you press Option.

5 Click **Library**.

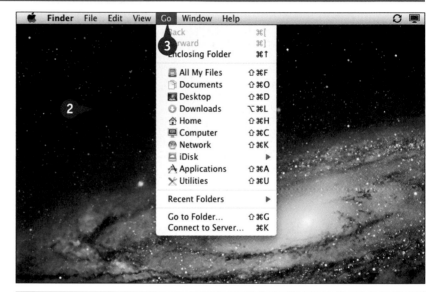

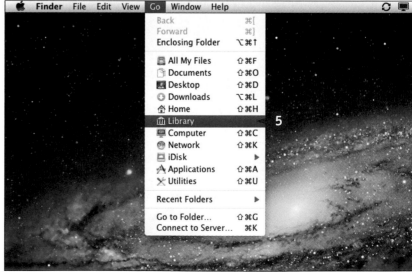

The contents of the Preferences folder appear.

6 Click the preference file for the problem application. See the tip for help on identifying the file.

Note: If the application has two or more preference files, move them all to the Trash.

7 Click ⚙▾.

The Action menu opens.

8 Click **Move to Trash**.

Mac OS X moves the file to the Trash.

9 Start the application.

The application creates a new preference file containing default settings.

10 Set preferences in the application. In most applications, click the application's menu and click **Preferences** to open the Preferences dialog.

The application saves your preferences in the new preference file.

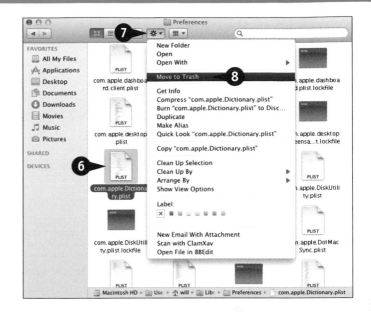

TIP

How do I find the right preference file to delete?
The names of most preference files use the format com.*company.application*.plist, where *company* is the manufacturer's name, *application* is the application's name, and .plist is the file extension for a properly list file. For example, com.apple.TextEdit.plist is the TextEdit preference file, and com.microsoft.Excel.plist is the Excel preference file.

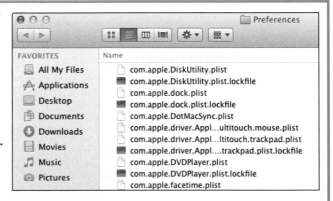

Troubleshoot Disk Permission Errors

To control what your iMac's users, applications, and different parts of the operating system itself can do, Mac OS X uses a complex system of permissions. Sometimes the permissions on some files become corrupted, which prevents Mac OS X or the applications from running as normal. When this happens, you can often fix the problem by repairing the disk permissions.

Troubleshoot Disk Permission Errors

① Click **Launchpad** (◉) on the Dock.

The Launchpad screen appears.

② Click **Utilities**.

The Utilities folder opens.

③ Click **Disk Utility**.

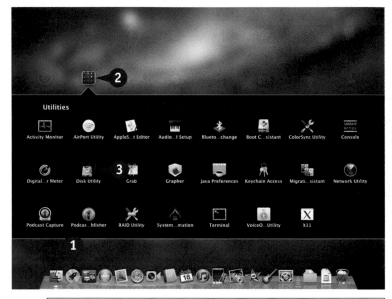

Disk Utility opens.

④ Click your iMac's hard disk.

The controls for manipulating the hard disk appear.

5 Click **First Aid** if the First Aid tab is not already highlighted.

6 Click **Repair Disk Permissions**.

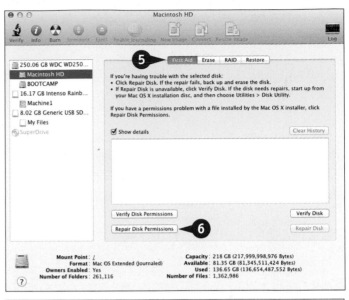

Mac OS X repairs the disk permissions. The process may take several minutes.

7 Click the **Disk Utility** menu and click **Quit Disk Utility** to close Disk Utility.

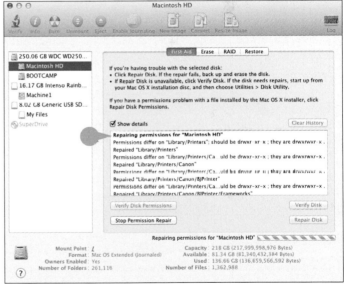

What are the symptoms of problems with permissions?

If your iMac has problems with permissions, it may run more slowly than usual. You may also find that applications quit unexpectedly or freeze so that you have to force quit them.

What causes problems with permissions?

The two main causes of problems with permissions are installing software and power outages. A badly written installation script can set permissions incorrectly on not only its own folder but also other folders. Power outages can leave files or folders with permissions temporarily changed to enable certain operations but not changed back as they would normally be.

Upgrade from Snow Leopard to Lion

Before upgrading to Lion, back up your files with Time Machine as discussed earlier in this chapter. If Mac OS X Lion came preinstalled on your iMac, you cannot burn an installation DVD as described here. To ensure you can recover from disaster, download the Lion Recovery Disk Assistant from the Apple website (http://support.apple.com/kb/DL1433) and use it to create a USB recovery drive for your iMac.

Upgrade from Snow Leopard to Lion

1 Download the Mac OS X Lion distribution file from the App Store.

2 When the download completes, the disk image opens.

3 Double-click the Mac OS X Lion icon.

The Install Mac OS X application opens.

4 Click **Continue**.

The Software License Agreement screen appears.

5 Read the license and click **Agree** if you want to proceed.

A screen appears showing the disk on which Mac OS X will be installed.

● If your iMac has two or more disks, you can choose a different disk by clicking **Show All Disks** and clicking the disk you want to use.

6 Click **Install**.

The installation runs, restarting your iMac so that it can install the files needed.

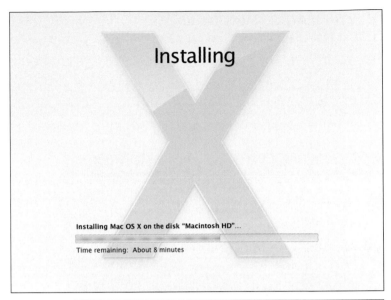

7 When the login screen appears, type your password and press Return.

Mac OS X logs you in.

Your desktop appears, and you can start using Mac OS X Lion on your iMac.

TIP

Can I buy the Mac OS X Lion upgrade on a DVD?

At this writing, the Mac OS X Lion upgrade is available only through the App Store.

After downloading the installation files, you can burn a DVD containing them. See the next task for instructions.

Create a Mac OS X Lion Installation DVD

I f your iMac came with Mac OS X Lion installed, you should have received a DVD containing the Lion installation files. You may need this DVD to troubleshoot problems or to reinstall Lion, so if you did not receive the DVD, ask your iMac's supplier for it.

If you downloaded Mac OS X Lion and installed it as an update to Snow Leopard, you can burn an installation DVD as described here. This is an important troubleshooting tool that you should create ahead of time instead of waiting until disaster strikes.

Create a Mac OS X Lion Installation DVD

1 Click the desktop.

The Finder becomes active.

2 Click **Go** and **Applications**.

The Applications folder opens.

3 Control +click or right-click **Mac OS X Lion**.

The context menu opens.

4 Click **Show Package Contents**.

The contents of the file appear.

5 Click **Contents**.

The contents of the Contents folder appear.

Note: In Icon view or List view, double-click to open each folder.

6 Click **SharedSupport**.

The contents of the SharedSupport folder appear.

7 Control +click or right-click **InstallESD.dmg**.

The context menu opens.

8 Click **Open With**.

The Open With submenu appears.

9 Click **Disk Utility**.

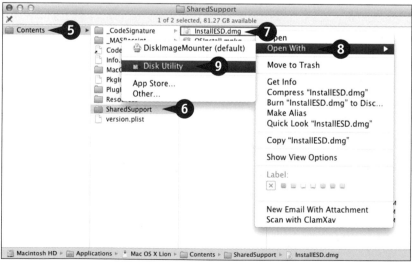

The Disc Utility window opens.

⑩ Click **InstallESD.dmg**.

⑪ Click **Burn**.

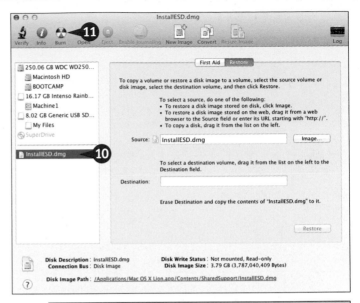

The Burn Disk In dialog opens.

⑫ Insert a blank recordable DVD in your iMac's optical drive.

⑬ Click **Burn**.

When the DVD is complete, eject it and label it.

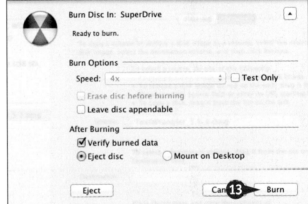

TIP

Can I install Mac OS X Lion from a USB drive?
If your iMac can boot from a USB drive, you can place the InstallESD.dmg on a USB drive by using Disk Utility. To boot your iMac from the USB drive, connect the drive and restart the iMac. At the startup chime, press and hold Option until the screen of startup disks appears. Click the USB drive, and then click the arrow button to start booting.

Repair Your iMac's Hard Disk

If your iMac does not start properly or if it crashes frequently, and repairing permissions does not fix the problem, you may need to repair the iMac's hard disk. To do so, you need to start your iMac using the Mac OS X recovery partition, and then run Disk Utility.

Repair Your iMac's Hard Disk

1 Restart your iMac.

2 At the startup chime, press and hold ⌘+R until the Apple logo appears.

Your iMac starts from the recovery partition.

The Mac OS X Utilities screen appears.

3 Click **Disk Utility**.

4 Click **Continue**.

The Disk Utility window opens.

5 Click your iMac's hard drive.

6 Click **First Aid**.

7 Click **Repair Disk**.

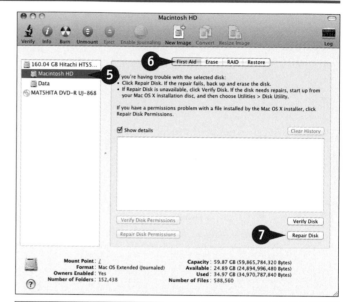

● Disk Utility repairs the disk, displaying its progress.

8 Click the **Disk Utility** menu and click **Quit Disk Utility**.

Disk Utility closes, and the Install Mac OS X dialog opens.

9 Click the **Mac OS X Utilities** menu and click **Quit Mac OS X Utilities**.

10 In the confirmation dialog, click **Restart**.

Your iMac restarts into Mac OS X from the hard disk.

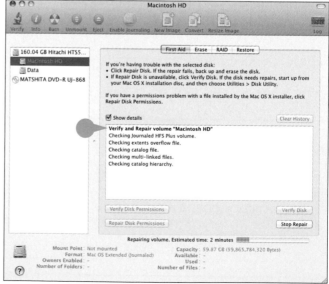

Reinstall Mac OS X to Solve Severe Problems

After a power outage or severe software damage, you may not be able to restart your iMac at all. When this happens, you need to reinstall Mac OS X to fix the problem. You can also reinstall Mac OS X if your iMac crashes frequently and you find that repairing the permissions and the disk does not help.

Normally, you can reinstall from your iMac's recovery partition. If the recovery partition has failed, use the original installation DVD that came with your iMac or a DVD you have burned from the Mac OS X Lion update you downloaded to upgrade Snow Leopard to Lion.

Reinstall Mac OS X to Solve Severe Problems

1 Restart your iMac.

2 At the startup chime, press and hold ⌘+R until the Apple logo appears.

Your iMac starts from the recovery partition.

Note: If your iMac cannot start from the recovery partition, insert the Mac OS X installation DVD in your iMac's optical drive. Restart the iMac. At the startup chime, press and hold C until the Apple logo appears. The Install Mac OS X screen then appears.

The Mac OS X Utilities screen appears.

3 Click **Reinstall Mac OS X**.

4 Click **Continue**.

The Software License Agreement dialog opens.

5 Click **Continue** and **Agree**.

6 Click **Agree**.

The Select the Disk Where You Want to Install Mac OS X screen appears.

7 Click the disk.

8 Click **Install**.

The Installer then installs Mac OS X.

9 After your iMac restarts, log in. You can then access your files as before.

Index